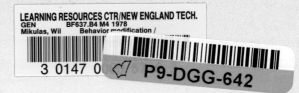

P9-DGG-642

Behavior Modification

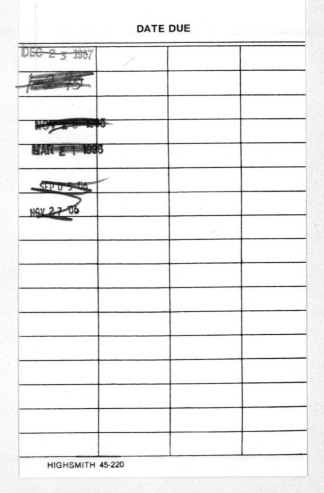

DATE DUE

DEC 2 3 1987			
NOV			
MAR 2 1 1996			
SEP 0 9 06			
NOV 2 7 06			

HIGHSMITH 45-220

Behavior Modification

William L. Mikulas
University of West Florida

Harper & Row, Publishers

NEW YORK   HAGERSTOWN   SAN FRANCISCO   LONDON

Sponsoring Editor: George A. Middendorf
Project Editor: Pamela Landau
Designer: Katrine Stevens
Production Supervisor: Kewal K. Sharma
Compositor: Bi-Comp, Incorporated
Art Studio: Danmark & Michaels, Inc.

BEHAVIOR MODIFICATION

Library of Congress Cataloging in Publication Data

Mikulas, William L
    Behavior modification.

    Includes bibliographies and index
    1. Behavior modification. I. Title.
BF637.B4M4   1978   153.8'5   77-13356
ISBN 0-06-044434-7

To Benita, my best friend
and a constant source of reinforcement.

Contents

Preface

This text is a brief overview of the whole field of behavior modification, including applications in schools, half-way houses, homes, businesses, and mental hospitals. The intent is to provide the reader with an integrated discussion of some basic principles and theories of behavior and behavior change across a wide range of settings and problem areas. I hope the book is useful as a supplementary text in courses in behavior modification, particularly those whose subject matter emphasizes a narrower domain of procedures or settings; as a supplementary text in courses in which behavior modification is one of many components; and as a brief survey for psychologists and other professionals who wish to know what has been going on in behavior modification and perhaps be directed to other readings and considerations.

There are currently many good texts on behavior modification, which was not so a few years ago in this relatively young discipline. Several texts deal with applications in clinical and counseling settings, operant applications in education and child rearing, or specialized topics, such as assertive training and self-control, to mention only a few topics. In addition, there are several specialized journals, thousands of relevant articles, and many edited books of original and reprinted articles. One of my purposes is to provide readers with sources of information so they may pursue areas of interest to them. I have included Suggested Readings (at the end of most chapters), Further Readings (Chap. 11), and many references.

Despite the texts currently available, none covers the whole field of behavior modification. Each is restricted by topic, settings of application, and/or procedures emphasized. This is fine; but a need exists, which I hope this book fills, for an overview of the entire field so that the reader develops an understanding of the breadth of behavior modification principles, as well as of some of the interrelationships among different approaches. By keeping the book relatively brief, I hope an overview can be offered without losing the reader in too much detail. For these reasons, I intend the book to be a supplement (as well as a core text) for courses in behavior modification and related approaches. For example, a course that is basically operant in nature could use the book to review non-operant procedures—such as desensitization and aversive counterconditioning. Or instructors emphasizing applications in clinical settings may wish to briefly expose their students to how the principles being discussed apply to other settings. Finally, many of my students in behavior modification have reported that first reading a brief chapter giving an overview of a topic, such as desensitization, aided their later understanding and made ease of learning of more detailed and more comprehensive readings on the topic.

This book may also be a supplement to courses that cover behavior modification as one of many topics—courses such as learning, abnormal psychology, clinical psychology, educational psychology, and counseling. Perhaps just some of the book will be read in some of these situations (one reasonable subset would be Chapters 1, 3, 7, 8, 9, and 10).

Behavior modification procedures could be organized in many ways, such as by settings of application or categories of problem behaviors. I have chosen an organization centering around general paradigms (e.g., respondent conditioning, operant conditioning, modeling). This has the advantage of providing some generality to change procedures, as well as suggesting relationships among various approaches, particularly as practitioners and theorists are generating new procedures and variations of procedures under an unwieldy mass of new terms. I think the organization I use is helpful in that it provides a conceptualization which may facilitate the reader's ability to see interrelationships among behaviors and the practitioner's ability to design a logical integrated change program drawing from the whole field of behavior modification. On the other hand, it is not always clear where a change procedure, such as covert sensitization (aversive counterconditioning? operant punishment?), should go. In such cases, I point out the different possibilities. And some approaches, such as assertive training, are a combination of many procedures and have to be put into a chapter where they best fit.

This book is a follow-up to an earlier book of mine, *Behavior modification: an overview* (1972). Since I essentially rewrote the whole book I do not see this book as a second or revised edition; but this is definitional. This book is somewhat more comprehensive than the 1972 book and reflects changes in the field of behavior modification, as well as changes in my knowledge and thinking.

A note to those involved in the current concern about sexist biases in our texts and language: Throughout the text I use the common grammatical convention of using male pronouns to refer to a person of either sex, intending to show no bias or preference for one sex or the other. I considered alternative ways of writing to avoid using this convention, but the alternatives seemed awkward and hindered communication of my material, which is my main concern. I tried to make sure my examples, real and fictional, did not contain a sex bias.

I am indebted to the many practitioners and theorists in behavior modification who are responsible for most of the material in this book, to my students and clients from whom I learned much, to the reviewers of my first draft, and to my wife-typist-best friend Benita who shares, supports, and pleases my being.

WLM

1 | Assumptions and Approach

Consider the following small sample of problems that psychologists, teachers, parents, and other change agents must deal with: What are effective ways of helping a person control or eliminate unwanted emotions such as some anxiety, anger, jealousy, aggression, and racial prejudice? What basic approaches are available to us to facilitate the reduction of nervous habits, epileptic seizures, stealing, and littering? What concrete things can be done when a person wishes to reduce overeating, smoking, or the consumption of alcohol or other drugs? How does one deal with insomnia and nightmares? If a client has a sexual dysfunction or is only sexually aroused by "inappropriate" objects, what can be done to eliminate the problem and facilitate desired sexual behavior? How can a person increase motivation in himself, a prison, a ward in a mental hospital, or a work organization? What are effective ways for a person to learn to relax, quiet his mind, and control unwanted thoughts? What constructive things can we tell a parent about child rearing, toilet training, and bedwetting? In school classrooms, what are effective ways of motivating the students, dealing with disruptive behavior, and individualizing instruction as much as possible? Given the enormous number of people seeking clinical and counseling help and the relatively small number of highly trained practitioners, how can we most effectively and efficiently help these people while maximizing the use of available human resources?

This book describes one approach, behavior modification, which deals with the above problems, among many others. The reason behavior modification can deal with such a wide range of problems, with varying degrees of effectiveness, is because the approach draws on several basic principles of human behavior that cut across many different problem areas and situations. Experimental studies are the main ways we refine our understanding of human behavior and evaluate and evolve our behavior modification practice.

BEHAVIOR MODIFICATION

Behavior modification is the application of experimentally established principles of behavior to problems of behavior. Currently, it draws most heavily from studies, not theories, in the areas of learning and motivation, although behavior modification is not restricted to these areas. When used in settings that are primarily seen as clinical, behavior modification is often called *behavior therapy* or *conditioning therapy*. Behavior modification is sometimes equated with applied operant conditioning (see Chapter 7), which is just a part of behavior modification and more accurately called *experimental analysis of behavior*.

In the last few years some writers have used the term *behavior modification* to refer to almost any practice that alters human behavior. But this is not the case. More specifically, behavior modification is not brainwashing or mind control, and behavior modifiers do not use psychosurgery or electroshock therapy and only occasionally use drugs as a temporary adjunct to a change procedure. Rather, behavior modification is structured learning in which new skills and other behaviors are learned, undesired reactions and habits are reduced, and the client becomes more motivated for the desired changes.

Behavior modification is experimentally based. The assumption of psychology is that there is a set of laws that describes factors which affect a person's behavior. If a person's behavior is changed, regardless of what the procedure is called (e.g., behavior modification, analysis, influence, nondirective counseling), the change must be based on these laws. And the closer the treatment procedure comes to using these laws, the more effective it is. It is not known exactly what these basic laws are, but the experimental psychologist believes that the information from experimental studies is the best approximation we have at present. The practice of behavior modification includes the technology of applying these principles to human problems. (Note that behavior modification is more a technology than a philosophy of the nature of human beings.) As various change procedures are developed, they too are experimentally studied in terms of such questions as how effective are different approaches for different problems and how can a specific procedure be improved. Therefore, behavior modification is continually evolving and improving. This book is intended to give the reader a brief conceptual overview of the whole field of behavior modification. Therefore, it is not possible or desirable to review all the related experimental research. However, I have included many references so the readers may be directed to that research literature they wish to inspect in more detail.

LEARNING AND MOTIVATION

Among the many factors that influence human behavior are genetic variables, physiological abnormalities, nutrition, and electromagnetic radiation. Treatment of some problems may thus involve changing the person's diet or removing a brain tumor. Other physiological factors such as genetic predispositions for some forms of schizophrenia, abnormally reactive nervous systems, biochemical imbalances in the brain, and mental retardation generally cannot be directly treated at present. Hence they must be considered part of the "personality" of the person (see Mikulas, 1974b, chap. 7) and seen as givens or constraints for whatever change procedures are applicable. Behavior modification may not be able to eliminate the retardation, but it can help the retarded person lead the most fulfilling life possible. Similarly, many problems that before were primarily treated by purely medical approaches are now seen to be best treated by coupling the medical approach with behavior modification (Katz & Zlutnick, 1974; Knapp & Peterson, 1976; LeBow, 1976).

However, when one looks at the range of psychological problems, such as those at the beginning of this chapter, one finds that the major variables responsible for the majority of most problems are variables related to learning and motivation. In some cases, this involves behaviors that were learned at one time or situation, but are considered undesirable at another time or place. Small children may be knocked down a few times by large dogs and develop a fear of dogs. If this fear persists into adulthood, persons with the fear may wish to rid themselves of it. People who began smoking cigarettes as teenagers for social approval may find several years later that they have learned a complex smoking habit which is difficult to eliminate for more than a short period of time.

On the other hand, many problems involve behaviors that the person has not learned, but needs to learn, such as how to study, relax, handle anxiety, or be more assertive. Behavior modification then draws strongly on learning and motivation, and much of the practice consists of helping people reduce undesired learned behaviors and learn new desired behaviors.

Throughout this book I will be conceptualizing behavior from a learning-motivation position. But psychology is overflowing with personality theories and clinical approaches that offer alternative ways of conceptualizing behavior. What are the relationships between these various models and why choose one over another? To some extent it is a matter of translation: How do the constructs and approaches of model A translate into the constructs and approaches of model B? Are the "strokes" of transactional analysis the same as "reinforcement" in behavior modification? In this context, many writers (Dollard & Miller, 1950; French, 1933; Kimble, 1961, chap. 14; Krasner, 1962; Sargant, 1959; Shoben, 1949; Truax, 1966) have attempted to show that what takes place in various forms of therapy and counseling can be explained from a learning orientation. However, the issue is much more than one of translation, for the various models often contain assumptions that lead to incompatibilities. In Chapter 10, after the reader has a better understanding of behavior modification, I will raise this issue again and suggest some relationships between behavior modification and other models.

There are a number of advantages to a learning-motivation based model. One is that the constructs are relatively "clean"; they are well defined with a minimum of excess meaning and associations. This facilitates an objective understanding of behavior. A second advantage is that learning and motivation, perhaps more than any other model, suggest complex interrelationships of the various constructs in a way useful in understanding and treating human problems that involve complex interweaving of many behaviors.

THE MEDICAL MODEL

From about the time of Freud until fairly recently the predominant way of thinking about and treating psychological problems has been the *medical model*. The assumption of this approach is that abnormal behaviors are products of more basic *underlying causes* within the psychological system, such as a subconscious conflict based on early childhood experiences. If a person reports a fear of snakes, this is merely a *symptom* of an underlying cause. In this case, the snake is usually seen as a sexual symbol; and the fear of snakes is based on sexual anxiety or castration fears. Similarly, one theory of alcoholism is that the drinking behavior is a result of a more basic cause of latent homosexuality. The medical model has so infused our culture that many people automatically assume it must be true. A disadvantage of this way of thinking is that undesired behaviors are often seen as a product of a basic pathology or psychological disease, an attitude which may lead to clients feeling more helpless or worse about themselves. A common early step in behavior therapy is reducing the client's beliefs and fears about being diseased or mentally ill in some sense.

Treatment based on the medical model requires procedures—such as psychoanalysis—aimed at the underlying cause, not the behavioral symptom. This usually involves the client gaining insight into the underlying cause and/or reliving and dealing with early experiences, often of a psychosexual nature.

Psychology as a science is very young, most of the information having been acquired in the last 30 years. Thus around the turn of the century, psychology was basically a subset of philosophy. Freud then built his medical model based on his medical training, his experiences with hysterical and neurotic clients, and his work with hypnosis. He and other medical model theorists generated a large number of creative and important ideas about human behavior, many of which have been refined and incorporated into the experimental literature and many of which have not held up and have been significantly altered or rejected.

Over time, many psychologists became dissatisfied with the medical model. One reason is that many of the basic concepts of the different theories (e.g., ego, id, power-striving, inferiority complex) were not defined so they could be adequately measured. Without adequate measures it is always questionable whether a construct is applicable to an individual or whether purported changes in a construct have taken place. This led to many different theories, all of which could explain people's behavior within their own theoretical constructs. But without better measures of the constructs it is difficult to choose between alternative explanations or alternative approaches to change procedures. Behavior modification defines its constructs in as measurable a way as possible.

A second question about the medical model concerns the idea of an underlying cause. Is a person's fear of snakes actually based on something like sexual anxiety? Medical models assume yes; learning-based models assume no. From a learning approach a person acquired a fear of snakes through some combination of experiences such as actual bad experiences with snakes; bad associations to snakes via stories, cartoons, religious tales, and the like (our culture is extreme in its bad treatment of snakes); and/or acquiring the fear from someone else, often a parent, who has the same fear (see Chapter 8). It is also likely that humans as a species have a predisposition to acquiring a fear of snakes (Seligman, 1971) or perhaps even some degree of an innate fear that is coupled with learning (Gray, 1971, p. 15).

This issue of the underlying cause is raised again below in the discussion of symptom substitution and again in Chapter 10 when considering the relationships between behavior modification and psychoanalysis. But if, in fact, there is no reason or need to trace an underlying cause, then one's treatment program can generally proceed significantly faster.

A major problem for all change agents, which is related to medical model types of conceptualization, is the tendency to explain behavior problems in terms of some characteristic of the person, rather than a functional understanding of the behaviors. A teacher might explain why a student misbehaves in class in terms of the student being a slow learner, or being from a broken home, or from a minority group. A foreman might account for a worker's poor work performance in terms of the worker being a loner or not identifying with the company. Behavior modifiers look at behavior more functionally—what are the conditions supporting this behavior? Being from a broken home does not make a child misbehave in class. Rather, when we functionally examine the behavior, we will probably discover something like the fact that the child gets peer approval for his misbehavior and has not learned other ways to get this attention. (Perhaps being from a broken home impaired his learning alternative behaviors.) We can easily help the child learn more acceptable and useful ways of gaining social approval; we cannot easily change the fact he is from a broken home. Similarly, by systematically studying the worker with poor work performance, we may find that he needs skill training related to his job or that the union would punish him for working harder.

BEHAVIORISM

Behavior modification then, as the name implies, is concerned with behavior, what does the person *do*. Behavior here is meant in the broadest sense, including overt behavior that is readily observable, covert behavior such as thoughts that are generally inferred from what the person tells us, various emotions, and subtle activity of the nervous system. In all cases we define the behaviors as objectively as possible within the confines of the practicality of the situation and the limits of our technology.

Behavior modification arose from the school of psychology called *behaviorism,* an approach that suggests the study of psychology should emphasize the understanding, prediction, and control of behavior. The first major statement of a behaviorist position was that of Watson in 1913. Watson's approach was a variation of *methodological behaviorism,* which argues that mental events cannot be scientifically studied since you cannot get agreement about what goes on in the mind. Watson held an extreme point of view in that he only considered the study of overt behavior as scientifically valid and attempted to reduce thinking to movements of the vocal cords and tongue. He emphasized the necessity for objective study of overt behavior, although he allowed for covert behavior. Many critics of modern behaviorism and behavior modification use Watson's form of behaviorism as a straw man. They suggest behavior modification disregards people's thoughts and feelings, treating them as empty organisms or white rats. In reality, although these criticisms may apply to some practitioners of many orientations, the field of behavior modification is not at all like that. Since its beginnings, behavior modification has been concerned with people's feelings, particularly anxiety. And Chapter 9 discusses the relationship of mental events to behavior and the application of behavior modification to thoughts.

Similarly, Skinner (1974) is the foremost spokesman for behaviorism today. He suggests a form of behaviorism called *radical behaviorism,* which recognizes and studies mental events as internal behaviors. Skinner's views and approach to behaviorism are not the same as all behaviorists practicing behavior modification. However, Skinner is important reading for students of behavior modification.

The type of behaviorism being suggested here is not an attempt to reduce all human behavior to a few simple reflexes or stimulus-response associations. Rather, it is an appreciation of the enormous complexity of human behavior and an attempt to understand this complexity in terms of interrelationships of component behaviors. Breaking behavior down into its components need not detract from an understanding of the person as a whole; instead it facilitates developing an effective change program. The component behaviors are not conceptualized as specific responses being learned to specific stimuli, but rather are classes of behaviors learned to classes of situations.

By focusing on behaviors, behavior modification provides practical information about what to *do* in real situations. While in school the student of clinical psychology may explore and debate various psychological-philosophical models of human behavior; but when sitting down with a client who is a sexually impotent alcoholic reporting general feelings of depression, what is the practitioner going to *do?* This client wants concrete, practical help now! A new teacher may have many creative ideas for educating fifth graders and individualizing instruction. But when he gets his first class he finds thirty different students with a wide range of academic backgrounds and behavior problems. He is spending much of his time as a policeman rather than an innovative educator. What is he to *do?*

Sometimes understanding a problem or seeing why he acts in some way may help a person deal with a problem. Perhaps the person has the skills to overcome a problem once the problem is understood. But usually this is insufficient. Thus behavior modification does not depend on understanding, insight, or being able to interpret behavior from some theoretical model as sufficient for behavior change. Rather, people may need help in learning alternative behaviors or skills that are not in their repertoire. A woman in a consciousness-raising group may discover she needs to be more assertive with her husband. But this knowledge does not teach her to be appropriately assertive without, for example, becoming too aggressive. In behavior modification we have specific ways of helping a person learn appropriate assertive behaviors (see Chapter 8). Or consider fears. Probably just about everyone reading this book has some type of undesired fear or source of anxiety, such as fear of spiders, fear of snakes, fear of heights, test anxiety, or anxiety about speaking before a particular group of people. Does your knowledge of this fear, your feeling the fear is irrational, or your ability to interpret the fear in terms of some theory eliminate the fear? Probably not. Behavior modification provides specific ways of helping people handle anxiety and eliminate fears.

This does not mean that understanding or insight is not present in behavior modification, only that it is often insufficient. In fact, behavior modification practices often encourage clients to observe and understand the causes of their behavior. This type of awareness or discrimination learning is often necessary for a thorough assessment and often is the first step in helping the person develop self-control of some behaviors. The relationship between understanding and behavior change will be covered in a little more detail in Chapter 9.

Working with behavior problems often involves a variety of different components. In some cases, there is a need for education or clearing up misconceptions. This is common in the treatment of sexual problems. Sometimes the client needs encouragement, permission, or a good listener. Sometimes the client needs medical aid, vocational training, driving lessons, or a new set of teeth. But beyond all of this the behavior modifier has a practical approach of what to *do* to deal with a range of behaviors that need to be increased or decreased.

SYMPTOM SUBSTITUTION

A concern of people from the medical model orientation is that behavior modification only treats the symptoms without getting at the underlying cause. If the underlying cause is not treated, it may simply manifest itself in terms of some other symptoms, a phenomenon called *symptom substitution*. This type of reasoning causes some people to reject a behavioral approach as only tinkering with symptoms.

The issue, however, is not as clear as it first seems. Symptoms and underlying causes have not been well defined. It is not clear exactly what constitutes a symptom, when substitution should occur, or when you have reached an underlying cause. It is not clear why one must make the assumption of symptom substitution; such an assumption is compatible, but unnecessary, from even a medical model or psychodynamic approach (Weitzman, 1967). Freud allowed this as just one possibility.

The issue becomes an empirical one: Does something such as symptom substitution follow treatment of behaviors? The answer appears to be no. A large number of studies (e.g., Baker, 1969; Lazarus, 1963; Nolan et al., 1970; Paul, 1967, 1968; Wolpe, 1961; Yates, 1958) has shown that if the treatment of the behaviors is adequately carried out, seldom does anything that resembles symptom substitution occur. The key word is "adequately," for if the practitioner does not treat all the relevant behaviors, then the untreated behaviors, or behaviors resulting from them, might be interpreted as symptom substitution (Cahoon, 1968). Some examples of this follow.

Many behaviors are maintained by anxiety. Consider, for example, a person who feels anxious in social situations and has adopted smoking as a means to reduce anxiety. If the behaviorist merely stopped the smoking behavior, the person might turn to some other anxiety-reducing behavior, for example, excessive drinking. Superficially, it would appear that symptom substitution had occurred. However, if the behaviorist treated the behavior of feeling anxious, as well as the smoking behavior, then there should not be a substitute symptom. Now the reader may wish to think of anxiety as some type of underlying cause in this case, and this is fine. But this is not how most medical model theorists would think of an underlying cause. And the anxiety in this situation is readily reduced from a behavioral position, as will be discussed in Chapter 3.

For treatment purposes, many people are taken from one environment and placed in another: A child is removed from a public school and placed in a special training school, an adult is taken from his home and institutionalized, or a drug addict is removed from society and placed in a treatment center. If, after treatment, clients are returned to their original environment, the old surroundings and friends may trigger some of the old behaviors, which may then be strengthened. A followup study might report relapse or symptom substitution, when in fact return of the undesired behavior was because of the environment the clients were returned to. This underscores the importance for all practitioners to systematically investigate and, if possible, alter any environments in which they place their clients.

The issue of symptom substitution was raised often in the early days of behavior modification, in the late 1950s and early 1960s. But it is not mentioned much anymore in the professional literature, primarily because of lack of empirical support. However, I still encounter it often when talking with lay people and undergraduates. It is an interesting example of the extent to which medical model assumptions have been accepted into large parts of our culture.

PROPERTIES OF BEHAVIOR MODIFICATION

1. Behavior modification is *ahistorical*. It does not matter how the individuals got where they are or acquired certain problems. The question is what do we do here and now? What currently elicits and maintains undesirable behaviors? What behavioral deficits currently exist? This does not mean we disregard historical information, for it is often useful. But historical information is used to help determine current variables affecting behavior. Sometimes historical information is unnecessary. If we had a case of a

student with test anxiety, it might take a long time to determine the events of the past that led to test anxiety. Fortunately, we can probably adequately reduce the anxiety in a few hours without knowing the genesis. Also, the genesis of some current problem may be another earlier problem that might now be resolved and need not be brought up again. Being ahistorical, behavior modification is often faster than approaches that require tracing down historical causes.

2. Behavior modification avoids labeling and categorizing people and the use of words such as "abnormal." Classification systems may be useful for some administrative and communication purposes and may suggest some variables to look at during assessment. But a label or category usually adds little to a functional analysis of the behaviors. On the other hand, labeling the person may be detrimental to the person (as will be discussed in the next chapter) or may cause the practitioner to overlook behaviors unique to that person.

Adjectives such as "abnormal," "deviant," and "mentally ill" are often used to describe people and behaviors. But these are basically social-political constructs by which people in a particular culture at a particular time define acceptable and unacceptable behaviors. Homosexuality in our culture is generally considered deviant. But this attitude has been changing in our culture; and in some cultures, such as some early Greek cultures, homosexuality was considered superior to heterosexuality. Similarly, some creative people and great leaders show behaviors that are infrequent (not normal) in our culture, but does this make them deviant or abnormal? Such terms are too poorly defined to be of much use. Behavior, regardless of how it is classified (e.g., normal versus abnormal), is acquired and can be modified by the same principles of learning and motivation. Whether the behavior is acceptable or not to some people or cultures is a separate ethical issue.

3. Behavior modification is sensible. The reasoning of behavior modification or some specific program can often be explained to clients, teachers, parents, ward attendants, and others in a way that "makes sense" to them. They need not accept some theoretical model or learn specialized terminology. When working with a client you can both know where you are going and why. When working with ward attendants in a mental hospital you get better results and cooperation when you reason with them. If you point out how one patient throws food in the cafeteria because it results in the nurse going and sitting with him, then it is possible to suggest reasonable ways to reduce the food throwing. On the other hand, if you describe the patient in nonsensical ways to the ward attendant, you should not expect much help from the attendant in your treatment program. If parents go to a child psychologist, they usually want some reasonable and specific sugges-tions for specific problems. They are probably not interested in

psychological-philosophizing or categorizing the child's behavior or developmental stage.

4. One of the greatest advantages of behavior modification is that it does not require a one-to-one relationship between the behavior modifier, who establishes and supervises the programs, and the clients. Thus the behavior modifier can train teachers to carry out programs in classrooms (Doerr, 1975) and parents to carry out programs with children (Berkowitz & Graziano, 1972; O'Dell, 1974; Sloop, 1975). This is more effective and efficient than trying to deal with all the individual children, particularly when the parents and teachers are often unknowingly responsible for the misbehavior they wish to change. In this context, numerous behavior modification books have been written specifically for teachers and parents (see Chapter 11). Similarly, ward attendants can learn to implement programs in mental hospitals (e.g., the token economies of Chapter 7). In one program working with juveniles, the psychologist supervises the behavior analysts who supervise the mediators who work with the youth (Tharp & Wetzel, 1969). And others are investigating how behavior modification procedures can be used in the training of people to carry out behavior modification (e.g., Loeber & Weisman, 1975). The importance of such programs is that more people and paraprofessionals can be effectively used in the treatment program, more people can be directly helped, and the behavior modifier can spend more of his time on general programs and specialized problems.

In addition, some behavior modification programs can be carried out with groups of people at a time. And in many situations, automation can do many of the tasks for people (Butterfield, 1974; Elwood, 1975; Schwitzgebel & Schwitzgebel, 1973). For all these reasons, plus the emphasis on self-control mentioned next, more people can be treated more efficiently and cheaper than approaches requiring a one-to-one relationship between the client and a highly trained practitioner.

5. Finally, a large part of behavior modification is concerned with self-control, approaches geared toward teaching people how to carry out change programs on themselves (see Chapter 11). This has many advantages, including freeing the practitioner's time and hence less expense to clients, greater attitude and behavior changes if clients attribute the changes to themselves, the clients learning general strategies that they can apply in a variety of situations, and the possibility of catching problems early or even preventing them from occurring. People may learn these self-control skills and programs from popularized magazine articles or books (e.g., Alberti & Emmons, 1975; Fensterheim & Baer, 1975; Robbins & Fisher, 1973), self-control clinics, television shows on self-control (Mikulas, 1976a), or individual counseling and training. In addition, several written self-control programs are being developed to help people learn by themselves such things

as how to improve study habits (Beneke & Harris, 1972); lose weight (Hagen, 1974; Hanson et al., 1976); and control premature ejaculation, the tendency of a male to ejaculate too quickly in intercourse situations (Lowe & Mikulas, 1975). Thus more and more behavior modification information is being distributed to people at large, so people can better understand, control, and direct their own behavior.

Overall then, behavior modification is a relatively new, evolving field that already contains a fast, efficient, and powerful technology for behavior change. It is an important literature for all change agents and people who wish to understand their own behavior, regardless of how they wish to incorporate this information into their own models.

SUMMARY

From experimental studies of behavior, including studies of learning and motivation, psychology is evolving an understanding of basic principles of behavior that may be seen in a wide range of situations. Behavior modification is the technology of applying these principles to problems of behavior, reducing undesired behaviors and teaching desired behaviors, while continually experimentally evaluating and improving the various approaches. As much as possible, the constructs of behavior modification are defined in ways that are readily measurable. The emphasis is on behavior, what does the person do, including overt and covert behaviors. The practitioner focuses on the complex interrelationships of current behaviors rather than on the historical causes or development of these behaviors. Behavior modification does not require a one-to-one relationship between practitioner and client. People can learn self-control skills and carry out programs on themselves; parents, teachers, and paraprofessionals can learn how to help implement programs with others; groups of people can often be treated at one time; and many aspects of different programs can be automated.

THOUGHT QUESTIONS

1. What are the strengths and limitations of trying to specify human behavior in terms that can be objectively measured?
2. Define "mental illness" and "abnormal". Discuss these definitions from a practical standpoint.
3. Define "behaviorism" in its broadest sense. What are the strengths and weaknesses of this approach? Why?
4. What properties must a change procedure have to be considered behavior modification as described in this chapter?
5. To what extent is or was your thinking about human behavior influenced by the medical model approach? Why?
6. When would understanding the nature or cause of a behavior problem be sufficient to eliminate the problem? When would it not be sufficient? Give specific examples. Think of examples from your own life.

7. Behavior modification, much of Gestalt therapy, and other change models are primarily ahistorical. Folk wisdom contains many suggestions such as "Don't cry over spilt milk" and "Today is the first day of the rest of your life." In Buddhism, an enlightened person comes to live more fully in the present. What is the common point among all of these? What are the practical implications of an ahistorical approach? When would collecting historical information or dealing with a historical problem be advantageous?
8. What is self-control? Can it be learned? Why?
9. Consider a form of therapy or counseling, other than behavior modification, with which you are familiar. To what extent can the change procedures of this therapy be thought of in terms of learning and motivation? What are the advantages of thinking about it in these terms? What does this mean about the relationships between this therapy and behavior modification?

Assessment and Objectives

The first task in behavior modification is to specify the problems and objectives in terms of measurable behaviors. It is not sufficient to say that a person is neurotic. Rather, it is necessary to specify which of the person's behaviors should be altered and which behaviors he does not have should be added. Similarly, it is not sufficient to choose as an educational objective that the student develop "an appreciation of history." Rather, it is necessary to specify exactly what behaviors are required of the student.

BEHAVIORAL ASSESSMENT

The purpose of behavioral assessment is to delineate behavioral deficits, inappropriate behaviors, and the frequency with which different behaviors occur in various situations. The first step is to specify the behaviors in such a way that there is little question about whether they occurred. For example, if the behavior modifier were interested in how afraid a person is of heights, he might measure change in heart rate when the person is at various heights and define fear in terms of this physiological response, or he might measure how high up a person will go by himself. If he wanted to measure how "tidy" a child is, he might define "tidiness" in terms of making the bed and hanging up clothes. The point is that the assessment focuses on objective, measurable behaviors.

Behavioral assessment deals with behaviors and their interrelationships. It avoids mapping people into constructs or categories that cannot be directly observed or measured, but only indirectly inferred from some of the behaviors. If a person reports being "generally uptight most of the time," behavioral assessment focuses on his behavioral strengths and deficits (including interpersonal skills, vocational skills, thoughts, emotions, etc.) that lead to the person being "uptight." There is no need in behavior modification to add to this assessment hypothesized conditions of such inferred constructs as ego-strength, self-concept, or psycho-sexual development.

Similarly behavioral assessment minimizes labeling or categorizing the person. The question is what does the person *do,* not what sort of person *is* he. Several possible problems may result from labeling a person: The practitioner may respond to the client too much in terms of the label and thus overlook some important behaviors or incorrectly assume the client to be similar in some ways to someone else with the same label. Other people, such as peers, teachers, and ward attendants may also respond and perceive the person too much in terms of how he is labeled. The label may saddle the person with an undesired social stigma. And if the person learns how he has been labeled, it may cause fear and anxiety and may result in the person acting in ways that match how he thinks a person so labeled should act (an example of self-fulfilling prophecy). Thus labels such as "paranoid schizophrenic," "socially maladjusted," and "slow learner" are generally avoided.

The way behavior modification assessment is carried out varies dramatically with the type of client and type of problems. It may involve sitting in the back of a classroom recording the behaviors of various students. It may be done indirectly from the reports of parents or teachers. It may involve measuring the amount of litter in a campground or the number of aggressive assaults following a particular television show. Or the assessment may be based on sampling the behavior of patients in a mental hospital, prisoners in their cells, or people at a political rally.

Many times the assessment will occur in a clinical or counseling situation in which the behavior modifier works in a one-to-one relationship with the client. Here, and in other situations, the relationship with the client is important; although the relationship is not seen as a necessary or sufficient condition for behavior change (see Chapter 10). Generally, it is desirable for the practitioner to have and demonstrate genuine and non-judgmental interest and concern for the client. The optimal practitioner is one who, as much as possible, can perceive, think, and feel from the client's position. From this vantage point the practitioner can draw on his knowledge of behavior modification and suggest to the client, in terms of the client's mode and vocabulary of thought and perception, possible courses of action to deal with the problems. The relationship with the client may facilitate such things as gaining accurate information, motivating the client, and setting up a program geared toward where the client psychologically is at the present. Thus behavior modifiers who work in such situations may often benefit from training in interpersonal and counseling skills.

ASSESSMENT PROCEDURES

Information for a behavioral assessment may come from a wide variety of sources, including direct observation of the client, as a student in a classroom or worker in a plant; self-report of the client, as in a counseling interview situation; role-playing, as when the practitioner assumes the part of the client's mother and with the client they role-play a recent interaction between the client and the client's mother; and physiological measures, such as measuring the amount of change in heart rate when the client imagines different fearful situations. Information may also be obtained from the client's peers, teachers, parents, doctor, or boss.

The client may be asked to write a brief autobiography or fill out a life history questionnaire (e.g., Lazarus, 1971, appendix A). Children may be asked what three wishes they would make in terms of changing things about their lives.

One of the best sources of information is to have the client keep a personal log or diary related to specific problems. A person with a lot of anxiety may keep a log including an exact description of each situation which made him anxious, how he responded in this situation, and what was the result of how he responded. Parents might keep a diary of their child's behavior, including the situations, how the child behaved, and how they and others then responded to the child. The clients themselves often learn much about their own behavior through such procedures, and this "know thyself" is often the first step toward self-improvement and self-control.

Numerous tests and questionnaires have been devised to aid behavioral assessment. The following is a sample. There are several variations of the *Fear Survey Schedule* (Geer, 1965; Wolpe & Lang, 1964) in which the client is given a long list of items (e.g., falling, automobiles, and dentists) and asked to indicate on a five-point scale the degree to which each item disturbs him. The answers are used to help determine situations that elicit anxiety. Suinn (1969) has developed a similar instrument to assess anxiety related to examination situations, test anxiety. The *Reinforcement Survey Schedule* (Cautela, 1972; Cautela & Kastenbaum, 1967) helps determine what situations, objects, and activities are pleasing or rewarding for the client. This includes things to eat, types of reading, music, sports, general activities, praise, and types of interactions with others. This information may be used to help establish rapport with the client (e.g., topics to talk about) and for specific programs, such as counterconditioning (Chapter 3) or operant conditioning (Chapter 7). A variation of this questionnaire has been developed specifically for children (Keat, 1974). Many assertive questionnaires have been developed to determine how non-assertive, assertive, or aggressive people are in various situations (e.g., Galassi et al., 1974; Gambrill & Richey, 1975; Gay et al., 1975; Rathus, 1973). These include how people respond in situations such as people pushing in front of them in a line or receiving an overdone steak in a restaurant. They help identify people who are over-apologetic, shy about dates, have trouble being open or frank, or have a hard time refusing unreasonable requests or generally just saying no. Such people often profit from assertive training (Chapter 8). The *Marital Pre-Counseling Inventory* (Stuart & Stuart, 1973) is a questionnaire completed by clients prior to beginning marriage counseling. This includes ways they get along and interact, likes and dislikes, goals, how time is spent, resources, interests, decision making, ways of communicating, sexual behavior, and ways of managing the children. A similar questionnaire for family counseling, the *Family Pre-Counseling Inventory* (Stuart & Stuart, 1975), has separate forms for adolescents, father, and mother. It covers similar topics as the marital inventory, as well as interactions among family members and perceptions of self and others.

The practitioner must be careful not to assign too much validity to the responses to questionnaires or tests, either those mentioned in this text or any others. Rather, the results should be perceived as more behavior, information, and sources of ideas and hypotheses to be pursued, qualified, and correlated with other behavior. For a client may understand a question differently from what a practitioner expects or mean something different by an answer than the practitioner would infer. There is also room for many cultural, social, age, and sex biases. For example, men often indicate less anxiety on the Fear Survey Schedule than women. This may be because they experience less anxiety and/or simply report it as less.

Information of this sort is used to determine what in the *present* affects the client's behaviors. What stimuli or situations elicit behaviors or make more probable certain behaviors will occur? What are the results or consequences of these behaviors? How do the various behaviors interrelate? What are the learning contingencies that are operative? What are the basic behavioral excesses and deficits?

All behavior or problems are broken down into component behaviors that are clearly defined and measurable. If a person reports being generally depressed, we do not have a standard treatment for depression. Rather, treatment depends on the behavioral assessment that may indicate the person receives inadequate reward from work, feels anxious in social situations, or gets taken advantage of easily.

Behaviors are defined in terms of how they are measured, objective descriptions that others can observe and verify. Rather than calling a child hyperactive, we may speak of how many times he leaves his seat during a class period. Ayllon and Azrin (1968b, p. 44) describe a case in which a social worker concluded on the basis of an interview that a female mental patient was incapable of independent functioning. Yet behavioral records from the ward showed the patient regularly bathed herself, brushed her teeth, dressed herself, made her bed, and worked six hours per day without disrupting others. What did the social worker mean by "independent functioning?" It would have been better if the social worker had stated the assessment in terms of measured behaviors.

A general issue is that it is often possible to change one set of behaviors without changing another set, even though they seem related or seem to be measures of a common problem. Fear, for example, may be measured by verbal report, *approach-avoidance behavior* (how close the client will go to the feared situation), and physiological measures. These behavioral measures of fear are relatively independent, and one can be altered without changing the others (Hodgson & Rachman, 1974; Rachman & Hodgson, 1974). Thus a person may report no longer being fearful of snakes, but refuse to get any closer to them. Or a person may handle a snake with no physiological increase in arousal, yet report still being afraid of snakes.

Realizing the independence of different behaviors, the practitioner should use a variety of different behavioral measures and be cautious about over-generalizing from one measure. This is particularly true of the client's verbal report, which can be easily altered without there being any other behavioral change. Rewarding a person for reporting changes in problematic behaviors may only be affecting the verbal behavior of reporting changes, when, in fact, such changes may not be taking place or are taking place to a lesser degree than reported. Verbal report is often biased by the client's attempt to maintain some image or please the practitioner.

It generally is desirable to measure the frequency with which the behavior to be modified occurs in different situations. With smoking, for example, the behavior modifier would want to know how much the person smokes in situations such as cocktail parties and after dinner. Such data provide *baselines* (relatively steady rates of behavior) that can be used later to judge the effectiveness of the modification procedure. The frequencies also provide information about which contexts or problems should receive the major emphasis and what would be a reasonable first step in the change program. Getting objective measures of the frequencies of behaviors may also reduce misperceptions. Without counting, a teacher may over-estimate how often a particular behavior occurs in a classroom, because the behavior is one he particularly dislikes. Without counting, a person may under-estimate the amount of alcohol he consumes each week. In *time-sampling* the frequency of a behavior is recorded during short intervals at various times. This way, we can occasionally measure a frequent behavior, rather than keep track of every time it occurs. Time-sampling also facilitates keeping information on a large number of people at one time, as in a classroom or hospital ward, as we can just sample each person's behavior at different times.

Often clients are asked to keep counts on their own behavior, a process called *self-monitoring*. This may be done using graphs, checklists, or marks in a pocket notebook. For example, a person may weigh himself each morning and put this on a graph on the refrigerator door. A popular self-monitoring device is a wristcounter, such as golfers use. This counter, worn like a wristwatch, can be used to count each occurrence of a behavior such as smoking a cigarette, pulling a beard, biting a fingernail, or thinking a self-depreciating thought. Sometimes self-monitoring is sufficient for some behavior change, although often it is not, for self-monitoring makes the person more aware of doing the behavior, a good first step to self-control. If this awareness is coupled with a dissatisfaction of the frequency the behavior is occurring plus the ability to change the frequency, then behavior change may result. Thus Maletzky (1974) was able to produce dramatic behavioral changes in a variety of behaviors (e.g., repetitive scratching, fingernail-biting, facial tics) by having the people count the behaviors using wristcounters and graph the frequencies and progress. Rozensky (1974) reported a greater effect on reducing cigarette smoking if the person recorded the cigarette before smoking rather than after. Thus self-monitoring is a useful assessment procedure, which may produce some behavioral change. In those cases where insufficient change results from the monitoring, we add the appropriate behavior modification program.

Kanfer and Saslow (1969) offer a diagnostic outline which consists of seven major components:

1. INITIAL ANALYSIS OF THE PROBLEM SITUATION. Determine (a) which behaviors are considered problematic because they occur in excess in frequency, intensity, or duration; (b) which behaviors are considered problematic because they fail to occur with sufficient frequency, adequate intensity, or appropriate form; and (c) which behaviors the patient can do particularly well.
2. CLARIFICATION OF THE PROBLEM SITUATION. Next, put the various behaviors into a more global picture by specifying the situations in which they occur, the consequences of the behaviors, and the probable effects of changing the behaviors.
3. MOTIVATIONAL ANALYSIS. Specify the events that are rewarding and punishing to the client and their effects in different situations.
4. DEVELOPMENTAL ANALYSIS. Delineate the effects of any physiologi-

cal limitations of the client, the effects of the client's current sociocultural milieu and any past changes in this milieu, and earlier behavioral problems.
5. ANALYSIS OF SELF-CONTROL.   Determine what behaviors the client can control and in which situations.
6. ANALYSIS OF SOCIAL RELATIONSHIPS.   Specify what people the client interacts with, how he behaves toward them, and how they behave toward him.
7. ANALYSIS OF THE SOCIAL-CULTURAL-PHYSICAL ENVIRON-MENT.   Analyze the client's environments in terms of the norms and the limitations they put on the client.

SPECIFYING TERMINAL BEHAVIORS

In a behavior modification program it is necessary to objectively specify the *target behaviors,* the terminal behaviors that are to be produced for different conditions. It is not sufficient, and it is ambiguous, for a clinician to say that his goal is "self-actualization" or "reorganization of self." The clinician must describe what behaviors the client would have to demonstrate for the clinician to attribute to the client something like self-actualization. Once the behaviors have been specified, it is much easier to decide on the procedures to produce the target behaviors, as well as to know when the goal has been achieved.

Similarly, it is a poor educational objective to say the terminal behavior is to be a "good understanding of algebra." Rather, the educator should specify exactly what behavior he wants—for example, being able to solve quadratic equations and to graph any linear equation. Mager (1962, p. 53) gives the following summary for preparing instructional objectives:

1. A statement of instructional objectives is a collection of words or symbols describing one of your educational intents.
2. An objective will communicate your intent to the degree you have described what the learner will be DOING when demonstrating his achievement and how you will know when he is doing it.
3. To describe terminal behavior (what the learner will be DOING):
   a: Identify and name the over-all behavior act.
   b. Define the important conditions under which the behavior is to occur (givens or restrictions, or both).
   c. Define the criterion of acceptable performance.
4. Write a separate statement for each objective; the more statements you have, the better chance you have of making clear your intent.
5. If you give each learner a copy of your objectives, you may not have to do much else.

The behavioral objectives should generally be stated in small, progressive steps—sequences of immediate goals on the way to long-range objectives. The target behavior for a nursery schoolboy may be for him to be "social"—that is, spend more of his time playing with others. The immediate goals may be a sequence such as (1) the boy watching the others playing games, (2) the boy playing for five minutes with another child, (3) the boy playing for ten minutes with another child, (4) the boy playing for ten minutes with more than one other child, and so forth. By taking small steps the behavior can be gradually changed and the amount of failure minimized, for the practitioner becomes quickly aware of any necessary changes in procedure.

ETHICS

All change agents, regardless of their theoretical model, are faced with a wide range of ethical questions. Choosing not to work with a client is an ethical issue. Choosing to minimize your influence on a client, and thus give greater weight to other sources of influence, is an ethical issue. Choosing a model or approach that does not deal with your influence as a change agent is an ethical issue.

The choice of terminal behaviors necessarily involves value judgments. Why is one target behavior chosen over another? Why is it better for the child to be social than non-social? Similarly, the choice of procedures to reach a goal often involves ethical issues. For example, if a person is an alcoholic who can be helped, but the treatment is unpleasant, such as aversive counterconditioning where electric shock might be paired with drinking (see Chapter 6), to what extent do the results of treatment justify the treatment procedures?

Basically, behavior modification does not specify a moral system. It is an amoral, not immoral, technology. It is concerned with variables affecting behavior change independent of the ethical issues that arise at various decision points. A strength of behavior modification is that it specifies its procedures and goals and thus clarifies and spotlights the ethical issues that must be confronted. Many behavior modifiers (e.g., Begelman, 1975; Davison & Stuart, 1975; Stuart, 1975) are raising and discussing a variety of ethical issues related to behavior modification practice. My personal bias is that at this level I cannot rationally defend any particular ethical system, but rather choose to emphasize the importance of being aware of the range of ethical issues that must be confronted.

The field of learning and motivation not only deals with behavior change once certain ethical decisions are made, but it is also concerned with how a person acquires a particular ethical system and how this affects his ethical behavior and decisions. This makes the discussion of ethical choices even more complex, for it carries us into the study of the influences on behavior that occur prior to the point we may have arbitrarily placed the ethical decision. Discussions of ethics are often controversial; but discussion of how a person may come to acquire certain ethical positions (e.g., Skinner, 1971) is often more threatening and controversial.

In practice, ethical decisions are made all along the way, perhaps according to some cultural or personal norms or some idea of how to help the client become happier or more fulfilled. The client can often be involved in the decisions about goals and procedures. Or the pratitioner may emphasize self-control and giving the client more skills, alternatives, and some sense of freedom. Finally, it is important to always keep in mind that although we may talk about undesirable *behavior,* meaning undesirable in terms of some ethical system, we do not want to go past there and talk about an undesirable *person.*

One important ethical issue that often arises is to what extent do you change a person to match a situation and to what extent do you change the situation. For example, in some cases it may be better to change the classroom materials and curriculum than to use behavior modification to increase the students' motivation in the existing system. In the last couple of years there have been a couple of poor programs, unfortunately called behavior modification, that were set up in prisons to coerce the prisoners into obeying the existing prison system, when actually the prison system needed to be changed. On the other hand, many cases exist in which the situation cannot be changed and/or it seems desirable to primarily change the person's behavior to the situation.

Another ethical issue that has been popular in behavior modification in the last few years concerns the treatment of homosexuality. Some people in our culture perceive homosexuals as deviants who need to be changed for their own good and the good of society. Some behavior therapists respond that they will only treat homosexuals who wish to change. Other behavior therapists, however, argue that in our culture there is such strong social prejudice and conditioning against homosexuality, that there is little free choice about being a homosexual or not, even if the client feels there is. Thus these practitioners prefer not to help a person change from being a homosexual, but prefer to help the person adjust better to being a homosexual (e.g., Davison, 1976). My bias is to try to remain aware of these arguments and the subtleties involved and consider each case individually.

Thus the choice of the goals for a behavior change program is sometimes more complex than it first seems. One must carefully consider the many implications of producing any behavior change, in terms of the person, the culture, and the related ethics. And of course, sometimes you run across things you did not consider. For example, one program (Goldstein, 1974) involved a counselor trying to increase "paying attention" in school in a Navajo child. The counselor began with trying to increase eye contact, a common first step in similar programs. But the child began running away from school. A probable reason for this is that in the Navajo creation account there is a terrible monster called He-Who-Kills-With-His-Eyes. So children learn to avert their eyes to avoid bringing harm to others; and in this culture a stare implies sexual or aggressive assault.

SUMMARY

Behavioral assessment involves specifying the problem in terms of behaviors, including behavioral deficits and excesses. The behaviors are defined, as much as possible, in ways that are readily observed and measured, being careful not to rely too heavily on any one measure, particularly verbal report. Assessment involves determining the frequencies with which behaviors occur in various situations, the consequences of the behaviors, and interrelationships among behaviors. Information for assessment comes from such possible sources as observation of the client, self-report of the client (including written reports such as assessment tests and daily logs), role-playing, physiological measures, and reports from other people who know the client. Similarly, goals of the change program are specified, as much as possible, in terms of measurable behaviors, often involving a sequence of intermediate steps leading to the final terminal behaviors. Ethical issues must be recognized all along the way from choosing whether to deal with a problem, to the choice of goals, to the choice of change procedures.

THOUGHT QUESTIONS

1. If as a clinician a client spoke of being generally depressed and feeling as a social misfit, what assessment procedures might you employ to behaviorally delineate the exact nature of the problem? What would be one possible example of a behavioral specification of this problem?
2. If as a school counselor a teacher reports that the students in his fourth grade classroom are too unruly, what procedures would you use to behaviorally assess this problem? Give examples of possible behavior problems you might discover.
3. Consider your answers to the first two questions. What would be examples of good behavioral objectives for each of these problem areas? Give sequences of steps leading to each goal.
4. Practice self-monitoring one of your behaviors for a few days. What did you learn? To what extent and in what way do you deceive yourself in the situations you monitored? Did the monitoring affect the frequency of the behavior? Why? What suggestions can you make to someone who will try self-monitoring?
5. To what extent can you interact with people without categorizing them in some sense? Spend a day trying not to lable or judge people. What did you learn from this? What are the practical implications of what you learned? For a very hard exercise, try spending a day in which you have no opinions about anything.

6. How reliable is a client's verbal report? What could be done to make it more reliable?
7. In a clinical setting where the practitioner works one-to-one with a client, what are important or useful properties of the counseling relationship? Express your answers in terms of well-defined measurable behaviors.
8. What is the best way for you to remain aware of the range of ethical issues you must consider in any change program?
9. Consider the various points of view discussed in the text about working with homosexuals. What is your position? Why? What if the client were 35? 20? 15? 10? What difference does it make if the client is male or female? Why?
10. How do you as a parent raise your children to do well in a culture that, from your ethical system, is different from what it should be?

SUGGESTED READINGS

Cautela, J. R. Behavior analysis forms for clinical intervention. Champaign, Ill.: Research Press, 1977.

Ciminero, A. R., Calhoun, K. S., & Adams, H. E. (eds.) Handbook of behavioral assessment. New York: Wiley, 1977.

Goldfried, M. R. & Kent, R. N. Traditional versus behavioral personality assessment: A comparison of methodological and theoretical assumptions. Psychological Bulletin, 1972, 77, 409–420.

Goldfried, M. R. & Sprafkin, J. N. Behavioral personality assessment. Morristown, N.J.: General Learning Press, 1974.

Hersen, M. & Bellack, A. S. (eds.). Behavioral assessment: A practical handbook. Elmsford, N.Y.: Pergamon Press, 1976.

Mager, R. F. Goal analysis. Belmont, Calif.: Fearon Publishers, 1972.

Mager, R. F. Preparing instructional objectives. Belmont, Calif.: Fearon Publishers, 1962.

Mash, E. J. & Terdal, L. G. (eds.). Behavior-therapy assessment. New York: Springer, 1976.

Thomas, E. J. (ed.). Behavior modification procedure: A sourcebook. Chicago: Aldine, 1974.

Wolpe, J. Theme and variations: A behavior therapy casebook. Elmsford, N.Y.: Pergamon Press, 1976. Section III.

# 3

Respondent Conditioning and Counterconditioning

Someone smiling at us produces a pleasant feeling. Pictures of good food may literally cause our mouths to water. In one type of fetishism a man is sexually aroused by the sight of a woman's shoe. A woman with an automobile phobia may become anxious when she sees a car. Why should these stimuli (smiles, pictures of food, women's shoes, automobiles) elicit these particular responses (a pleased feeling, salivation, sexual arousal, anxiety)? It is not instinctual that these stimuli elicit these responses; hence it probably is learned.

Perhaps one reason a smile now elicits a pleased feeling is that in a person's learning history the stimulus of a smile was associated with other stimuli, such as affection, which produced a pleased feeling. The stimulus of the image of the food was associated with the stimulus of the taste of the food, with the taste eliciting salivation. Eventually the image of the food came to elicit salivation. Similarly, the sight of a woman's shoe may have been paired with sexually arousing stimuli such as from masturbation. The image of an automobile may have been paired with an anxiety-producing stimulus such as seeing a close relative die in an automobile accident. The learned associations may have been gradually built up over time, as in the case of the smile and affection, or may have followed a single dramatic learning experience, as in the case of the automobile accident.

RESPONDENT CONDITIONING

This type of learning is called *respondent conditioning,* the learning model in which one stimulus, as the result of being paired with a second stimulus, comes to elicit a response it did not elicit just previously. Usually this new response is similar to the response previously elicited only by the second stimulus. In this model the first stimulus is called the *conditioned stimulus* (CS) and the response it comes to elicit is called the *conditioned response* (CR), while the second stimulus is called the *unconditioned stimulus* (UCS) and the response it already elicited is called the *unconditioned response* (UCR). Figure 1 illustrates this for the case of the child who is gradually

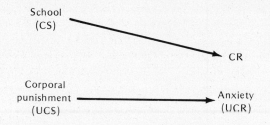

School
(CS)

CR

Corporal
punishment   Anxiety
(UCS)   (UCR)

FIGURE 1.   Respondent Conditioning of Anxiety

developing a dislike for school (CS) because the teacher emphasizes the use of corporal punishment (UCS), which makes the child anxious and fearful (UCR). I have had a couple of cases in which this was the first step for the children developing school phobias.

Numerous theories account for respondent conditioning (see Mikulas, 1974b, p. 98); but the following is satisfactory for our present purposes: Through association of the CS and UCS, the CS comes to provide information about the occurrence of the UCS. The more probable it is the UCS will follow the CS, the stronger the respondent conditioning and the more probable it is the CR will follow the CS. After the CR begins to occur, it may be rewarded or punished (Chapter 7), which affects its occurrence. In this sense the CR is often a response the person makes to prepare for the UCS. I was in a restaurant in which the lights would dim (CS) just before you would feel a blast from the air conditioner (UCS) because of the high energy requirements for the onset of the air conditioner. The scantily clad waitresses would shiver or cover their shoulders (CR) automatically when the lights dimmed. Respondent conditioning is often called *classical conditioning* and sometimes *Pavlovian conditioning,* although there is ambiguity in these terms (Hebb, 1956).

It is important to realize how prevalent respondent conditioning is in human behavior, particularly as it relates to emotional affect. Consider all the things that please or displease you and all the situations that elicit emotions such as affection, sexual arousal, anger, anxiety, or frustration. Consider how you differ in these areas from other people you know or people from different times or different cultures. Although some of these responses may be largely innate, such as some reactions to physical pain, most of these reactions are learned, primarily by respondent conditioning. Respondent conditioning in humans often is mediated by language. If a friend tells you that George is a "racist," then perhaps some of your emotional affect to the word "racist" will become associated to your image or memory category of George. Respondent conditioning is often complex, involving more than associations between one particular CS and one particular UCS. Thus a person may have negative feelings around older, male authority figures based on experiences with his father, two elementary school teachers, and a local policeman. Or a person may have bad associations to bars in one part of town based on one personal experience, stories from friends, and newspaper accounts. A person's present reactions to certain situations may be based on such a complex set of experiences that the person can not readily remember them, and they may be extremely difficult to trace back historically. Fortunately, since behavior modification is ahistorical, this is not necessary. Rather, we would determine the person's current reactions to specific situations and use our knowledge of respondent conditioning to change undesired reactions.

Let us consider a few more examples. In a classic study Watson and Rayner (1920) made a loud noise behind 11-month-old Albert whenever he reached for a white rat. This noise (UCS) was frightening (UCR) to Albert and resulted in a fear (CR) of rats (CS), as well as of other furry objects. A woman had two painful childbirths, so that she became anxious when she learned she was pregnant again. Some teenagers take up smoking tobacco even though the initial reaction to smoking may be aversive. Here the associations to smoking, through sources such as peers and advertisements, make smoking desirable. Chapter 7 deals with the effects of rewards (reinforcement) and punishments on behavior. In human behavior most of the things that are rewarding (e.g., attention, approval, money, good grades) or punishing (e.g., ostracism, criticism) acquired their affect through respondent conditioning and are called *conditioned reinforcement* and *conditioned punishment* (see Mikulas, 1974b, p. 103).

Three important variables affecting respondent conditioning are (1) temporal order of the stimuli, (2) interstimulus interval, and (3) response dominance. *Temporal order* refers to the fact that you generally get the best conditioning if the CS precedes the UCS *(forward conditioning);* while you generally get little or no conditioning if the UCS precedes the CS *(backward conditioning).* Early attempts at treating alcoholism involved making the person sick and then having him drink an alcoholic drink. This is backward conditioning, which probably decreased the effectiveness of the program.

Backward conditioning, however, does work in some situations, such as those discussed below under response dominance; but the best approach is to establish forward conditioning. Also in some situations, the CS and UCS occur together, not one before the other. This may be inevitable, as when you cannot separate a person from one of his characteristics, and may readily produce respondent conditioning.

Assuming forward conditioning, the *interstimulus interval,* refers to the amount of time from the onset of the CS to the onset of UCS. Generally, with many exceptions, you usually get the best respondent conditioning with an interstimulus interval of about one-half second. Although conditioning may occur with much longer intervals (e.g., nausea from food poisoning may condition to the taste of the food that occurred many hours earlier), in most behavior modification programs, one-half second seems optimal.

Before conditioning, both the CS and the UCS elicit responses. However, people seldom list the initial response to the CS, for it is usually relatively minor in importance to the UCR and the later CR. *Response dominance* refers to the relative strengths of the responses elicited by the CS and UCS before they are paired, the relative strengths of R_1 and UCR in Figure 2. Now what happens when we pair the CS and the UCS? If R_1 and UCR are

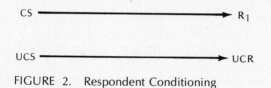

FIGURE 2.   Respondent Conditioning

compatible, both stimuli may come to elicit both responses. If the responses are incompatible, the conditioning will tend toward both stimuli eliciting the dominant response. Since the UCR is usually dominant to R_1, R_1 is usually not even mentioned and we have the result shown in Figure 1. However, if R_1 were dominant to the UCR, the conditioning may go the other way, backward conditioning. If you have a fear of snakes and I throw a snake in your lap and tell you to relax, I will probably get anxiety associated with the word "relax" rather than relaxation associated with snakes. Response dominance is the critical component to counterconditioning, which is discussed later. Although the concept of response dominance is important in respondent conditioning, there is currently little research on it.

Other variables of respondent conditioning include that the more times the CS and UCS are associated (CS predicts UCS) the more the learning; within limits you often get better learning with a strong UCS than a weak UCS; and you get poorer learning if you have the learning trials (CS-UCS pairing is a trial) too close together.

APPLIED RESPONDENT CONDITIONING

Establishing a new response by respondent conditioning is often part of a behavior modification program. Consider a person who is not sexually aroused by what he considers desired heterosexual cues, but is only aroused by cues he considers undesirable, such as an unusual sexual fantasy or homosexual stimuli. If such a person is not offended by masturbation, we may gradually pair the desired heterosexual cues (e.g., imagined scenes, photos) with the sexual arousal associated with masturbation (e.g., Marquis, 1970). We would probably begin with the stimuli that already elicit sexual arousal and gradually change from these to the new desired stimuli. Then as the person later engages in sexual behavior in the presence of the desired stimuli, the natural forms of respondent association will take over. The respondent conditioning here is used to overcome an initial obstacle, get things started, and turn the process over to the regular course of events.

Enuresis (bedwetting) is a problem affecting many children at all ages, including about 10 percent of six-year-old children. In addition to being a problem by itself, it also leads to other problems such as anxiety and guilt. A possible component of some enuresis is that the child has a small bladder capacity and poor development of related muscles so that the child urinates more both during the day and at night (Yates, 1975, chap. 3). Treatment then often involves teaching the child to have a larger bladder capacity by rewarding him during the day for going for longer and longer times without urinating. In a few cases the enuresis is because of excessive anxiety in the child and reducing the anxiety eliminates the enuresis.

But the most common approach for dealing with enuresis is the *bell and pad* or *urine-alarm* procedure (Mowrer & Mowrer, 1938). The logic is that internal cues of the bladder and related muscles are too weak to awaken the child at night so that he may go to the bathroom before wetting the bed. Treatment uses a specially constructed bed pad that when moistened by urine sounds a bell or buzzer and wakes the child up. (Such devices are sold by Wards and Sears.) The child now also begins inhibiting more urination as the bell rings. Since increased muscle tension (CS) precedes urination and bell (UCS), which wakes up the child and inhibits more urination (UCR), then by respondent conditioning eventually the muscle tension alone will wake the child and inhibit bedwetting. Thus the child is taught to respond to the internal cues that most people use to control urination. This is a fast and relatively effective procedure by itself and couples well with training in increasing bladder capacity. It has also been successfully used with enuretic adults (Turner & Taylor, 1974). There are other explanations for how the bell and pad procedure works (see Doleys, 1977; Lovibond, 1964), such as the child learning to wake up to avoid the bell or buzzer.

Azrin, Sneed, and Foxx (1974) improved on this urine-alarm method by adding training in inhibitory control, rewards for correct urination, training in rapid awakening, increased fluid intake to increase the response rate, self-correction of accidents, and practice in toileting. They reported significantly reducing bedwetting after one night of such intensive training.

A spectacular example of respondent conditioning is Efron's (1957) report of treating an epileptic. Most epileptics can detect the onset of a seizure by a subjective aura that precedes the seizure. Efron found that one of his female clients could inhibit her seizures by inhaling the odor of jasmine during the early stages of the aura. Efron then respondently conditioned the smell to the sight of a bracelet. Then she could inhibit the seizure by staring at the bracelet. Eventually, just thinking about the bracelet could inhibit seizures. Interestingly, looking at or thinking about the bracelet also elicited a subjective sense of smelling jasmine. In terms of latency of effectiveness, the direct odor was faster than seeing the bracelet, which was faster than thinking about the bracelet. Eventually, the client would just have spontaneous experiences of the odor of jasmine; but by then she was no longer having any seizures. This suggests the whole process moved further back so that pre-seizure cues triggered off the sense of jasmine and inhibited seizures. (This is a common sequence in many self-control programs in which initially conscious components eventually slide out of consciousness.) Finally, the occasional smell of jasmine disappeared and there were still no more seizures. The generality of this case study to other epileptics needs considerable more research.

Although there are situations, such as those above, in which a new response needs to be established by respondent conditioning, more often in behavior modification it is a matter of changing or eliminating an undesired behavior. In respondent conditioning there are two ways of dealing with undesired behaviors: extinction and counterconditioning.

EXTINCTION

Respondent conditioning is accomplished by establishing a contingency (relationship) between the CS and the UCS: the CS predicts to a certain degree the onset of the UCS. If we terminate this contingency so that the CS is not associated with the UCS, eventually the CS will no longer elicit the CR. This process is called *extinction*. If a small child is scratched (UCS) by a cat (CS) and hurt (UCR), then the child may develop a fear (CR) of cats. If the child now encounters cats without anything bad happening, the fear may extinguish. Sometimes following extinction, the CR may gain in strength over time. This is *spontaneous recovery*. However, in practical situations, this is usually minimal; and with further extinction the CR will no longer reappear.

There are basically two ways of carrying out extinction: gradual and not gradual. The gradual approach consists of moving through a sequence of steps, called a *hierarchy*, toward the object or situation that elicits the strongest CR. The alternative is to bypass most of these intermediate steps and confront the final situation right away. (Actually these are not two different approaches, but two points on a continuum of how many steps there are until approaching the final situation.) For example, if a child had a fear of the water at the beach, a gradual approach would involve slowly approaching the water, perhaps first playing on the beach 20 feet away from the water, then playing 10 feet away, then at the edge of the water, then putting feet in the water, and so forth. The non-gradual alternative may be to put or carry the child into the water until the fear extinguishes.

Although extinction is applicable to any respondently conditioned response, it is most used with anxieties and fears. People are continually confronted with situations that elicit some anxiety, such as standing up to the boss, making a presentation before a class, or talking about something personal. If the person can approach and be in the anxiety situation without anything unpleasant happening, then some of the anxiety should extinguish. The following are some general guidelines for using a gradual approach to the extinction of anxiety and fears: First, it is necessary to establish a hierarchy of steps toward the feared object or situation. It is generally better to have too many steps than too few. Second, it is desirable to encourage, motivate, or reward the person for going through the hierarchy. However, the person should move through the hierarchy at a comfortable pace, extinguishing most of the anxiety at each step before moving on. Finally, it is often useful to provide the person with a way to reduce the anxiety while all this is taking place—perhaps by teaching the person how to relax, having the person imagine pleasant scenes, or having the person pretend to be someone who would not be anxious in this situation. These aids, plus any rewards the person receives, help to reduce anxiety, provide motivation, and produce some counterconditioning, as discussed later. A good variation of the above is to first have the person gradually go through the hierarchy of steps in his imagination and then in real life, the latter called *in vivo*.

The non-gradual approach to extinguishing fears involves immediately confronting the feared situation. If a child learning to ride a bicycle falls off and hurts himself, his parent may have him get right back up and try again. If a person feels anxious about dancing in front of others in a nightclub, he may force himself to get up and do it. This approach often works, but sometimes the resulting anxiety is too great and the person ends up more anxious rather than less anxious. Therefore, my bias is to generally favor the gradual approach, which although slower is also safer. A variation of the non-gradual approach involves bombarding the person with the anxiety-producing stimuli and/or keeping the person in the anxiety situation without escape. This approach is called *flooding* and will be discussed in Chapter 4.

As will be seen throughout this text, most behavior modification procedures can, to some degree, be carried out in the imagination (see Chapter 9).

Extinction carried out in this way is called *covert extinction* (Cautela, 1971). There is currently little research in this area, but the following is an example: Götestam and Melin (1974) used covert extinction with four female amphetamine addicts (who were mainlining 100–200 mg., 3–5 times per day). They had the clients imagine situations in which they would inject themselves and had them imagine they felt no effect from the drug. Following one week of this treatment, about 100 trials, there was a decrease in the effect of the drug, even to the extent of the clients getting no effect when actually taking the drug. At a nine-month follow-up, three of the four women were not using amphetamines.

Respondent extinction can be seen to be a critical component of many therapeutic or change programs, although it is not conceptualized as extinction. Therapists, while maintaining a non-judgmental or permissive attitude, may encourage their clients to recall or discuss emotionally laden ideas or memories. Psychoanalysts, scientologists, and primal scream therapists may encourage their clients to recall and relive early painful experiences, perhaps real or unintentionally fabricated to suit the theory. People who feel uptight about some aspect of their body may attend a weekend marathon in which everyone goes around nude and each person tells sympathetic listeners about a problem that brings on uptightness. Peer-evaluation counseling may involve two non-professionals sitting down and gradually telling each other more and more personal-emotional things. As a spiritual tool, Ram Dass (Richard Alpert) may say to people, "anything you can think, feel, desire, fear, anything you can bring to your mind about any of these, that you have difficulty with, are embarrassed by, are made uncomfortable by sharing with me—share it with me." Some forms of meditation help people free themselves from emotional attachments by letting their thoughts and behaviors run their course while holding in a calm conscious space. My bias is that all these examples contain respondent extinction as a component and realizing this can facilitate whatever is to be accomplished.

COUNTERCONDITIONING

Counterconditioning is the reduction of undesired elicited responses by respondently conditioning incompatible responses to the eliciting situations. The first step is to determine the situations that elicit the undesired responses, as spiders may cause excessive anxiety in some people. The second step is to determine or establish ways to elicit a response incompatible with and dominant to the undesired response, such as some forms of relaxation may be to the spider anxiety. Finally, the incompatible response is respondently conditioned to the stimuli eliciting the undesired response, as stimuli producing relaxation may be paired with stimuli related to spiders. This counterconditioning is continued until the undesired response has been adequately reduced, usually until it no longer occurs.

Counterconditioning is often used to reduce unwanted emotional reactions such as anxiety, anger, or jealousy. Most clinical cases have an anxiety component that needs to be handled in some way. *Desensitization*, discussed in Chapter 5, is the counterconditioning of anxiety with relaxation. In other situations, the undesired response is a rewarding, approach response, as occurs in some aspects of alcoholism, drug-addiction, and over-eating. The sight of a bar may elicit a craving for a drink or the taste of one cigarette may lead to smoking another. In these cases, counterconditioning may involve conditioning in an unpleasant or aversive response to the stimulus situations eliciting the approach response. This is called *aversive counterconditioning* and will be discussed in Chapter 6.

It is important in counterconditioning that the incompatible response be dominant to the undesired response. Sometimes this is not a problem. For example, in aversive counterconditioning the aversiveness of electric shock or imagining unpleasant scenes may be dominant to the pleasing effects of having a second piece of pie. However, response dominance is often an issue. The way to insure the incompatible response is dominant is through the use of a hierarchy, similar to the gradual approach of respondent extinction. That is, rather than immediately starting with counterconditioning to the situation that most strongly elicits the undesired response, we begin with a situation which weakly elicits the undesired response. We then apply our counterconditioning to a sequence of situations, the hierarchy, that gradually approximates the situation which most strongly elicits the undesired response. In the case of a person with a fear of spiders, our counterconditioning using relaxation would begin with items low on the hierarchy (such as the word "spider"), work up the hierarchy through intermediate items (such as a picture of a spider), on to items at the top of the hierarchy (such as touching a live spider). The assumption is that the effects of the counterconditioning generalize (carry over to similar stimuli) up the hierarchy, thereby gradually reducing the strength of the undesired response elicited by the various situations. In the example of the spider anxiety, it may be that at the beginning of treatment the anxiety elicited by a picture of a spider or touching a live spider is dominant to any relaxation we can produce. But our relaxation is dominant to the anxiety elicited by the word "spider"; so we begin our counterconditioning there. Now as we countercondition out the anxiety to the word "spider" it is assumed the counterconditioning carries up the hierarchy and reduces somewhat the anxiety to the picture and the live spider. By the time we get to the picture, our relaxation is dominant to any remaining anxiety, which we can now countercondition out. And this counterconditioning generalizes up the remainder of the hierarchy. Thus if we choose a hierarchy of related items, have a sufficient number of items in our hierarchy, and do not move through the hierarchy too fast, we can insure that the incompatible response is dominant to the undesired response and counterconditioning will move in the desired way. This approach will be seen in greater detail when discussing desensitization (Chapter 5), but it is important to remember it applies to all counterconditioning.

Counterconditioning is not simply replacing the undesired response with the incompatible response. Rather, it is a matter of moving along a continuum from the undesired response toward the incompatible response. Counterconditioning may be stopped anywhere along the continuum with the usual stopping point being some neutral middle point. Thus with the spider anxiety we would probably countercondition until the person felt neutral (not anxious, not relaxed) toward spiders, although we could countercondition less and leave some anxiety or countercondition more so we get relaxation. Aversive counterconditioning may be part of a program with a female homosexual to reduce sexual arousal to females. We would probably stop at the point the client felt neutral to females rather than continuing until she felt aversion. On the other hand, if we had a male client who would go to jail if he exposed himself at a playground again, it may be desirable to continue the counterconditioning until aversion is elicited in this situation.

Although the explanation of counterconditioning used in this discussion is practical for behavior modification, on a theoretical level it should be considered highly tentative until considerable more research is done related to the basic assumptions. Guthrie (1935) was one of the first major theorists to consider counterconditioning, and his conceptualization was similar to how counterconditioning is described above. Wolpe (1958) introduced the concept of *reciprocal inhibition,* borrowed from physiology, to account for counterconditioning, primarily desensitization. The assumption is that counterconditioning generally involves one part of the nervous system physiologically inhibiting another part, as desensitization may involve the parasympathetic nervous system inhibiting the sympathetic nervous system. Critics (e.g., Wilson & Davison, 1971) of this concept of reciprocal inhibition to account for counterconditioning suggest that the concept is an unnecessary addition to our explanation and not well supported by physiological research. However, "reciprocal inhibition" is a common expression in behavior modification related to counterconditioning.

In both respondent extinction and counterconditioning, the client is presented with the CS or a gradual sequence of approximations to the CS. Procedurally, the only difference between the approaches is that in counterconditioning we present stimuli or training that leads to an incompatible response to be associated with the CS. This similarity between the two approaches allows some theorists to assume they are the same. Thus it is possible to argue that counterconditioning is simply extinction. The purpose of the incompatible response is for motivation and/or to facilitate the extinction process. Desensitization, as the most common example, may be seen as extinction rather than counterconditioning (e.g., Wilson & Davison, 1971). The role of relaxation is a way to motivate the client to work through the hierarchy and/or reduce anxiety so the client is in a better state for extinction.

On the other hand, my bias and the position of theorists such as Guthrie is that respondent extinction is counterconditioning. The assumption is that extinction is not the passive weakening of a behavior, but the learning of new, perhaps incompatible, behaviors. If this position is correct, then in counterconditioning you are providing the client with an incompatible behavior, while in extinctcon you are relying on the incompatible behavior occurring some other way. Hence counterconditioning is potentially more effective.

But whatever the theoretical explanation for counterconditioning and how it differs from extinction, it is clear what to do procedurally in applied situations. Next I turn to relaxation, the most commonly used response for counterconditioning anxiety.

RELAXATION

Teaching a client how to relax is often a powerful and needed therapeutic approach just in itself, for our culture provides more and more potential sources of stress and anxiety; and few people ever learn effective ways to relax. Thus many people report they are often anxious or uptight. This may be associated with specific fears, a racing mind, or inability to get to sleep easily. Also each year more research (e.g., Holmes & Masuda, 1972; Seligman, 1975) relates many physiological problems, such as colds, ulcers, and cancer, to the stress a person experiences and how the stress is handled. Thus relaxation training is a common part of many programs. It is often useful to introduce this training early in clinical sessions because it calms the client down, shows him you have some powerful tools at your disposal, and gives the client a sense that there are things *he* can do about his own behavior.

Thus several programs have been geared toward teaching people how to relax and use this as a self-control skill (Goldfried & Trier, 1974; Mikulas, 1976a; Sherman & Plummer, 1973). The people learn how to sense when they begin to feel anxious and learn how to relax instead. They learn how to handle stressful situations, as well as how to reduce specific problems such as tension headaches, nervous muscle movements, and anxiety-produced distortions in thought and perception. Learning to relax is also an important component in treating insomnia (Borkovec et al., 1975; Nicassio & Bootzin, 1974). For these reasons, the best type of relaxation procedure is one in which the client learns a skill of relaxing rather than has something done to him to make him relax (e.g., drugs).

The most-used relaxation training in behavior modification is some shortened variation (see Bernstein & Borkovec, 1973) of the muscle relaxation procedure developed by Jacobson (1938). This involves the client alternately tensing and relaxing various muscles while focusing his attention on the different feelings. With instruction and practice, the client learns how to relax himself "at will"; identify the onset of stress or anxiety earlier, which facilitates self-control; and generally become more aware of the muscles in his body, which may reduce a variety of problems, such as unconscious chewing on the tongue, headaches resulting from muscle tension in the neck and head, excessive wrinkling of the face, and poor posture.

A variation on this relaxation training is *cue-controlled relaxation* (Russell & Sipich, 1973) in which the person, while relaxed via muscle relaxation and focusing on his breathing, associates a word such as "calm" or "control" with the relaxed state. The person can then use this word to help cue in the relaxed state.

There are many other ways of training and producing relaxation (White & Fadiman, 1976) that may be useful with different clients, problems, or situations. Hypnosis, in addition to facilitating relaxation, can also be used to increase the client's motivation for parts of the program and may improve visualizing scenes in the imagination, if this is part of the treatment. On the other hand, hypnosis varies in effectiveness with clients and involves many dangers for the practitioner lacking substantial training. Autogenic training (Lindeman, 1973; Luthe, 1969) is a form of relaxation training similar to self-suggestion. It involves giving yourself such suggestions as "My right arm is heavy," "My heart beats calm and regular," and "My forehead is cool." Autogenic training packages well with biofeedback. Biofeedback (Chapter 7), as it relates to relaxation, involves the use of machines to tell clients how anxious or aroused they are in terms of some physiological measure such as muscle tension, skin resistance, or skin temperature. This biofeedback information helps the clients learn to relax and is particularly useful when a set of muscles requires specialized attention. Meditation is being used more in behavior modification (e.g., Berwick & Oziel, 1973; Boudreau, 1972); and besides facilitating relaxation it is also useful when the client needs to learn to calm his mind (e.g., insomnia, racing mind) or just generally get a little more perspective on his life.

Finally, drugs such as tranquilizers or breathing a mixture of oxygen and carbon dioxide (Ley & Walker, 1973) may be used to produce relaxation. Ideally, they would only be used as a temporary adjunct to the treatment program and would gradually be phased out. But however relaxation is produced, once a person is relaxed or can relax on cue, we can use relaxation to countercondition anxiety.

COUNTERCONDITIONING ANXIETY

Anxiety is the most common emotional reaction that is counterconditioned; relaxation is the most common incompatible response used to countercondition anxiety; and desensitization is the most common way to countercondition anxiety with relaxation. However, many other incompatible responses, elicited or facilitated by the practitioner, may be used to countercondition anxiety, such as laughter, assertive behavior, anger, music-elicited responses, eating, emotive imagery, and aversion relief. An incompatible response other than relaxation may be chosen because it is difficult to get the client to relax, the other response is already strong in the client's repertoire, or the other response is one that independently needs to be strengthened.

Laughter is a good response for counterconditioning anxiety, if the person can learn to laugh at himself or the situation. At first, it may be necessary for the client to alter the situation in his imagination to facilitate making it seem humorous. Ventis (1973) described a case of a coed who was anxious about attending a banquet at which she would encounter her ex-boyfriend. A humorous image involving the boyfriend was used for counterconditioning. After one session and a brief hierarchy she was able to attend the banquet that evening with little discomfort.

Assertive behavior is often used to overcome anxiety, for many people are anxious in situations in which they are unassertive. Learning to be appropriately assertive (see Chapter 8) may be an important part of social skill training with the client, as well as being a source of behaviors that will countercondition anxiety.

When using anger to countercondition anxiety we generally do not want to condition the person to feel anger in the anxiety situations. Rather we use the principle of counterconditioning that lets us stop at the intermediate neutral point. Goldstein and associates (1970) begin by having the client in the consulting room pair anger-arousing imagery, plus vocal and motor behavior, with imagined situations that elicit anxiety. Later, the client uses the anger-arousing imagined images for counterconditioning *in vivo* (real life) situations. The anger-arousing scenes can be used both for counterconditioning and as a self-control procedure for handling anxiety, these two functions often going together in counterconditioning. Butler (1975) used anger to countercondition a variety of fears in his client, including a fear of traveling more than about eight blocks from home (a form of agoraphobia, fear of open spaces). Treatment involved the client imagining an anxiety-provoking scene and responding with anger, angry verbalizations, plus vigorous muscular activity.

Lowe (1973) used the excitatory responses elicited by music to countercondition anxiety in a client who had trouble learning to relax. The client was a former rock guitarist who would get excited by particular music and could augment the excitement by imagining such things as he was performing the music.

In a classic study, Jones (1924) used eating as one of the responses to countercondition a fear of rabbits in three-year-old Peter. The rabbit was introduced in a cage in the far part of the room where Peter played and ate. Each day the rabbit was brought closer (a hierarchy) until it was out of the cage and in Peter's lap. This counterconditioning generalized to other furry objects that Peter had also been afraid of. (Jones was a student of Watson, whose conditioning of little Albert was mentioned at the beginning of the chapter.)

Emotive imagery is the counterconditioning of anxiety with images that arouse feelings such as pride, affection, self-assertion, or mirth. Therefore, it obviously overlaps with other counterconditioning approaches being discussed. So far it has primarily been used with children who are not easily trained to relax. With adults, emotive imagery may combine well with desensitization. The originators of the approach, Lazarus and Abramovitz (1962), treated a ten-year-old boy who feared the dark by using his passion for the radio series "Superman" and "Captain Silver." Treatment involved the boy imagining a story involving himself, Superman, and Captain Silver. In the story he imagined himself in situations that gradually became darker. At the end of the third session he was able, without anxiety, to picture himself alone in his bathroom with all the lights turned off, awaiting a communication from Superman. This treatment eliminated the fear of the dark and was accompanied by an improvement in school work and a decrease in insecurity.

Aversion relief refers to the offset of an aversive event, such as the offset of electric shock. This offset, assumed to be pleasant, can be paired with words such as "calm" or used to countercondition anxiety by pairing the offset with an anxiety situation. This approach has not been used much, particularly with the number of preferable alternative approaches. It comes up the most in situations where the onset of an aversive event is being used for aversive counterconditioning (Chapter 6). A form of aversion relief is *respiratory relief,* which is based on the relief following holding your breath. Treatment of anxiety would involve having the person hold his breath and then begin breathing when presented with an anxiety situation (e.g., Orwin et al., 1975).

New approaches to countercondition anxiety continually come up in the literature, and creative practitioners will find many other ways that suit their particular cases. Kass, Rogers, and Feldman (1973) report several cases in which they counterconditioned anxiety with responses specific to the different individuals. One woman became distressed at being called names, which then led to fighting. Treatment involved her imagining herself laughing at the person calling her names. Another client was anxious about being alone, rejected, or in crowds. This was counterconditioned with a scene in which she was lying in bed looking at new drapes. And in another case, job anxiety was counterconditioned with sitting up exercises.

OTHER COUNTERCONDITIONING

All of the logic and examples that apply to counterconditioning anxiety with relaxation also apply to the counterconditioning of other unwanted emotional responses such as anger, jealousy, or frustration. For example, Hearn and Evans (1972) used a desensitization-type approach in which relaxation was used to countercondition anger in student nurses. And Cotharin and Mikulas (1975) used a desensitization-type approach to reduce racially related emotional responses in high school students. Following this, white students could interact pleasantly with black students whom before they felt uncomfortable with and had to avoid.

Now relaxation is just one of many incompatible responses we can use to countercondition these unwanted emotional responses. We could use many of the incompatible responses mentioned above for counterconditioning anxiety. For example, Smith (1973) describes a case in which he used humor to countercondition anger. The client was a 22-year-old female who could not control her extreme anger responses with her husband and three-year-old son. The child's misbehavior generally elicited extreme rage, including screaming, breaking things, and physically attacking the child. A hierarchy of situations was constructed, and the items of the hierarchy were greatly exaggerated to make them humorous. Counterconditioning with this hierarchy reduced the anger the situations elicited, gave the client control over her temper, and allowed her to view anger eliciting situations more objectively.

In general then, we can probably countercondition any unwanted, conditioned, emotional response (e.g., anxiety, anger, racially related emotional responses) with any incompatible response (e.g., relaxation, humor). Since we can stop our counterconditioning at a neutral point, it often may not matter whether the incompatible response is desirable or not. All this gives the practitioner enormous flexibility in tailoring a counterconditioning program to his client's specific problems and skills. The choice of what incompatible responses to use for counterconditioning depends on which such responses the client already has in his repertoire or could readily learn and which responses would be profitable to learn for reasons more than counterconditioning (e.g., relaxation, assertive behavior), My bias is that most, if not all, changes in affect that occur in any non-physiological treatment program, regardless of the theory behind the treatment, is because of respondent extinction and/or counterconditioning. Seeing it from this perspective may result in the practitioner being more aware of the need to strengthen or establish incompatible responses and perhaps use a hierarchical approach.

Masters and Johnson have determined more about the human sexual response and its dysfunctions than anyone else in history. Their program for the treatment of sexual dysfunctions (Belliveau & Richter, 1970; Masters & Johnson, 1970) is still the classic work in this field; and many other programs (e.g., Hartman & Fithian, 1972) have drawn on their work in varying degrees and added other treatment components. The Masters and Johnson treatment program has basically two overlapping parts, educative counseling and behavioral assignments. The educative counseling involves general sex education, discussion of motivation to change, discussion of basic problems, and instruction in the treatment approach. This is coupled with history taking, general assessment, and physical examinations. The behavioral assignments consist of programs, geared toward the specific type of dysfunction, that the couple carries out with each other in private.

Although Masters and Johnson conceptualize their treatment program as a form of psychotherapy, the behavioral assignments are much like behavior modification with counterconditioning playing a large role. A major part of most of the treatment consists in eliciting the sexual response in a non-coital situation, then gradually moving through a hierarchy of steps leading to coitus while maintaining the sexual response. The implicit assumption is that the sexual response will gradually countercondition the responses (e.g., anxiety) which are impairing the sexual response in coitus. Thus a man with impotence, often unable to achieve or maintain an erection sufficiently for coitus, will first be stimulated to erection in a non-coitus situation. Then while maintaining and restimulating the erection, the male is gradually moved through a sequence of steps leading to coitus. A similar approach is used with a female with orgasmic dysfunction, seldom or never experiencing an orgasm. First the woman's sexual response is elicited in non-coitus situations. Then she moves through a sequence of stages toward coitus. Other things are involved in the treatment of these and other sexual dysfunctions, but counterconditioning seems to be a significant component.

Viewing the Masters and Johnson program from the behavior modification position suggests several ways the program can be improved (see Murphy & Mikulas, 1974). For example, in many cases anxiety is impairing the sexual response. Now Masters and Johnson are using the sexual response to countercondition the anxiety that is impairing the sexual response. This may often work, particularly with a good hierarchy. But sometimes the anxiety is too great. Many of the cases they report as failures are cases in which too much anxiety exists. This suggests the addition of something like desensitization to first reduce some of the anxiety. There is also a need for more individualizing of the hierarchies. For many people the first step in the behavioral assignment may be too anxiety producing. For others, the items in the hierarchy need to be geared more toward their specific problems. Masters and Johnson believe the sexual response will naturally occur if they can just remove the obstacles. A behavior modifier may go further and initiate or strengthen the sexual response to specific situations. This would probably involve respondent conditioning and perhaps the use of sexual fantasies, masturbation, vibrators, or pornography.

A case study by Davison (1968) will finish this section as it illustrates various aspects of counterconditioning. The client was a 21-year-old, unmarried male who was only sexually aroused by sadistic fantasies, involving torturing women, which he masturbated to about five times a week. He dated little and showed no interest in girls. The first step was for the therapist to argue against any disease interpretation of the client's unusual behavior.

This is common as the behavior modifier often has to reduce his client's fears about being inherently sick, abnormal, or evil. Davison's next step was counterconditioning: The client was instructed to masturbate while looking at pictures of sexy, nude women, using his sadistic scenes to occasionally help initiate or maintain arousal and erection. From these pictures the client slowly moved along a sequence of pictures of women with more and more clothes on and finally to imagined situations from real life. Now Davison was helping and encouraging the client to begin asking out girls. Finally, aversive counterconditioning was used to reduce the sexual arousal to the sadistic fantasies. This involved associating in the imagination a sadistic fantasy with an unpleasant image, such as drinking from a bowl of urine and feces. All of this produced a decrease in sadistic fantasies and a positive sexual feeling toward girls. Six months after treatment ended, the client used what he had learned to return to sadistic fantasies for a while and then reverse it back. At this point he found he had no need for sadistic fantasies and was involved in a relatively vigorous program of dating.

SUMMARY

Respondent conditioning is the learning model in which a stimulus situation comes to elicit a relatively new response or increase in response because of association with other stimulus situations. Formally, the conditioned stimulus (CS) comes to elicit the conditioned response (CR) because of the person learning that the CS is associated with (provides information about) the unconditioned stimulus (UCS), which elicits the unconditioned response (UCR). In most situations, respondent conditioning is best when the CS comes on about one-half second before the onset of the UCS and the UCR is dominant to the response originally elicited by the CS. Respondent conditioning is sometimes used in behavior modification to establish or strengthen a response, as in the treatment of enuresis or in building in sexual arousal to a situation. Undesired respondent behavior is changed by respondent extinction or counterconditioning, both of which may or may not be done gradually with a hierarchy of intermediate steps. Extinction consists in presenting the CS without its being paired with the UCS until the CR is suitably reduced. Counterconditioning consists in conditioning a desired response to the CS to gradually replace the undesired response, with a hierarchy often used to control response dominance. Practically, extinction and counterconditioning only differ in the degree to which the practitioner facilitates the occurrence of an incompatible response. Relaxation training, a useful procedure in itself, is also part of programs for the self-control and counterconditioning of responses such as anxiety. Anxiety can be counterconditioned with a range of incompatible responses, including relaxation, laughter, assertive behavior, anger, music-elicited responses, eating, emotive imagery, aversion relief, physical exercise, and sexual responses. Similar responses can be used for the counterconditioning of many other behaviors, including anger, jealousy, frustration, racially related emotional responses, and aspects of sexual dysfunction. Aversive counterconditioning is counterconditioning in which a response to an unpleasant stimulus, such as electric shock or imagining an aversive scene, is gradually conditioned to stimuli that elicit undesired, but pleasant approach behavior, as in parts of alcoholism or addiction to other drugs.

THOUGHT QUESTIONS

1. Define respondent conditioning, respondent extinction, and counterconditioning. What are the practical and theoretical differences among them? For each give a real life example you have observed.
2. Discuss the variables of respondent conditioning as they may relate to a case in which you are reducing anxiety with emotive imagery.
3. Describe at least five different ways to teach or produce relaxation in a client. For each give a situation in which this method would be the preferred approach.
4. Describe a hypothetical case in which you countercondition anxiety with a response other than one of those mentioned in the chapter. Why would you use this particular response for this case?
5. Describe a hypothetical case in which you use humor to countercondition jealousy.
6. Describe covert extinction using a hierarchy for the reduction of test anxiety.
7. Consider any of the things you value. To what extent may respondent conditioning have been involved in the learning of this value? Give possible examples. Does understanding part of the cause of the value affect the value itself? Why?

SUGGESTED READINGS

Bernstein, D. A. & Borkovec, T. D. *Progressive relaxation training: A manual for the helping professions.* Champaign, Ill.: Research Press, 1973.

Eysenck, H. J. & Beech, R. Counterconditioning and related methods. In Bergin, A. E. & Garfield, S. L. (eds.), *Handbook of psychotherapy and behavior change: An empirical analysis.* New York: Wiley, 1971.

Salter, A. *Conditioned reflex therapy.* New York: Farrar, Straus & Giroux, 1949. Capricorn paperback, 1961.

4 Flooding

In the last chapter I described two basic ways to change behavior based on respondent conditioning: counterconditioning and extinction. And each of these may be done gradually, using a hierarchy to slowly approach the situation that elicits the strongest response; or non-gradually, confronting the situations high on the hierarchy right away. This chapter deals with a variation of non-gradual extinction. Remember that respondent extinction consists of presenting the CS to the client over and over without pairing it with the UCS until the CR no longer occurs. The first time Carl was on a merry-go-round (CS) he fell off and hit his head on the pavement (UCS) causing much pain and discomfort (UCR). Now Carl has a basic fear (CR) of getting on a merry-go-round. A non-gradual extinction approach would consist of getting Carl on the merry-go-round and keeping him there while ensuring nothing bad happens to him.

FLOODING

The non-gradual extinction approach of *flooding* consists of rapidly exposing the client to the CS, while minimizing the client's escape from the CS. Hence the approach is sometimes called *response prevention*. Nesbitt (1973) reported the case of a 24-year-old female with an intense fear and aversion of escalators, which she had for seven years, originating from the time her relatives forced her on an escalator. Treatment consisted of getting her on an escalator, the first ride with the therapist and then alone. One half hour of this treatment reduced her fears. Six months later she experienced little anxiety when on escalators.

The key to flooding is the rapid exposure to the CS rather than more spaced presentations. This would correspond to continually keeping the woman on the escalator rather than taking breaks between rides. The assumption is that this approach will facilitate the extinction, perhaps because the person becomes too physically exhausted for the CR to occur, perhaps because the response prevention helps break down avoidance responses which do not have the time or opportunity to occur.

To date, flooding has almost exclusively been used with situations that elicit anxiety. A major advantage of flooding is that it is much faster than gradual approaches such as desensitization. A major disadvantage is that often it will increase the strength of the CR rather than extinguish it. If a child has a fear of dogs, forcing him to confront a lot of dogs may increase his fear rather than extinguish it. We do not know enough yet to be always able to predict whether the anxiety will increase or decrease. Hence my bias is to generally favor a gradual approach.

Although there has been a moderate amount of research on flooding (Morganstern, 1973; Smith et al., 1973), many unanswered questions still exist in a confounded, contradictory literature: What is the effect of how anxious the client is? What is the effect of the amount of anxiety elicited during treatment? What is the optimal duration of presentation of different anxiety situations? What are the differences between an imagined CS and an in vivo CS? To what extent may flooding be accomplished without letting anxiety occur? To the extent that flooding can be carried out with little or no anxiety, it may be possible to reduce some of the possible disadvantages of flooding, such as increasing the associated anxiety. Finally, flooding can be used to reduce avoidance responses without reducing the associated anxiety (Rachman & Teasdale, 1974). That is, because of the response prevention component, a person may learn via flooding not to avoid an anxiety situation, but still feel some anxiety. When would this be a desirable thing to do?

One problem area in which flooding initially seems effective is the treatment of obsessive-compulsive neurosis, conditioned anxiety generally associated with repetitive fixed thoughts (obsessions) and/or ritualistic motor behavior (compulsions) (Boulougouris & Bassiakos, 1973; Rachman et al., 1973). Rachman and his associates (1973) used a combination of flooding and modeling (Chapter 8). The modeling involved the therapist as a model doing the feared act. One of their cases was a 22-year-old female who for five years had a fear of "contamination" by dogs, which generalized to many areas of London. She avoided areas around London where she had been contaminated, and her fears led her to move repeatedly (five times in three years). She washed her hands at least 50 times a day, threw away large amounts of contaminated clothing (especially boots), and cleaned her whole house every day (including curtains, carpets, floors, and shelves). The treatment involved complete contamination of her environment in the treatment hospital, shopping expeditions in areas of the town she avoided, and response prevention of excessive washing. At the end of treatment, there was no evidence of excessive washing or cleaning rituals, but she still had some thoughts about contamination.

Flooding is a component of the treatment procedures of a variety of different therapies, including aspects of encounter groups, gestalt therapy, and primal therapy. It arises when clients are continually confronted with situations, memories, thoughts, impressions and criticisms by others, or any other source of anxiety they are not permitted to escape from, physically or psychologically. This is often accompanied by strong emotional reactions by the clients. In psychoanalysis, some of these reactions may be interpreted as *abreaction* or *catharsis,* both meaning the reduction of emotional tension because of reliving the experience that caused the tension. In different settings and with different client expectations, the emotion of the clients and/or the following emotional exhaustion may be associated with what are interpreted as early childhood memories, memories of previous lives, or metaphysical or religious experiences. Sargant (1959) suggests that in situations such as these, as well as in many types of religious and political conversion, the effect is because of emotion-produced suggestibility. That is, if a person has his emotions worked upon until he reaches an abnormal condition of anger, fear, or exaltation, and if this condition is maintained for a while, then the person may become more open to suggestions about new beliefs and behaviors.

Although flooding has primarily been used with anxiety-producing situations, it can also be used with other respondently elicited emotions. (Remember the generality of the respondent extinction and counterconditioning in the last chapter.) For example, Blanchard (1975) reported the case of a 27-year-old woman who had unpleasant experiences associated with the death of her fetus. This led to hatred and revulsion for pregnant women. The treatment included two one-and-a-half hour flooding sessions, which extinguished her hatred and fear.

IMPLOSIVE THERAPY

A variation of flooding developed by Stampfl and Levis (1967) is *implosive therapy* or *implosion* (Ayer, 1972; Frankel, 1972; Morganstern, 1973; Stampfl, 1970, 1975). Implosive therapy is flooding with these characteristics: (a) All presentations of anxiety situations are done by having the client imagine scenes. (Remember throughout this text that treatment based on imagined situations generalizes surprisingly well to in vivo situations.) (b) The imagined scenes are often ones of exaggerated or impossible situations designed to elicit as much anxiety as possible. (c) The scenes are often based on hypothesized sources of anxiety, some of which are psychodynamic in nature. These hypothesized sources of anxiety center around such things as hostility toward parental figures, rejection, sex, and dynamic concepts like Oedipal complex and death wish.

Treatment usually consists in first having the client imagine an anxiety-producing scene and realize that, although unpleasant, the anxiety is not unbearable. Then the client is given a sequence of high anxiety scenes to imagine, often in order of increasing anxiety, hence a hierarchy to some degree. This treatment, generally accompanied by strong emotional reactions of the client, is continued over a few treatment sessions until the anxiety is assessed to have extinguished.

A person with a fear of spiders might be told in detail to imagine a scene in which, when he bites into a sandwich, spiders come out of the sandwich and go into his mouth. The scene may continue with detailed descriptions of the spiders crawling around in the client's mouth and nose. Or a person who is afraid to fly in airplanes may be told to imagine a scene in which he is flying in a plane, the plane blows up, his body is torn into a lot of pieces, and he experiences the pieces of his body falling to the ground. The scene may continue with the person's funeral and a trip to hell. Hogan (1968) has described the types of scenes he uses in the treatment of snake phobias. These scenes include such images as a snake crawling in your lap, the snake biting your fingers, blood dripping from the fingers, squeezing the snake, the snake biting your face, the snake pulling your eye out and eating it, and the snake crawling into your eye socket and nose. Another scene might involve falling into a pit filled with thousands of snakes. Assuming the snake is a symbol of male sexuality, Hogan might have a female client imagine a large snake sexually violating her and mutilating her sexual organs.

There are two major problems in the use of implosive therapy. First, from the orientation of behavior modification, as discussed in this text, it is not clear why one would use hypothesized or psychodynamic sources of anxiety. Scenes of snakes attacking a female's sexual organs may make sense from a psychoanalytic orientation, but they do not currently follow from a behavioral-experimental orientation. The second problem, as would be expected from the discussion of flooding, is that although some clients are reported to improve following implosion (e.g., Hogan & Kirchner, 1967, 1968; Smith & Sharpe, 1970) other clients end up with more anxiety being built-in (e.g., Barrett, 1969; Fazio, 1970). For example, Barrett (1969) used implosion for the treatment of snake phobias in college students. For one student, the images of snakes became conditioned to having her eyes shut, as she did during treatment. She then consistently visualized snakes when she shut her eyes, had trouble sleeping, and could not attend course lectures. The literature and research on implosion is mixed (e.g., Morganstern, 1973); and it is difficult to determine the results of different variations of implosion by different practitioners with different problems in different types of clients.

An important issue is why implosive therapy, and related flooding procedures, is effective in some cases. The following are possible explanations: To a certain extent implosive therapy may be extinction as intended. But if it is extinction, why use such horrible scenes rather than real life ones? To what extent do these more anxiety scenes facilitate extinction? In practice implosion often involves the use of a small hierarchy; and the client is often asked to imagine alternative ways of responding to the anxiety scenes. This suggests that part of the effect may be due to counterconditioning. The client is often encouraged and given incentives to continue steps of the treatment, thus introducing elements of operant conditioning (Chapter 7). The high emotion experienced during treatment may make clients more suggestible, as discussed above, perhaps including suggestions they are improving. The high emotions may also produce a contrast effect between imagined and real life situations (Hodgson & Rachman, 1970). If you have just spent some time imagining spiders doing horrible things to you and are emotionally exhausted, you may not react much to the small spider on the sidewalk outside the clinic. Finally, there is "flight into health," meaning the sooner you get better, the fewer of these unpleasant treatments you will get. Suggestibility, contrast, and flight into health effects are generally transient, decreasing over time.

Overall, flooding and related procedures, such as implosive therapy, are fast approaches to extinguishing emotional reactions, primarily anxiety. However, in some cases more anxiety is built-in rather than extinguished. Research on when flooding is an effective and desirable treatment, the best way to carry it out, and how it works is contradictory and incomplete.

SUMMARY

Flooding is non-gradual respondent extinction in which the client is rapidly exposed to the CS while minimizing his escape from the CS. It has been primarily used in the treatment of anxiety, including some favorable initial results with obsessive-compulsive neurosis. Implosive therapy is a flooding procedure using exaggerated imagined scenes, often drawing on hypothesized (e.g., psychoanalytic) sources of anxiety. Flooding is usually faster than gradual approaches such as desensitization, often elicits various images and emotional reactions, and in some cases results in the clients becoming more anxious. Considerable research is needed on situations in which flooding is applicable and the optimal flooding procedures. When flooding appears effective, the results may be because of phenomena such as extinction, counterconditioning, operant conditioning, suggestibility, contrast, and flight into health.

THOUGHT QUESTIONS

1. What are the differences among counterconditioning, respondent extinction, flooding, and implosive therapy?
2. Give three different situations in which you would consider using flooding. Why?
3. Outline a flooding program for a person who is afraid of heights, using both imagined scenes and in vivo situations.
4. Describe the use of flooding with a hypothetical case in the reducing of an emotion other than anxiety, fear, or anger.
5. What are the pros and cons of using hypothesized sources of anxiety in imagined scenes, as in implosive therapy?
6. List three relatively unanswered questions about flooding. What is your best guess about the answers to these questions? Why?
7. Describe an experiment in which you could separate the following possible effects of flooding procedures: extinction, emotion-induced suggestibility, and contrast effects.

SUGGESTED READINGS

Morganstern, K. P. Implosive therapy and flooding procedures: A critical review. *Psychological Bulletin,* 1973, *79,* 318–334.

Smith, R. D., Dickson, A. L., & Sheppard, L. Review of flooding procedures (implosion) in animals and man. *Perceptual and Motor Skills,* 1973, *37,* 351–374.

Stampfl, T. G. & Levis, D. J. Essentials of implosive therapy: A learning-theory-based psychodynamic behavioral therapy. *Journal of Abnormal Psychology,* 1967, *72,* 496–503.

Desensitization

Although defined in various ways, *desensitization* (also called *systematic desensitization*) is basically the gradual counterconditioning of anxiety using relaxation as the incompatible response. The procedure, originally developed by Wolpe (1958), is one of the most powerful tools in behavior modification. It is not uncommon for a severe phobia or source of anxiety of long-standing to be removed in a few weeks. It is also one of the most researched procedures, resulting in a continual honing down of the approach, as well as the development of specialized variations and theoretical accounts (Bandura, 1969; Davison & Wilson, 1973; Kazdin & Wilcoxon, 1976; Paul, 1969; Rachman, 1967; Wilson & Davison, 1971). Desensitization has three basic components: training in relaxation, construction of hierarchies, and counterconditioning. This chapter assumes the reader has a good understanding of the relaxation and counterconditioning procedures discussed in Chapter 3.

TRAINING IN RELAXATION

Since relaxation is to be used as the incompatible response in counterconditioning anxiety, one of the first steps is teaching the client how to relax,

49

usually using a shortened version of Jacobson's (1938) muscle relaxation method (see Chapter 3). If this is not effective, then relaxation may be trained or elicited by some other means such as biofeedback, hypnosis, or drugs. Or the practitioner may decide to countercondition the anxiety with one of many other incompatible responses.

In practice, the amount of relaxation produced by muscle-relaxation training is usually more than is necessary for desensitization. In fact, some evidence exists that desensitization can be effective if the person can just maintain a general feeling of calmness or mental relaxation (Marshall et al., 1972; Rachman, 1968). However, training in something like muscle relaxation is still desirable because it provides learning a useful self-control skill and provides a level of relaxation that allows for the client's gradually becoming less relaxed during a counterconditioning session.

CONSTRUCTION OF HIERARCHIES

During assessment (see Chapter 2), it is necessary to determine what stimuli (situations and thoughts) elicit anxiety. This is accomplished through a variety of assessment procedures, possibly including interviews, daily logs, questionnaires (such as the Fear Survey Schedule), approach-avoidance behavior (how close the client will come to the feared situation), and physiological measures.

After the anxiety-eliciting stimuli have been determined, they are divided into groups according to common elements. Some stimuli can be grouped according to a central theme, as in a *thematic hierarchy*. For example, one person may feel anxious about being criticized, about being self-conscious, and about being misunderstood. For this person these fears may center around the general theme of fear of adverse social evaluations. Some stimuli may be grouped according to a specific event, such as a death of a loved one or a divorce. Such a group would be the basis for a *spatio-temporal hierarchy*.

The main pitfall is that the behavior modifier may group stimuli according to an inappropriate theme or event. Fears of being in filled buses, crowded elevators, and rush-hour traffic jams may be grouped according to a theme of a fear of crowds of people. The real theme, however, may be a fear of being confined in a small area. Determining the common elements or themes is a problem-solving skill that comes with practice and is aided by supervision.

After the fears and sources of anxiety have been generally grouped, it is necessary to decide which need to be treated. Some fears are adaptive fears and need to be left alone. A high school client of mine felt anxious about smoking marijuana with friends in the school bathrooms. This fear should not be decreased, primarily because of the local laws and enforcement at the time. Some fears can be left alone or treated later because they are not of immediate importance to the client's main problems. Some fears are based on misconceptions or faulty perceptions and are best handled by an educative approach. This arises often in areas related to sexual behavior and causes of mental illness. Other fears are unadaptive fears, based more on experiences and emotional associations than misconceptions. These are the fears for desensitization. In most cases there will probably not be more than one or two categories or themes of anxiety that require fairly immediate desensitization. Wolpe suggests that it is unusual for a client to have more than four such categories.

The next step is to take each category of anxiety stimuli and arrange them into a hierarchy, a rank ordering of the stimuli according to the amount of anxiety they elicit, with the items producing the most anxiety at the top of the hierarchy. Physiological measures are useful in doing this ranking, but most practitioners rely on the client's subjective estimate about how much anxiety he would experience in each actual situation. To facilitate this subjective report, Wolpe uses an anxiety scale in which the top of the scale (100) corresponds to the worst anxiety the subject can imagine and the bottom of the scale (0) corresponds to no anxiety. The unit of the scale is a *sud* (subjective unit of disturbance). The subject can then report his feeling of anxiety in terms of suds. A report of 25 suds would correspond to the point on the scale one-quarter of the way between no anxiety and maximum anxiety.

For desensitization, the items in the final hierarchy should not be too far apart in terms of the anxiety they elicit. Wolpe suggests that the difference between successive items should not be more than 5 to 10 suds. Thus it will often be necessary to add more items to the hierarchy than were originally found in the first assessment. The following is a hierarchy that Emery (1969) used in treating a 27-year-old law student with a fear of eating in a public place:

suds	Item
(95)	1. Having dinner at a girlfriend's house with her parents present
(85)	2. Having dinner out with a girl
(80)	3. Having breakfast out with a girl
(70)	4. Having dinner out with your parents
(60)	5. Having dinner alone at an unfamiliar restaurant
(50)	6. Having dinner at the university cafeteria with some classmates
(45)	7. Having dinner at the university cafeteria by yourself
(40)	8. Having dinner alone in a familiar restaurant
(35)	9. Having dinner at an old friend's house
(30)	10. Having lunch at the cafeteria
(25)	11. Having breakfast at the cafeteria
(15)	12. Having breakfast at a familiar restaurant on Saturday morning
(10)	13. Having lunch with a long-time friend
(5)	14. Having lunch in your apartment

VISUALIZING SCENES

After the appropriate hierarchies have been constructed and the client has learned to relax to the extent that he can relax relatively well and quickly, then the anxiety may be reduced through counterconditioning (see Chapter 3). This consists of slowly moving up through the hierarchy while keeping the client relaxed. The items in the hierarchy may be approached by putting the client in the actual situations (in vivo); but generally in desensitization the client merely imagines being in the situation, "living" it as realistically as possible. Usually the practitioner begins by describing the scene in some detail while the client imagines the scene. One reason for using imagined situations is that they generally produce less anxiety than the in vivo ones and hence are a better starting point. A second reason is that the use of imagined scenes gives the practitioner greater flexibility, for any situation can be created in the imagination, while for many situations it may be impractical or inefficient to go out to them or simulate them in the clinic.

Desensitization involving only imagined scenes generalizes well to in vivo situations. The client may then experience no anxiety in vivo, or he may experience a small amount of remnant anxiety, which he counterconditions or lets extinguish. Therefore, many practitioners use only imagined scenes during desensitization. An alternative is to have the client, after he has gone through most or all of the hierarchy in his imagination, go through the hierarchy in vivo using the same gradual counterconditioning approach he learned in the clinic using imagined scenes.

Some problems occur in using imagined scenes, for ideally the client is able to live the situation as if actually in it, rather than merely visualize it as if watching a movie. Although many clients can do this readily, a few cannot and need a different approach. A second problem is that the client may not visualize the scene presented—perhaps imagining a scene more, or less, anxiety producing. Finally when a person is imagining a scene he is not holding a constant image in his mind. Rather a continuous flow of imagery occurs (Barrett, 1969; Weitzman, 1967). Thus the counterconditioning involves themes and associations within the client's cognitive system, rather than simple specific stimuli.

COUNTERCONDITIONING

Assuming we have a client who can relax and visualize scenes, we are ready to begin the actual counterconditioning. During counterconditioning it is necessary to have a measure of how much anxiety an item from the hierarchy elicits; this measure is the basis for deciding when to move to the next item. The two most common measures are physiological measures and subject reports. When the client is reporting anxiety, it is important that he not disrupt the relaxed state. Wolpe has the client report anxiety by lifting a finger. The amount of anxiety can be determined by asking the client to lift his finger to questions about how many suds the item elicited.

The first item presented is a neutral item. If the client reports anxiety to this item, there probably is something about the particular desensitization setting that is producing anxiety. And this anxiety will have to be dealt with before continuing with the specific hierarchies.

Following a no-anxiety presentation of the neutral item, the client is presented with the lowest item on the hierarchy. He imagines this until he signals, as by lifting his right index finger, that he is beginning to feel anxious. When he signals anxiety, he is told to "Stop the scene and relax." Relaxation here may be facilitated by having the client shift to imagining a personally pleasurable scene. If the client imagines the hierarchy scene for about ten seconds without signaling anxiety, he is again told to "Stop the scene and relax." Because great individual differences occur between people concerning how quickly they can begin imagining scenes, some practitioners have clients signal, as by lifting the left index finger, when they begin clearly imagining the scene. The ten seconds, or whatever amount of time is appropriate, is then measured from this point.

After a scene has been stopped and the client has relaxed briefly, the same scene, or a variation of it, is presented to the client again. Each item on the hierarchy is presented repeatedly until it no longer elicits anxiety, a common criterion being for clients to be able to imagine the scene two successive times without signaling anxiety. At this point, the next item on the hierarchy is presented until it is counterconditioned and so on through the whole hierarchy. Through his signaling the client determines the rate at which he goes through the hierarchy, a very reassuring fact to many clients who do not want to be pushed into unpleasant situations too fast. A safe and sure approach is to stay with each item until it elicits no anxiety. However, desensitization may be accomplished by substantially reducing the anxiety associated with each item, but not to 0 (e.g., reducing it from 40 to 15 suds), before moving to the next item. This probably depends on generalization of the counterconditioning down the hierarchy as well as up. In one case, reducing the anxiety of each tiem by only 50 percent was found effective (Rachman & Hodgson, 1967).

The following is part of the first counterconditioning session that Emery (1969) had with the subject whose hierarchy is given above:

> First, I'd like you to imagine as vividly as possible that you are having lunch in your apartment (pause of 5 seconds—no signal). Stop imagining that and continue relaxing, just enjoying the calm, soothing feelings associated with relaxation (pause of 10 seconds). O.K., once again, imagine yourself, as realistically as possible, having lunch in your apartment (pause of 10 seconds—no signal). Stop imagining that and now imagine yourself in one of your personal forms of relaxation just letting yourself relax further and further (pause of about 20 sec-

onds). Now, stop imagining that and imagine yourself as vividly as possible in the following situation . . . you are having lunch with a long-time friend (pause of 3 seconds—no signal). Stop imagining that and continue relaxing while concentrating on the looseness and heaviness of your body (pause of 10 seconds). O.K., once again, imagine yourself eating lunch in your apartment (pause of 20 seconds—no signal). Stop imagining that now and switch over to one of your personal forms of relaxation while you continue to relax and enjoy yourself (pause of 20 seconds). O.K., stop picturing that and imagine yourself as vividly as possible having lunch with a long-time friend (pause of 8 seconds—client signals). Stop imagining that; in order to help you relax even further I am going to count from 1 to 10 and with each count you'll feel yourself sinking into a deeper, more complete state of relaxation, further and further, so that when I reach the count of 10 you'll feel completely relaxed. . . .

The length of counterconditioning sessions and the number of sessions per week vary greatly and should be geared to the client. Some clients have been desensitized in one session lasting several hours. However, it is usually wise to start with short sessions (15 to 30 minutes) and gradually build up to longer sessions (45 to 60 minutes) with about two sessions per week. It is usually suggested to end a session with the successful completion of a scene. Also at the beginning of a session, it is best to start lower on the hierarchy than where you left off the session before. This allows for some therapeutic loss or spontaneous recovery between sessions. Finally, to help the client maintain attention, it is desirable during a session to slightly alter the scenes and switch back and forth between different hierarchies.

The practitioner needs to be flexible during desensitization. Feedback from the client during or after a session may alter how the practitioner presents scenes or how much time he allows the client to imagine a scene before stopping. It is also common to alter or add to the hierarchy along the way. For example, a client may rate one item as 50 suds; but when imagining it during desensitization, it is 80 suds. With experience the whole desensitization procedure can become fluid.

After the client has completed most of the hierarchy using imagined scenes, he may be instructed to gradually go through the hierarchy in vivo. For a person with a fear of flying an item low on this hierarchy might be simply driving up to the front of the airport terminal. When doing this in vivo, the client would keep himself relaxed while driving up to the terminal. If he starts to feel anxious, he would merely stop and relax or drive away if necessary. This would be continued until he could drive up to the front of the terminal without feeling anxiety.

Drugs are sometimes used to facilitate relaxation for counterconditioning using imagined scenes (e.g., Friedman, 1966) or in vivo situations (e.g., Munjack, 1975). In these cases it is best if the client is gradually phased off the drugs, another form of hierarchy. In some cases this is the only hierarchy: The client, while relaxed via drugs, is allowed to encounter anxiety-producing situations in the natural order they arise. Then the medication is gradually reduced.

DESENSITIZATION PROBLEMS

One problem in carrying out desensitization is that the client may not learn muscle relaxation sufficiently for counterconditioning. If this is the case, relaxation may be produced by other means such as drugs or hypnosis. Or it may be better to use a counterconditioning approach based on an incompatible response other than relaxation.

A second possible problem may be that the client cannot visualize scenes well enough to use imagined scenes. This can sometimes be helped by having the client practice imagining neutral scenes or by presenting the scenes via hypnosis. If not, then it may be desirable to switch from imagined scenes to slides, videotapes, or in vivo stimuli. In some cases, these alternatives may be preferable to imagined scenes even if the client can visualize well.

Sometimes the client may visualize all right, but it is suspected he is visualizing incorrect scenes (perhaps you find that none of the scenes elicit anxiety). In these cases it is often desirable to have the client verbalize what he is imagining for a few times. It may be necessary to pace the client through the whole scene rather than just tell him basically what to imagine.

Another problem is the use of an unsuitable hierarchy, often noticed when desensitization goes too slow or too fast. Possible problems include a hierarchy based on the wrong theme, an insufficiently weak starting point, or a client that does not consider this an irrational fear, but rather something truly dangerous.

THEORIES OF DESENSITIZATION

Desensitization is described in this text in terms of counterconditioning. Relaxation is conditioned to stimuli that previously elicited anxiety. The overall effect of this conditioning is gradual, moving from anxiety through neutral toward relaxed. Conditioning is generally terminated when the client feels neutral, that is, no anxiety (0 suds). The purpose of the hierarchy is to maintain relaxation dominant to anxiety.

However, as discussed in Chapter 3, any counterconditioning procedure can also be interpreted as respondent extinction. Wilson and Davison (1971) have made such an argument for desensitization. They suggest that desensitization is basically extinction, the client approaches feared situations, in imagination or in vivo, without adverse effect. This results in respondent extinction of the anxiety. However, desensitization research has suggested the important facilitative effects of relaxation training and the use of hierarchies, neither of which is needed for extinction (e.g., McGlynn, 1973). Wilson and Davison suggest that the facilitative effects of relaxation and use of hierarchies are because of the fact that they encourage the client to approach and be exposed to the feared stimuli. If this is the case, then we can use other types of incentives to get the client to approach feared stimuli. These may include money or praise. In fact, there are several reports (e.g., Leitenberg & Callahan, 1973) in which fears are reduced by operant procedures (see Chapter 7) that consist of rewarding the client for gradually approaching a feared situation. A counterconditioning theorist would see these rewards as having a counterconditioning effect in addition to the incentive effect.

There are also several other sources of reward that occur during desensitization and may be incorporated into a theoretical explanation. The practitioner may reward the client with attention or praise for progress in desensitization. (Remember that if the practitioner is not careful here he may only be changing the client's report of progress of no anxiety, rather than more general changes.) Also in desensitization, as in many other change programs, the client's perception of his own progress is often a powerful source of reward. This reward probably facilitates carry-over from the clinic to other settings.

Another interpretation of desensitization is that it is based to some degree on learning controlled attention shifts (Wilkins, 1971; Yulis et al., 1975). That is, the desensitization procedure teaches the client how to shift his attention away from the feared object. Currently little research delineates the role of this variable, although it seems of minimal importance, for most phobics are already skilled at shifting away from anxiety sources, and this often impairs their work in desensitization when they should attend to the anxiety scene.

Finally, several theorists suggest that desensitization is best interpreted and carried out as a form of self-control of anxiety (Goldfried, 1971; Zenmore, 1975). That is, desensitization is not counterconditioning to specific situations which then generalizes to other situations. Rather, it is learning a general coping skill for dealing with anxiety situations. The client learns how to sense anxiety and switch into a more relaxed state. The use of the hierarchy is merely providing the client gradual practice in his self-control skill with a relevant and important anxiety source. Thus it is better during desensitization to emphasize the self-control approach rather than rely on counterconditioning; and evidence exists to suggest this is the case (e.g., Spiegler et al., 1976). However, even if adding a self-control component or emphasis to desensitization does improve treatment effectiveness, this does not mean that the results are not due to counterconditioning or extinction.

Working from the self-control approach, Suinn and Richardson (1971) developed a procedure called *anxiety-management training* that uses no hierarchies. Anxiety is treated as stimuli to which the client learns to respond with responses that reduce or remove the anxiety. This is done by having the client visualize past events that arouse anxiety and learn to detect the onset or increase in anxiety. He then learns to reduce the anxiety with competing responses such as relaxation or feelings of success or competency caused by an imagined scene.

Despite the different theoretical interpretations of desensitization, what the practitioner should *do* seems to be the following: During relaxation training emphasis should be put on the client learning to discriminate fine differences between relaxation and non-relaxation (e.g., anxiety, tension). The client should learn how to use relaxation as a self-control skill in dealing with anxiety. This should be done in a variety of ways, including during counterconditioning with imagined scenes and later in vivo assignments. Otherwise, desensitization should be carried out as described above.

VARIATIONS OF DESENSITIZATION

There are many variations of desensitization and combinations with other procedures. The following sample of variations includes group desensitization, mechanization of desensitization, self-desensitization, dealing with pervasive anxiety, and contact desensitization.

Group desensitization

An advantage of behavior modification is that in many situations it can be applied to groups of people at a time, thus saving time and expense. To apply desensitization in groups it is necessary to have a hierarchy common to all the clients. This is usually easiest accomplished if the fear is relatively common, specific, and not complicated with other psychological problems. The second requirement is that the rate through the hierarchy should be geared toward the slowest client for each item; you do not advance to the next item until everyone in the group has been desensitized to the current item. Lazarus (1961) was one of the first to do group desensitization of a variety of phobias, including acrophobia (fear of heights), claustrophobia (fear of enclosed places), and sexual fears. Other group desensitization includes treatment of fear of public speaking (Paul & Shannon, 1966) and fear of spiders (Robinson & Suinn, 1969).

Mechanization of desensitization

Several researchers have devised procedures for mechanizing various parts of desensitization and thereby freeing more of the practitioner's time. Migler and Wolpe (1967) describe a case in which the client, under the behavior modifier's supervision, made a tape of the hierarchy items and relaxation instructions. Then with a slightly modified tape recorder, the client was able to desensitize himself at home. Donner and Guerney (1969) were able to treat test anxiety in a group of clients by administering the desensitization through a tape-recorded set of instructions.

Lang (Lang et al., 1970) has computerized much of desensitization with equipment called DAD (Device for Automated Desensitization). DAD presents, via tapes, instructions in hypnosis and relaxation and a pre-recorded hierarchy of items. When the client becomes anxious, DAD gives instructions to stop visualizing the scene and relax. DAD carries out desensitization effectively and the clients do not object to working with DAD.

Self-desensitization

Related to mechanizing desensitization are a variety of studies in which the client carries out much of the desensitization procedure on himself. We have already seen some of this above in the use of tape recorders and in vivo assignments. Self-desensitization carries it a little further, and several manuals have been written for this purpose (e.g., Rosen, 1976; Wenrich et al., 1976). A common approach is the client learns to relax primarily from tapes, the practitioner helps the client construct the hierarchies and instructs him in the desensitization procedure, and then the client desensitizes himself perhaps with the aid of tapes (Baker et al., 1973; Morris & Thomas, 1973). One study with highly fearful snake phobics (Rosen et al., 1976) found that clients could successfully desensitize themselves using only a desensitization manual and a record of relaxation instructions. In this study, the self-desensitization was as effective (moderate treatment effects) as therapist administered desensitization.

The research on group desensitization, mechanization of desensitization, and self-desensitization shows that in at least some situations a one-to-one relationship with a human practitioner is not necessary and perhaps inefficient or undesirable.

Pervasive anxiety

Desensitization requires being able to specify the stimulus situations that elicit anxiety. Sometimes a client seems to be anxious most of the time. This is often called *pervasive anxiety* or *free-floating anxiety*. When such a state is not caused by organic disorder, there are two basic possibilities: (1) There are a few common situations or stimuli that elicit anxiety, which are easily dealt with by desensitization. (2) There are many different stimuli that elicit anxiety, perhaps making standard desensitization impractical. The most common way of dealing with this latter situation is to emphasize general self-control approaches to anxiety control, perhaps aided at first by drugs that facilitate relaxation. This then amounts to self-control training, plus in vivo counterconditioning.

Cautela's (1966a) more general approach to pervasive anxiety consists of four procedures:

1. REASSURANCE.   The client is reassured that the practitioner will always be ready to help.
2. DESENSITIZATION.   The client is desensitized to abstract concepts (e.g., people or responsibility) related to the anxiety.
3. IN VIVO RELAXATION.   The client is taught how to relax himself and to use this in situations that cause anxiety.
4. ASSERTIVE TRAINING.   The client is taught to assert himself in situations in which he was inappropriately passive (see Chapter 8).

Contact desensitization

A variation of desensitization called *contact desensitization* is a combination of in vivo desensitization and modeling (see Chapter 8). It is also called *participant modeling* and *modeling with guided participation*. Since desensitization and modeling are both effective ways of dealing with fears, their combination is quite powerful. Contact desensitization, which was developed by Ritter (1968), consists of three basic steps:

1. The client watches someone else (the model) approach the feared object.
2. The model helps the client approach the object.
3. The model is gradually faded out as the client approaches the feared object.

In an unpublished report of 1965, Ritter described her treatment program for a female undergraduate (S) who was unable to perform the required dissections in a biology course:

PHASE I   The subject made no attempt to perform during the first phase of treatment, but merely observed the dissection procedures of her classmates. S located herself as far from the activities as was comfortable and watched for brief periods while occasionally reminding herself that the dissection animal, a foetal pig, was a dead nonsensing object. S gradually extended the time she observed and also gradually moved closer to the dissection scene as she became more comfortable.

PHASE II   S obtained the assistance of a sympathetic female student who served as a co-therapist (T). S momentarily placed her hand on T's while T was performing a dissection movement; S gradually extended the time she rested her hand on T's. When the foregoing could be done with ease, S progressively slid her hand forward on T's thereby approaching contact with the dissection instrument. This was continued until S had her fingers directly on the dissection instrument while T was also still holding it. Finally, when S was comfortable with this arrangement she asked T to remove her hand but to remain watching in case assistance was needed.

PHASE III   S practiced dissecting alone, first while T observed and then independently.

Research on contact desensitization suggests that it is often more effective than just modeling (e.g., Lewis, 1974; Röper et al., 1975) and often faster and as effective as standard desensitization (e.g., Bandura et al., 1969; Litvak, 1969). A limitation is that contact desensitization can only be applied in situations which can be readily modeled and gradually phased into. Thus some cases, such as fear of childbirth, are better treated by other approaches. Research to date that has attempted to factor out the relative importance of the different components of contact desensitization (modeling, contact with feared object, participation, active versus passive treatment, verbal instructions) has yielded mixed results that need further clarification (Blanchard, 1970; Lewis, 1974; Murphy & Bootzin, 1973).

In working with snake phobics, Bandura and his associates (1975) found that they could improve the effects of contact desensitization by adding an additional hour in which the subjects continued on their own, interacting with the snake as they did during treatment. Contact desensitization has also been used with groups for snake phobias (Ritter, 1968) and fear of heights (Ritter, 1969).

Thus desensitization and related procedures are powerful ways of dealing with fears and anxiety. As the practitioner becomes more familiar with this approach he can alter it and interweave it with other approaches in ways that best fit his client and treatment approach. Also this chapter should be seen as a detailed example and perhaps model for the more general counterconditioning procedures discussed in Chapter 3.

SUMMARY

Desensitization, the gradual counterconditioning of anxiety with relaxation, basically consists of three components: (1) teaching the client to be able to relax; (2) constructing hierarchies, rank orderings of sources of anxiety according to common elements; and (3) gradually counterconditioning the anxiety by slowly moving through the items of the hierarchy, in imagination and/or in vivo. Treatment is often most effective if the client also learns to discriminate subtle differences between being relaxed and not and learns basic self-control skills for dealing with anxiety. Theoretical interpretations of the desensitization procedure include such components as counterconditioning, extinction, operant conditioning, controlled attention shifts, and self-control of anxiety. Desensitization can often be carried out with a group of people at one time, can be mechanized in varying degrees, and can often be done by people on themselves with the help of a practitioner and/or special materials. Contact desensitization is a powerful change procedure combining modeling and in vivo desensitization.

THOUGHT QUESTIONS

1. List the sequence of steps for carrying out desensitization from initial assessment through use of imagined scenes to in vivo assignments.
2. For each of the following, give two assessment procedures you would use to help identify and specify possible sources of anxiety: a six-year-old with a school phobia, a college student with test anxiety, a non-verbal mental patient who does not like to be touched.
3. Devise and describe a hypothesis-testing procedure to determine the correct theme underlying situations eliciting anxiety in your client.
4. Make up a possible hierarchy with suds for a person with a fear of being at home alone. What is the theme of this hierarchy? Give an example of an alternative theme that would generate some of the items on the hierarchy.
5. List three possible problems in doing desensitization and what you would do to try to avoid them.
6. Outline a possible course of self-desensitization you could take to eliminate one of your sources of anxiety. Will you actually do this? Why?
7. Using the desensitization procedure as a model, outline a program for a hypothetical case using emotive imagery to countercondition anger.
8. How do the following differ procedurally: desensitization, counterconditioning, flooding, and contact desensitization?
9. As a behaviorist, discuss the use of suds and imagined scenes in desensitization.
10. What are the advantages and disadvantages of using a computer, with direct input from the client's physiological responses, rather than a human practitioner to carry out desensitization with a client?
11. List five common fears that would lend themselves to group desensitization. Should group desensitization for any of these fears be part of our high school programs or educational television programming? Why?
12. Describe an experiment that would differentiate between two of the theories of desensitization.

SUGGESTED READINGS

Davison, G. C. & Wilson, G. T. Processes of fear-reduction in systematic desensitization: Cognitive and social reinforcement factors in humans. *Behavior Therapy,* 1973, 4, 1–21.

Goldfried, M. R. & Davison, G. C. *Clinical behavior therapy.* New York: Holt, Rinehart & Winston, 1976. Chapter 6.

Paul, G. L. & Bernstein, D. A. *Anxiety and clinical problems: Systematic desensitization and related techniques.* Morristown, N.J.: General Learning Press, 1973.

Rosen, G. *Don't be afraid: A program for overcoming your fears and phobias.* Englewood Cliffs, N.J.: Prentice-Hall, 1976.

Wenrich, W. W., Dawley, H. H., & General, D. A. *Self-directed systematic desensitization: A guide for the student, client and therapist.* Kalamazoo, Mich.: Behaviordelia, 1976.

Wolpe, J. *The practice of behavior therapy.* 2d ed. Elmsford, N.Y.: Pergamon Press, 1973. Chapters 6 & 7.

Aversive Counterconditioning

In the last chapter on desensitization it was seen how counterconditioning can be used to reduce aversive-avoidance reactions to situations. In this chapter is the opposite, use of counterconditioning to reduce unwanted positive-approach reactions. This is the procedure of *aversive counterconditioning,* the counterconditioning of positive reactions using the response to an aversive (unpleasant) situation as the incompatible response (Feldman, 1966; Hallam & Rachman, 1976; Rachman & Teasdale, 1969). For example, a person addicted to some drug (e.g., heroin, alcohol, tobacco) has positive associations to many aspects of taking the drug, including such things as pleasant associations to a particular bar and drinking friends, a calming effect associated with lighting up a cigarette, a reduction of withdrawal symptoms after taking more heroin, or socially approved relaxing of inhibitions associated with drinking alcohol. These types of positive associations continually make it more probable the person will again use the drug, thus strengthening the addiction even though the long range effects of using the drug are undesirable and even aversive. The logic of aversive counterconditioning is to pair situations that elicit the undesired positive response (e.g., the handling and taste of a cigarette) with stimuli that elicit a dominant, incompatible, aversive response (e.g., the reaction to electric shock) as a way of reducing the positive reaction.

Aversive counterconditioning follows the general approach of counterconditioning described in Chapter 3: First, we identify those stimuli that elicit the undesired response, in this case a pleasant-approach response. Next, we determine or establish ways to produce an incompatible response, in this case an aversion response. Then we gradually apply our counterconditioning, using a hierarchy to control response dominance. In aversive counterconditioning, a hierarchy is often unnecessary because the aversion response may always be dominant to the undesired response. However, this is not always the case and practitioners sometimes overlook the importance of a hierarchy in some aversive counterconditioning. Finally, remember that in counterconditioning we can stop at any point along the way between the two incompatible responses. Thus in aversive counterconditioning we can stop while the client still has a positive reaction to the stimuli, continue on and stop when the client feels neutral to the stimuli, or continue further until the client feels aversion to the stimuli.

Aversive counterconditioning is primarily used with self-rewarding behaviors. The person smoking an undesired amount of marijuana is reinforced (rewarded) for smoking by the results of smoking. The person who is sexually aroused by specific stimuli (e.g., people of the same sex, young children, certain types of clothes) is reinforced by the sexual arousal and resulting sexual fantasies and behaviors. This self-reinforcing aspect of the behaviors makes them difficult to treat by most counseling-therapeutic approaches. Behavioral treatment involves aversive counterconditioning to reduce some of the positive associations resulting from the natural source of reinforcement, as well as helping the client develop alternative reinforcing behaviors. For example, aversive counterconditioning may involve electric shock paired with photos of young children that elicit undesired sexual arousal.

This is a good place to see the importance of temporal contingencies on behavior. Consider an alcoholic who often gets drunk, feels happy, has a good time with his drinking friends, and withdraws from his daily problems. As a result of this, he later wakes up with hangovers, is slowly losing his job, and is involved in marriage problems, all related to his drinking. Now why do these bad effects from drinking not have a greater influence on his drinking? Part of the reason is that they are too distant in time to the actual drinking. The positive associations, which occur close in time to the drinking, have a stronger effect on the drinking behavior than the more distant negative associations. In fact the negative associations may act as stimuli for more drinking. Thus a purpose of aversive counterconditioning is to bring to bear immediate aversive associations to stimuli associated with the undesired behavior.

Behavior modifiers frequently use a combination of procedures to increase treatment effectiveness. This is particularly true for the types of behaviors treated with aversive counterconditioning. It would be unusual if aversive counterconditioning were all that was necessary. Usually treatment would involve other components such as desensitization, training in social skills, or vocational training. For example, it would be a disservice to a homosexual to merely help him reduce his sexual arousal to people of the same sex. In addition, it may be desirable to help him develop his heterosexual arousal and social skills, as well as deal with many problems associated with the change in life-style.

Because aversive counterconditioning is often unpleasant, it is generally restricted to behaviors that are difficult to treat by other means and to situations in which the advantage of cure more than offsets any disadvantages of procedure. In reality, many clients have reported they found aversive counterconditioning less unpleasant than interpersonal probings, interpretations, and evaluations they experienced in some other forms of therapy. However, the use of aversive events certainly raises ethical questions and creates problems such as some clients disliking treatment, some clients becoming more aggressive or more anxious, and the fact that some procedures cannot be used with some clients (such as electric shock treatments with some cardiac patients).

COMPARED WITH OPERANT PUNISHMENT

In most of the current literature, the material covered in this chapter is subsumed under the term *aversion therapy,* which includes two distinct, and often confused, models: aversive counterconditioning and operant punishment. Aversive counterconditioning, discussed in this chapter, is based on respondent conditioning, the systematic pairing of two sets of stimuli, one which elicits the undesired response and one which elicits the aversion response. The stimuli are paired independent of what responses the client makes. The client's responses are only a measure of the progress of the conditioning. Operant punishment, discussed in the next chapter, is based on operant conditioning. Here the aversive stimulus is presented contingent upon a particular response of the client and usually occurs if and only if the client makes the response. Consider the use of an unpleasant odor in the treatment of over-eating. In aversive counterconditioning, the odor would be paired with cues that tend to elicit or encourage over-eating, as a way of weakening the support for over-eating. In operant punishment, the odor would be paired with the response of over-eating as a way to suppress the act of over-eating.

Keeping in mind the distinction between the two approaches is important for a number of reasons: The aversive stimulus is contingent on stimuli in one case and responses in the other. This leads to significant differences in the occurrence and timing of the aversive stimulus. The types of results and changes in behavior that follow from the two procedures are different. And the literatures on respondent and operant conditioning suggest different optimal ways of conditioning.

In practice or in reading many of the reports of aversion therapy, it is often difficult to separate aversive counterconditioning from operant punishment, with many situations having components of both. In reality, it is impossible to have one without the other. For whenever the aversive stimulus occurs the person is doing something (doing "nothing" is doing something; a live person is always behaving) and hence is punished for what he is doing. And whenever the aversive stimulus occurs, it will be associated with whatever stimuli are present at that time. The key then becomes the contingencies the practitioner emphasizes in his treatment program.

EXAMPLES

Examples of aversive counterconditioning are found in a variety of settings. A common way to break a dog of killing chickens is to hang a dead chicken around the dog's neck for a while. Pliny the Elder suggested part of treatment for alcoholism might involve putting spiders in the bottom of the person's glass. And aversive associations are often established at the verbal level as when a person says "Bob is a gossip."

Most of the early clinical reports and experimental studies of aversive counterconditioning used drugs or electric shock to produce aversion. Much of the early treatment of alcoholism used chemically induced nausea (Lemere & Voegtlin, 1950). Treatment may consist of pairing the taste of the person's favorite alcohol with a drug that makes him nauseous. A common practice today is to keep an alcoholic on the drug antabuse (disulfiram), which, combined with even a small amount of alcohol, causes nausea and vomiting that may last a couple of hours. However, the use of antabuse is seldom sufficient by itself and generally needs to be part of a more comprehensive treatment program.

Raymond (1964) reported several cases of aversive counterconditioning using apomorphine-induced nausea. One case was a 63-year-old alcoholic man who was given two treatments a day for 31 days. This was sufficient to produce abstinence from alcohol for the three years of follow-up. A second case involved a 14-year-old boy addicted to cigarettes. Ater three treatments he stopped smoking and even the smoke from his father's cigarette made him feel ill. Thompson and Rathod (1968) employed drugs that would partially stop respiration for a short time. They were able to reduce the use of heroin by associating this aversion with the taking of heroin.

Many practitioners and researchers came to prefer electric shock to drugs as the aversive stimulus. One reason is that with electric shock it is easier to control many of the variables which are important in conditioning, such as onset, offset, duration, and intensity of the aversive event. Fewer trials per day can generally be given with drugs than shock. Drugs, such as those that produce vomiting, are often more unpleasant to the client and staff than electric shock. Greater individual differences and side effects occur with drugs. And some of the drugs depress the central nervous system and hence retard learning and treatment effectiveness.

Lubetkin and Fishman (1974) used shock in the treatment of a 23-year-old heroin addict. The client imagined and described behavior sequences leading up to and including heroin intake, while receiving electric shocks along the way. Shifting to imagining a scene of a drug-free situation was paired with the offset of the shock. Following treatment the client remained drug free during the eight-month follow-up.

It is also possible to use portable shock units, which then permit in vivo aversive counterconditioning (McGuire & Vallance, 1964). This permits counterconditioning to important environmental stimuli, allows the client to carry-out much of the treatment himself, and makes it possible to gear part of the treatment to internal cues, such as a craving for a drug, which may be difficult to reproduce in the clinic.

Aversive counterconditioning has become broader and more flexible as a wider range of aversive stimuli have been employed. Other sources of aversion include cigarette smoke, unpleasant odors, aversive pictures or sounds, social and personal criticism, and aversive imagined scenes.

Lichtenstein and his associates (1973) reduced smoking by having a machine blow warm cigarette smoke in their clients' faces while they were smoking. This produced a significant reduction at the six-month follow-up with about 60 percent of the clients totally abstinent.

Morganstern (1974) took advantage of the fact that smoking a cigarette is aversive to many non-smokers. His client was a 24-year-old obese female who ate much in addition to her regular meals (pizza and ice cream one to three times per day, almost 200 pieces of candy and dozens of cookies and doughnuts per week). Treatment, in the clinic and self-treatment at home, consisted of pairing eating junk food (e.g., candy) with taking a drag of a cigarette and then spitting out the food and exclaiming, "Eating this junk makes me sick." Through this the client was able to loose 53 pounds.

Colson (1972) successfully worked with a 24-year-old male homosexual. Treatment involved the client relaxing and visualizing a homosexual experience while presented with an unpleasant odor, primarily smelling salts (aromatic ammonia).

Mandel (1970) has been working with male homosexuals by having them concentrate on a color slide of a naked man. Counterconditioning was achieved by transposing on this slide a color slide of hideous running sores which cause disgust.

Serber (1970) has described what he calls "shame aversion therapy," which he uses to treat sexual deviants who are ashamed of their acts. Treatment consists in having the subject perform the act in front of the practitioner and/or others. Thus a male transvestite who is sexually aroused by wearing women's clothes in private would be required to put on and wear these clothes in front of the practitioner. To the extent that the person feels ashamed doing this, it may have a counterconditioning effect.

OFFSET OF THE AVERSIVE STIMULUS

The onset of an aversive stimulus is unpleasant by definition. It is the onset that is paired with other stimuli in aversive counterconditioning and with a response in punishment. The offset of the aversive stimulus is pleasant by contrast. This offset can be associated with stimuli (called *relief stimuli*) to which we wish to respondently condition a positive effect. Or the offset can be used to reward a desirable behavior. For example, in treating male homosexuality, male homosexual slides may be paired with the onset of shock, while female heterosexual slides would be paired with offset of shock. Variations of this procedure were used by Feldman and MacCulloch (1965), and by Thorpe and his associates (1964). In treating alcoholism, the drinking of alcohol can be paired with shock followed by drinking of orange juice during the relief time (McBrearty et al., 1968).

Feldman (Feldman, 1966; Feldman & MacCulloch, 1965) argues that the offset of the aversive stimulus should be used to reward a desired behavior such as avoidance of the inappropriate object and/or approach to the appropriate object. The main reason is that the learning under the operant model (particularly avoidance responses) generally takes longer to extinguish than learning under the respondent model.

Although the various suggestions for use of the offset of the aversive stimulus are reasonable, to date there is a lack of research systematically evaluating the effect of this variable. There is also a need to separate respondent from operant variables. For example, Rachman and Teasdale (1969, p. 137) argue that the effective process in Feldman's procedure is not the development of an avoidance response, but rather the respondent conditioning of anxiety to the homosexual stimuli.

GENERALIZATION

An interesting question often raised is why should the effects of aversive counterconditioning generalize to situations in which clients know they will not encounter the aversive stimulus. If people are undergoing aversive counterconditioning in a clinic for alcoholism, why should this affect them when they are at the corner pub away from the clinic and practitioner? The facts are that aversive counterconditioning does generalize, in varying degrees, to non-clinic situations. One possibility is that the conditioning takes place at a level outside of cognitive control (see Chapter 9). That is, as a result of conditioning, alcohol-related cues elicit specific responses in or out of the clinic. Although people are aware they are not in the clinic, this awareness has a minimal effect on their conditioned reactions. In this sense, it is like a phobia in which specific situations trigger anxiety even though the person knows the anxiety is unreasonable and undesired. Bandura (1969, chap. 8), on the other hand, accounts for the generalization in terms of self-control. He suggests that as a result of aversive counterconditioning clients can stop the unwanted behavior in vivo by reinstating in imagination the aversive reactions they experienced in treatment.

But whatever the explanation, several things can be done to facilitate generalization: The clinic can be arranged to match the real world as much as possible. Many behavioral treatments of alcoholism use simulated bars set up in the clinic. Any possible in vivo conditioning should be emphasized. Part of the treatment should help establish self-control skills, such as mentioned above relative to Bandura and discussed below relative to covert sensitization. Finally, it is often desirable to have the client return periodically to the clinic for booster sessions, additional conditioning sessions to minimize loss of treatment effects.

THEORIES

Several problems exist in developing a theoretical account of the effects of aversive counterconditioning (Hallam & Rachman, 1972, 1976). One problem, discussed earlier, is that aversive counterconditioning and operant punishment are often confused and confounded in practice and in explanations. A second problem is that most of the literature consists of case studies and treatment programs in which aversive counterconditioning is just one component. This is useful for developing effective treatment approaches, but more research is necessary for factoring out the relative importance of different components. There has also been little parametric research, systematically varying different variables such as the onset and intensity of the aversive stimulus. Of the many applied counterconditioning approaches, aversive counterconditioning lends itself better than most for such parametric studies, which would help factor out such things as the operant and respondent components. There is also a need for research related to many other variables, including the client's motivation to change and the expectancies the client has for the effects of the treatment. Given these qualifications let us consider four basic theories, counterconditioning, extinction, state theory, and cognitive theory.

Counterconditioning

According to the counterconditioning explanation (Chapter 3), aversion reactions gradually become respondently conditioned to stimuli that previously elicited the positive or approach responses. Thus through aversive counterconditioning the taste and smell of a cigarette, which were pleasing and reinforcing, are gradually neutralized or made aversive. There are currently two problems with this theory. First is that laboratory studies on conditioning emotional reactions in humans suggest that these conditioned reactions extinguish quickly. This could mean that the counterconditioning in aversive counterconditioning also extinguishes quickly and thus long-term treatment effectiveness may depend on other treatment components. Or it may be that, for reasons yet to be determined, the aversive counterconditioning in clinical situations is longer lasting than the quite different laboratory studies.

The second problem with the counterconditioning explanation is to account for the generality of results that often follows fairly specific conditioning. For example, treatment of alcoholism may involve aversive counterconditioning in the clinic to a specific set of stimuli related to specific drinks and the cues of the simulated bar. It would not be unusual if the treatment effects carried over to a wide range of different drinks and situations. The question is how to account for such a generality of results. A simple counterconditioning explanation would account for these results in terms of generalization, the carry-over of the conditioning from specific stimuli to similar stimuli. However, what constitutes "similar" probably depends on cognitive processes of the client, rather than simple physical properties of the stimuli. Critics of the counterconditioning theory say the theory cannot adequately account for the generality of the results.

Extinction

As discussed earlier (Chapter 3), anything that can be interpreted as counterconditioning can also be interpreted as extinction, although I am not familiar with anyone yet advocating an extinction theory for what is covered in this chapter. According to an extinction theory, stimuli are presented during treatment without letting them be paired with the pleasant result, thus producing extinction. For example, a person might taste a martini, but spit it out before getting effects from the alcohol. Such a hypothesis would need to account for the effect of the aversive event. One possibility is that the aversive event prevents the usual pleasant reaction from occurring and hence facilitates extinction.

State theory

Hallam and Rachman (1976) have proposed a tentative "state theory," which is based on a change in general responsiveness (sensitization), rather than changes in specific stimulus-response associations. According to this theory, aversive counterconditioning has two effects: (1) a general sensitization, a tendency simply to be more reactive to the types of stimuli encountered in treatment; and (2) a suppression of the undesired behavior, with the suppression diminishing over time. The success of the treatment depends on how long the suppression lasts, what alternative reinforcing behaviors are developed during suppression, and the amount of reinforcement from the success in suppressing the undesired behavior.

Cognitive theory

According to cognitive theories of aversive counterconditioning (e.g., Bandura, 1969), the effects of treatment are based on such elements as expectancy of treatment results and the learning of self-control. Cognitive theorists essentially suggest learning is more cognitive or central than is their conceptualization of conditioning theories such as counterconditioning. The generality of results following specific treatment is often offered as support of this position. Another possible cognitive aspect of aversive counterconditioning is based on cognitive dissonance. The argument is that because the treatment is aversive clients will change their behavior following treatment to "justify" (avoid dissonance) going through such aversion (Carlin & Armstrong, 1968). A critical test for many cognitive theories would be to see if aversive counterconditioning generalizes to situations where the client knows he won't encounter the aversive stimulus and is motivated away from such generalization.

Because of the many confounding variables discussed at the beginning of this section, it is not possible to currently separate the various effects. Probably different treatment programs are based on and emphasize different combinations of the various factors suggested by the different theories.

COVERT SENSITIZATION

A variation of aversive counterconditioning is *covert sensitization* (also called *verbal aversion* and *aversive imagery*) in which the stimuli to be counterconditioned and the aversive event are imagined scenes (Cautela, 1966b, 1967, 1970c; Cautela & Wisocki, 1971). Here a person imagines a situation in which the undesired behavior would occur, imagines beginning to do the undesired behavior or intending to do it, and then imagines a scene that is aversive, such as vomiting, falling into a cesspool, or social criticism. For example, Polakow (1975) used covert sensitization as part of a program in treating a 24-year-old, female barbituate addict. Imagined scenes of thinking about barbituates, making contact with a dealer, and ingesting pills were associated with images of being attacked by hordes of large sewer rats (which she had indicated on the Fear Survey Schedule as being a strong source of fear).

Although little research has been done on optimizing covert sensitization, Cautela, who has done much of the work in this area, suggests several guidelines for effective treatment: The emphasis of the treatment should be on the intent to do the behavior, rather than the behavior itself. This catches the problem earlier in the behavior chain, and Cautela believes it minimizes overgeneralization. That is, the covert sensitization may involve conditioning related to the client's intent on drinking alcohol, rather than anyone drinking alcohol or alcohol in general. Cautela also suggests alternating the aversive scenes with scenes in which the client performs an alternative desired behavior and experiences relief. The imagery may be enhanced through the various senses, as by having the client smell or hear something related to what he is imagining. Finally, as is true of most aversive counterconditioning, covert sensitization is often most effective when combined with other procedures such as relaxation training. The following is part of Cautela's (1970c) treatment of smoking for a client:

> You are sitting at your desk in the office preparing your lectures for class. There is a pack of cigarettes to your right. While you are writing, you put down your pencil and start to reach for a cigarette. As soon as you start reaching for the cigarette, you get a nauseous feeling in your stomach. You begin to feel sick to your stomach, like you are about to vomit. You touch the package and bitter spit comes into your mouth. When you take the cigarette out of the pack, some pieces of food come into your throat. Now you feel sick and have stomach cramps. As you are about to put the cigarette in your mouth, you puke all over the cigarette, all over your hand, and all over the package of cigarettes. The cigarette in your hand is very soggy and full of green vomit. There is a stink coming from the vomit. Snots are coming from your nose. Your hands feel all slimy and full of vomit. The whole desk is a mess. Your clothes are full of puke. You get up from the desk and turn away from the vomit and cigarettes. You immediately begin to feel better being away from the cigarettes. You go to the bathroom and wash up and feel great being away from the cigarettes.

There are many advantages to covert sensitization, in general and in comparison to other forms of aversive counterconditioning. One advantage is that it requires no apparatus or drugs. A second advantage is that it can be made very specific, such as gearing it toward eating the *second* piece of pie or drinking the *second* manhattan when the treatment is geared toward reducing over-eating or excessive drinking. Perhaps most important is that the client can utilize the procedure on himself, permitting in vivo counterconditioning and the development of a powerful self-control skill.

Consider a female college student who has trouble with over-eating. The cafeteria, snack bar, vending machines, and food in her room all provide cues that cause her to eat excessively and unwisely. Part of her treatment may involve covert sensitization, perhaps with aversive scenes such as seeing her boyfriend with his arm around another girl, laughing at how fat the client is. Now after a few treatment sessions, the client may use these scenes in a self-control fashion. When a candy bar in a vending machine calls out to her, she can switch to an imagined scene to stop her desire for, or intent to get, the candy bar. With practice, she may find that eventually she does not need to call up the whole aversive scene, but can do it indirectly through a subjective feeling of "willing" not to buy or eat something. With more time, she may find that her willing becomes automatic and the whole process slides out of consciousness.

There are many problems, primarily lack of research, in experimentally evaluating covert sensitization and deciding among various theoretical explanations (see Mahoney, 1974a, p. 93–103). Most of the literature is case studies reporting varying degrees of success. There are few systematic controlled studies; and covert sensitization is often used with, and hence confounded with, other procedures. The fact that the whole treatment takes place in the client's imagination makes evaluation of exactly what is going on very difficult. All the problems and theories related to aversive counterconditioning, discussed earlier, apply here. In this context, I have described covert sensitization as an example of aversive counterconditioning, while Cautela sees it as an example of operant punishment. In practice it is usually possible to find elements of both of these. The issue is which you emphasize.

The following is a sample of some of the mixed reports on covert sensitization: In cases of overeating covert sensitization is often part of a successful treatment program (e.g., Cautela, 1966b). But some controlled studies have questioned its usefulness (e.g., Diament & Wilson, 1975). Foreyt and Hagen (1973) compared covert sensitization and a placebo control (imagining a pleasant scene rather than an aversive one) for weight reduction. Both groups showed a significant decrease in their perceived palatability of the foods imagined during treatment, but no significant weight loss. The results were explained in terms of factors such as suggestion and attention. Janda and Rimm (1972) found covert sensitization effective in reducing eating and weight, but the results at the end of treatment were only significant for those subjects reporting the highest degree of arousal when presented with the aversive scenes. At a six-week follow-up the changes for the entire group of covert sensitization subjects were significantly greater than for the controls. Barrett and Sachs (1974) studied the effects on smoking of covert sensitization. They compared four groups, a forward group (smoking scene, then aversive scene), a backward group (aversive scene, then smoking scene), a backward interval group (backward plus 60 seconds between scenes), and a non-associative group (aversive scene only). They found all treatments to be equally effective. They suggested their results were best explained in terms of such variables as motivation or cognitive changes. In evaluating all such research studies, it is important to keep in mind that covert sensitization is probably most effective when coupled with other treatment procedures, particularly when dealing with complex self-reinforcing behaviors such as over-eating, smoking, and excessive drinking.

Overall, aversive counterconditioning appears to be a potentially useful component in the treatment programs for some difficult behaviors. Evaluation, explanation, and improvement of aversive counterconditioning awaits further research.

SUMMARY

Procedurally, aversive counterconditioning is the counterconditioning of situations that elicit positive-approach behavior using an aversive event, such as unpleasant reactions to certain drugs, electric shock, pictures, odors, sounds, and responses of other people. Covert sensitization is aversive counterconditioning in which the stimuli to be conditioned and the aversive event are imagined scenes. In aversive counterconditioning, the aversive event is primarily respondently associated with stimuli that tend to elicit aspects of the undesired behaviors; while in operant punishment, the aversive event is primarily associated with the occurrence of the undesired behaviors and is usually used to suppress these behaviors. The offset of the aversive event may be used to respondently condition positive effect to some stimuli and/or operantly reinforce some desired behavior. Theories of aversive counterconditioning include counterconditioning, extinction, state theory, and cognitive theory. Although considerable more research is needed, aversive counterconditioning appears to be an effective component of many change programs, particularly when coupled with other approaches. This is especially true in dealing with self-reinforcing behaviors that are difficult to reduce by other means.

THOUGHT QUESTIONS

1. Give three examples of aversive counterconditioning occurring naturally, that is, without someone specifically setting up the contingencies.
2. Give two different hypothetical clinical examples of aversive counterconditioning using aversive events other than those mentioned in the chapter.
3. Outline an aversive counterconditioning program for smokers who come to your clinic. How would you maximize generalization to situations outside the clinic?
4. Outline an aversive counterconditioning program for a hypothetical case of heroin addiction, using hierarchies, in vivo conditioning, and respondent use of the offset of the aversive event.
5. Outline a covert sensitization program for a hypothetical problem drinker. What other approaches (e.g., desensitization) may be part of your overall program? Why?
6. Using a table or diagram, show the relationships among respondent conditioning, counterconditioning, desensitization, and aversive counterconditioning.
7. What are the implications of the fact that whenever you have aversive counterconditioning you also have operant punishment? Give an example in which this would be a serious problem.
8. Are there any problem behaviors that are not self-reinforcing which you would change by aversive counterconditioning? Explain your answer.
9. How important in aversive counterconditioning is the client's motivation to change? How would a counterconditioning theorist answer this question differently from a cognitive theorist?
10. There have been several times in which a sex offender is offered the choice of going to jail or going through aversive counterconditioning. Discuss the ethical and practical issues involved.

11. Describe an experiment that would distinguish, at least for one situation, between a counterconditioning and state theory explanation of aversive counterconditioning.
12. Construct a theory of aversive counterconditioning that incorporates counterconditioning, sensitization, suppression, and self-control.

SUGGESTED READINGS

Davison II, W. S. Studies of aversive conditioning for alcoholics: A critical review of theory and research methodology. *Psychological Bulletin,* 1974, *81,* 571–581.

Hallam, R. S. & Rachman, S. Current status of aversion therapy. In Hersen, M., Eisler, R. M., & Miller, P. M. (eds.), *Progress in behavior modification. Vol. 2.* New York: Academic Press, 1976.

Rachman, S. & Teasdale, J. *Aversion therapy and behaviour disorders: An analysis.* Coral Gables, Fla.: Univ. Miami Press, 1969.

7

Operant Procedures

The last four chapters have emphasized learning based on associations between stimuli. This chapter is concerned with learning and motivational changes based on events that follow behavior and generally are a result of the behavior. A worker receives his salary following completion of a certain number of hours of work. A student receives a particular grade on a test as a result of achieving a certain test score. A child is reprimanded for using certain words. In these cases there is some relationship, called a *contingency*, between the person's behavior (working a number of hours, achieving a test score, using certain words) and some resultant or *contingent* event (salary, grade, reprimand). *Operant conditioning* (also called *instrumental conditioning*) is the learning model based on the effects on behavior of contingent events and the learning of the nature of the contingency. Skinner is the current major authority on operant conditioning.

OPERANT CONDITIONING

If the contingent event makes it *more* probable that the person will behave in a similar way when in a similar situation, the event is called a *reinforcer*. Occasionally, when Bobby was put to bed before he wanted, he would cry. His parents dealt with this by reading him a story to quiet him down. Over time, Bobby cried more often when put to bed. In this situation, the parents' reading him a story was a reinforcement for Bobby's crying. On the other hand, if the contingent event makes the behavior *less* probable, then the event is called a *punisher*. For a while, Susan did all her banking at the neighborhood bank. However, because of poor service there, she gradually shifted most of her business to another bank. Here the poor service is a punishment for using the neighborhood bank.

Following the behavior, the contingent event may come on or increase *(positive);* or the contingent event may go off or decrease *(negative)*. This produces four combinations: positive reinforcement, negative reinforcement, positive punishment, and negative punishment.

Positive reinforcement is an increase in the probability of a behavior due to an increase in the contingent event. Carol, a new manager in a company, began praising workers for submitting their reports on time. In a couple of weeks, this reinforcement by praise greatly increased on-time reports. Positive reinforcement, when appropriately used, is one of the most powerful of all behavior change tools.

Negative reinforcement is an increase in the probability of a behavior due to a decrease in the contingent event. A person learns to use his relaxation skills to offset anxiety, with the decrease in anxiety being a negative reinforcer. A client in aversive counterconditioning (see Chapter 6) is reinforced for putting out his cigarette by the negative reinforcer of the offset of the hot smoke in his face. Thus negative reinforcement is based on the decrease of something undesired such as pain or anxiety. Negative reinforcement is not punishment; reinforcement is an increase in the probability of behavior, while punishment is a decrease.

Negative reinforcement is the basis of *escape conditioning,* learning to escape an aversive situation and being reinforced by the decrease in aversion. Scotty may learn to leave a neighbor's house when the neighbor gets drunk and obnoxious. Escape conditioning may lead to *avoidance conditioning* in which the person learns to avoid the aversive situation. Scotty may learn to avoid going to his drinking neighbor's house. Many politicians avoid important political issues in which no matter what position they take a moderate number of people will get mad and perhaps later vote against them. Votes and money are two strong reinforcers accounting for much political behavior.

Positive punishment is a decrease in the probability of a behavior due to an increase in the contingent event. This is what most people mean when they use the word "punishment." If every time Al tells his algebra teacher he is having trouble keeping up with the class he is then given extra remedial work, then the extra work may act as a punisher resulting in a decrease in asking for help.

Negative punishment is a decrease in the probability of a behavior due to a decrease in the contingent event. This corresponds to a decrease in something desirable following some behavior. If every time a person stutters it briefly turns off a movie he is watching and describing and if this results in a decrease in stuttering, then the offset of the movie is a negative punisher for stuttering.

These four types of contingent events are shown in Figure 3. Note that the onset and offset of the same event may function differently depending on what behaviors they are contingent on. Thus if the onset of a pleasing event results in positive reinforcement, its offset often results in negative punishment. If the onset of an aversive event produces positive punishment, its offset will often produce negative reinforcement. (This is why negative reinforcement is so often confused with punishment.)

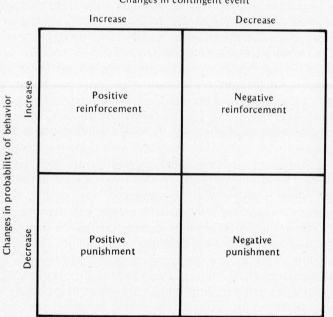

Changes in contingent event

	Increase	Decrease
Increase	Positive reinforcement	Negative reinforcement
Decrease	Positive punishment	Negative punishment

Changes in probability of behavior

FIGURE 3.   Effects of Contingent Events

If we record how probable a behavior is, such as how often it occurs, before we establish one of the above four contingencies, this initial probability is called a *baseline*. Operant conditioning is the establishing of a behavior-event contingency that alters the probability of a behavior away from its baseline. If we now terminate the operant contingency, then the behavior will often return toward the baseline level, a process called *extinction*. Thus reinforcing a behavior increases its probability from the baseline; while later withholding the reinforcement extinguishes the behavior back toward baseline. Punishing a behavior reduces its probability from the baseline; while withholding the punishment lets the behavior extinguish back toward the baseline. Extinction may be slowed or prevented if other variables, such as other reinforcement, come to support the behavior at its new level. For example, an unassertive person may learn to be more assertive with the help of social reinforcement and encouragement from the members of his assertive training group. If the client's new assertive behavior is useful and pleasing (reinforcing) to him in his daily life, then it may continue without the group support.

Sometimes after a behavior has been extinguished its probability drifts back in the pre-extinction direction. This is called *spontaneous recovery*. For example, on Monday and Tuesday David may get his teacher's attention (reinforcement) by playing with the books in the case near his desk. On Wednesday through Friday the teacher extinguishes this behavior. Then on Monday David gives the books another try (spontaneous recovery). Fortunately, this can then be easily extinguished.

From an operant position it is important for the behavior modifier to learn to ask questions such as the following: What is the function of the behavior? What supports or reinforces the behavior? In what situations is the behavior most likely to occur? Learning to identify sources of reinforcement is one of the most powerful skills a behavior modifier can cultivate. Sources of reinforcement are often unexpected. For example, you might be using desensitization (Chapter 5) to reduce a fear in a client and having little success or having trouble getting sufficient motivation or cooperation from the client. Then when pursuing the function of this fear in the client's life, you may find that having the fear is reinforcing and hence the resistance. Perhaps having the fear results in the client receiving special attention or favors from his peers. Or perhaps having the fear keeps him from having to deal with more difficult problems you were not aware of. In such a case these sources of reinforcement and other problems may have to be dealt with before removing the fear. Often this involves helping the client learn other ways to get the reinforcement now received for the undesired behavior. In the clinical literature the expression *secondary gain* is used when discussing reinforcing aspects of apparently undesired behaviors.

Now we turn to behavior change strategies that are based on operant conditioning. This includes altering the stimulus situations in which behaviors occur *(stimulus control)*, getting desirable behaviors to occur and reinforcing them, extinguishing and/or punishing undesired behaviors, reducing the reinforcing effects of events that support undesired behaviors, and combining operant procedures with other approaches.

STIMULUS CONTROL

Operant behaviors do not occur in a vacuum; they occur more in some situations than others and are triggered by external and internal cues. That is, for all operant behaviors there are stimuli, called *discriminative stimuli* and abbreviated S^D, which tend to cue the response. Discriminative stimuli do not elicit the behavior, as the CS elicits the CR, but rather set the occasion for the behavior, making it more or less probable the behavior will occur. Thus we can often alter operant behavior by altering discriminative stimuli.

One approach is to remove discriminative stimuli that cue undesired behaviors. As part of a program to reduce smoking we might remove those stimuli that increase the tendency to smoke, such as ashtrays on the table. When trying to lose weight we might change the route from work to home so it does not pass the doughnut shop.

A second stimulus control approach, called *narrowing,* involves restricting behaviors to a limited set of stimuli. A person who overeats probably is eating in many situations. This results in many discriminative stimuli (e.g., reading, watching TV, having a drink, socializing) cuing the tendency to eat. To cut back on this, we might restrict the eating to one place and certain times. Or in reducing smoking, we might restrict smoking to when the client is sitting in a particular chair in the basement.

Eliminating cues and narrowing are often combined. For example, in improving study habits an important component is establishing good study areas. If a student sits on the sofa when studying, eating, listening to music, and interacting with dates, then the sofa will cue thoughts, feelings, and behavior tendencies that may be incompatible with studying. It is preferable to set up an area in which nothing takes place except studying (perhaps a desk in a corner), get out of the area when doing things like daydreaming, and remove from the area stimuli (e.g., pictures, food) that cue behaviors incompatible with studying. Similarly, treatment of insomnia might involve only going to bed when sleepy; leaving the bed when not falling asleep; and not reading, eating, or watching TV when in bed.

A third stimulus control approach involves introducing stimuli that tend to inhibit the undesired behavior and/or cue behaviors incompatible with the undesired behavior. A person trying to lose weight might put signs and pictures on the refrigerator door.   Or a person who has quit smoking may tell all his friends he has quit. Then the presence of one of his friends may be a stimulus to not smoke.

Because a person's behavior gets tied into the stimuli and patterns of his daily life, it is often desirable to alter as many of these cues as possible. This *stimulus change* may involve a wide range of things such as rearranging furniture, buying new clothes, painting a wall, eating meals at different times, having sexual intercourse at different times and places, or joining a new club. Stimulus change is useful in situations such as part of marriage counseling or when a client is ready to significantly alter his life-style. Similarly, removing a person from his usual life situation until the change program is accomplished is often useful, particularly if coupled with stimulus change of the environment the client returns to.

Stimulus control deals with the antecedent side of operant behavior; the following sections deal with the consequence side.

REINFORCING DESIRABLE BEHAVIORS

The most common operant approach consists of reinforcing desirable behaviors. And this should generally be a component of all operant programs, even when the emphasis is on some other approach, such as extinction.

Nature of reinforcement

There is no theoretical agreement on the nature of reinforcement (see Mikulas, 1974b, p. 130). It is also not clear whether reinforcement affects learning and/or motivation. That is, does the reinforcement somehow strengthen the learning, such as facilitating the physiological changes that underlie the learning, and/or does the reinforcement change the person's motivation, such as providing incentives for certain behaviors? The areas of learning and motivation subtly blend together; so in this text I have related behavior modification to learning-motivation rather than just learning.

Fortunately, these theoretical issues do not impede practical application. For in behavior modification we can take an empirical approach to reinforcement, an approach favored by Skinner. Here we merely identify events that function as reinforcers and use them. An important, but surprisingly often overlooked, point is that we must identify what actually is reinforcing to the person, not what we expect should be reinforcing to him. A good approach to determining reinforcers is to ask the person what is reinforcing, as with a Reinforcement Survey Schedule (Cautela & Kastenbaum, 1967). Similarly, events we may consider not to be reinforcing in fact are. A common example is the teacher who yells at a student as an intended punishment, when really the teacher may be reinforcing the student with attention and/or causing the student to receive social reinforcement from his peers for getting the teacher mad.

Sometimes something will not be reinforcing to the client unless he has had some moderately recent experience with it. Talking on the telephone to a relative may not be reinforcing to a mental patient who has not used the telephone for years. Playing a game may not be reinforcing to an elementary student who is unfamiliar with the game. In these cases, it is often desirable to prime the client by giving him some free experience with the reinforcer before the operant contingencies are established. This procedure is called *reinforcer sampling* (Ayllon & Azrin, 1968a). Sampling of the reinforcer may be increased by having the client observe another person doing the sampling.

Praise is a common and powerful reinforcer. When appropriately used, it has made dramatic changes in a variety of settings, including elementary classrooms and businesses. Money is another powerful reinforcer already affecting much of our behavior. One study used money as a reinforcer to reduce litter in a park in Utah (Powers et al., 1973). A sign notified visitors that for each bag of litter turned in they would receive a choice of 25¢ or a chance to win $20.00 in a weekly lottery. Over 12 weeks, $200.00 in lottery money and $8.50 in quarters were paid out and more than twice as much litter was turned in as before the reinforcement contingency. Another study used money to increase the punctuality of six workers who were chronically late to work in a Mexican manufacturing company (Hermann et al., 1973). For each day they arrived on time, the workers were given small daily bonuses, about 16¢.

Reinforcers for patients on a mental ward may include a visit with the social worker, choice of whom to eat with, a trip to town, candy, cigarettes, new clothes, or gradually earning more privileges. Reinforcers for students may include longer recess, opportunity to be the teacher's aide, field trips, dances, or time in a special reward area filled with different things to do. To date there have only been a few applications of behavior modification in business settings and related organizations (e.g., Luthans & Kreitner, 1975; Mager & Pipe, 1970; Whyte, 1970); but this is changing rapidly. Potential reinforcers in these settings include recognition and praise, bonuses, equipment and supplies, additional staff, added privileges, participation in decision making, option for overtime, and days and hours off.

One theory of reinforcement that has had some impact on behavior modification is that of Premack (1965). Basically, this theory suggests that high-probability behaviors can be used to reinforce lower-probability behaviors. (More formally: If the onset or offset of one response is more probable than the onset or offset of another response, the former will reinforce the latter, positively if the superiority is for the "on" probability and negatively if for the "off" probability.) Thus telling a child he must eat his vegetables (low probability) before he can go out and play (high probability) is using Premack's principle, also sometimes called "Grandma's rule," because grandmothers and others have been using this approach for a long time. The historical importance of this theory in behavior modification is that it focused attention on opportunity to engage in various activities as sources of reinforcement. And some of these activities may be desirable in themselves. For example, students may work on math problems (low probability) in order to work on an ecology project in the library (high probability). Here we not only motivate the students to do more math, but we use a reinforcer that is educationally desirable and perhaps was already part of the program. Goldstein (1974) found that for Navajo children reinforcing activities included learning to weave, silversmithing, leather working, traditional dancing, and storytelling.

To date, however, most of the research related to Premack's theory has been animal studies; research with humans is incomplete and inconclusive, particularly applied studies (Danaher, 1974; Knapp, 1976). The Premack theory also predicts many non-obvious sources of reinforcement from high probability behaviors such as answering a telephone when it rings, opening a door whose handle you have your hand on, and drinking from a glass you have lifted to your mouth. Although these have been used as reinforcers in some behavior modification programs (i.e., coverant control discussed in Chapter 9), little evidence exists relative to their reinforcing effects.

A variation of reinforcement, called *covert reinforcement* (Cautela, 1970b), involves the client imagining a pleasing scene, such as skiing down a mountain, as the reinforcement. Cautela uses covert reinforcement to reinforce behaviors which are also imagined. (Note the parallels to covert sensitization.) Cautela has his client imagine a sequence of steps of the desired behavior. As the client imagines each step Cautela says "reinforcement" and the client then imagines his pleasant scene. Later the client learns how to do this on his own. Research on the effectiveness of this procedure is mixed and lends itself to a variety of explanations (see Mahoney, 1974a, p. 104). Many of the studies seem to be best interpreted in terms of counterconditioning. For example, in one study (Marshall et al., 1974) covert reinforcement was used to successfully reduce fear of snakes in female subjects. Treatment involved having the subjects imagine snake scenes, then relax, and then imagine their reinforcing scene. The relaxation and imagining the pleasant scene may countercondition some of the anxiety associated with snakes. Other studies include successful treatment of test anxiety (Guidry & Randolf, 1974) and a rodent phobia (Blanchard & Draper, 1973). Landouceur (1974) reduced fears of rats, but the group that imagined reinforcement after the anxiety response was not significantly better than the group that imagined the reinforcement before, a result contrary to operant conditioning.

Cautela (1970a) has also suggested *covert negative reinforcement,* which is the same as covert reinforcement except that the client terminates imagining an aversive scene contiguous with imagining a desired behavior. This, however, results in the reinforcement preceding the desired behavior, rather than following it as is required by operant conditioning. An example of treatment would be a homosexual imagining a snake approaching his neck (aversive scene) and then shifting to a scene of hugging a naked girl. Again this may be primarily counterconditioning (e.g., aversion relief). There is currently little evidence on the effectiveness of covert negative reinforcement. One study (Marshall et al., 1974), mentioned earlier, found that covert negative reinforcement was not as effective as covert positive reinforcement in reducing fear of snakes.

A final variation of reinforcement is *self-reinforcement,* reinforcement people give themselves. This may be a form of covert verbal reinforcement (e.g., "That was good work.") or a more tangible reinforcer such as buying yourself some treat. Self-reinforcement is often an important part of self-control processes in which people reinforce themselves for desired behaviors (e.g., Bandura, 1971b; Kanfer, 1971; Mahoney, 1974b).

Initiating behavior

To reinforce desirable behavior the behavior must first occur. If a catatonic has not said anything for five years, it would not be an effective approach to wait for him to say something to reinforce his talking. Thus an important part of the operant approach is to use ways to help initiate the behaviors to be reinforced. There are many ways to do this, including shaping, modeling, fading, punishment, and guidance.

Shaping, also called *successive approximation,* is the reinforcing of behaviors that gradually approximate the desired behavior. The key to shaping is the use of successive approximations that are small enough steps so that there is an easy transition from one step to the next. If one is cultivating the ability to meditate for long periods of time, it may not be desirable to start trying to meditate for an hour. An alternative would be to begin at ten minutes and add one minute every other day, gradually shaping meditation for longer periods of time.

Ayllon (1963) treated a female schizophrenic who wore an excessive amount of clothing, including several sweaters, shawls, and dresses. Before each meal the patient was weighed to determine the weight of the clothing (total weight minus patient's body weight). To receive her meal, the reinforcement, the weight of the clothing had to be less than a set value. At first the patient was allowed 23 pounds of clothing, but this was gradually decreased until she was only wearing 3 pounds of clothing.

The following is a common sequence in shaping language in non-verbal children (Harris, 1975): The child is taught to attend to the teacher. The child learns non-verbal imitative behaviors, going from gross movements such as clapping to more refined movements including use of the mouth. The child learns verbal imitation; first all vocalizations are reinforced, then vocalizations that more and more closely match those of the teacher. Finally, the child's vocalizations are shaped toward functional speech.

Shaping involves starting where the client is, taking small enough steps so the client's behavior smoothly changes, providing reinforcement and support for the changes, and catching mistakes or problems early because of the small steps. Practitioners often also need to use shaping when trying to change the philosophy or programs of the agency or organization where they work.

Modeling, discussed in Chapter 8, involves a change in a person's behavior as a result of observing the behavior of another person, the model. Thus a way of initiating a behavior, particularly with a child, is to have the person observe someone doing the desired behavior and encourage imitation of the behavior. A client who is learning how to interview for a job may first watch the practitioner model appropriate behaviors in a simulated job interview. Or a teacher who praises one student for good behavior may find other students imitating this behavior.

Modeling and shaping combine together well. For example, in *model-reinforcement counseling* the client listens to a tape recording of a counseling interview in which another person is reinforced by a counselor for making a certain class of statements. Then the client is reinforced for making these types of statements. This approach has been used to increase information seeking of high school students engaged in career planning (Krumboltz & Schroeder, 1965) and deliberation and deciding about majors by college students (Wachowiak, 1972).

Azrin and Foxx have shown how the operant approach can dramatically facilitate toilet training in retarded (Foxx & Azrin, 1973b) and "normal" children (Azrin & Foxx, 1974). Their approach with normal children, involving modeling and shaping, includes these components: A wetting doll is used as a model; the child teaches the doll to potty in the same way the child is learning to potty. The child is given extra drinks to increase urination and then through instructions and shaping learns complete toilet procedures, including removing and putting on clothes, use of the toilet, and cleaning up. The child is continually reinforced with praise and treats for maintaining dry pants. Wet pants lead to disapproval, toilet practice, and the child changing the pants. It is important that the child be ready to learn such skills (usually about 20 months old), and Azrin and Foxx give specific tests for this readiness. It is also important that the parent devote himself full time to the program to facilitate shaping and catching accidents immediately. When testing the effectiveness of this program, Azrin and Foxx found that most children could learn the complete toilet-training skills and procedures in less than one day, with the average amount of time being less than four hours. After training, pants inspection and reinforcement are continued for a few days.

Fading involves taking a behavior that occurs in one situation and getting it to occur in a second situation by gradually changing the first situation into the second. A small child might be relaxed and cooperative at home, but frightened and withdrawn if suddenly put into a strange classroom. This fear can be circumvented if the child is gradually introduced to situations that approximate the classroom. Fading is particularly important when a client learns new behaviors in a restricted environment, such as a clinic, hospital, or half-way house. Taking a person out of such a setting and putting him directly back into his home environment may result in a loss in many of his new behaviors and skills. It is preferable to gradually fade from the therapeutic environment to the home environment. Shaping involves approximations on the response side, while fading involves approximations on the stimulus side. And both are similar to the use of a hierarchy in countercondi-tioning (chapter 3).

Punishment of one behavior suppresses that behavior and results in other behaviors occurring. Perhaps one of these other behaviors is a desirable behavior that can be reinforced. This is not a particularly efficient or desirable approach in most cases.

Guidance consists of physically aiding the person to make some response. Thus as part of contact desensitization (Chapter 5) or flooding (Chapter 4), the client may be guided to touch a feared object. Guidance may be used to help a client learn a manual skill or help a child who is learning to talk how to form his lips to make specific sounds.

Variables of reinforcement

Several variables affect the effectiveness of reinforcement. The three most important are amount of reinforcement, delay of reinforcement, and schedule of reinforcement.

Amount of reinforcement refers to both the quality and quantity of reinforcement. Within limits, and with many exceptions, as the amount of reinforcement is increased, the effect of the reinforcement increases.

Delay of reinforcement refers to the amount of time between the person's behavior and the reinforcement for that behavior. As a general rule, you get the best results if the reinforcement occurs right after the behavior. Praising a child for sharing with a friend is generally most effective if the praise occurs right after the sharing than if it is mentioned later in the day. A strength of the toilet-training program described above is that the reinforcers and punishers occurred right after the behaviors. This facilitates the child learning exactly which responses are reinforced and which are punished.

As the delay of reinforcement increases, the effectiveness of the reinforcement decreases. If a student turns in an essay and two weeks later gets it back with the grade of *A,* the reinforcing effects of the *A* on the student's paper writing behavior are much less than if the paper were returned the next day. If a child is required to do specified tasks around the home for his allowance on Friday, we may find the child lax in doing the chores at the beginning of the week, but working well by Thursday or Friday.

Learning to do things that have a long delay of reinforcement is a complex part of the social learning in our culture. We start as children who want immediate gratification and are gradually socialized to function under long delays of reinforcement, such as working for two weeks before getting a paycheck or going to school for many years before reaching a desired position. Learning to respond to long-term contingencies over short-term contingencies is a major aspect of self-control (Rachlin, 1974). You do not eat the extra piece of cake now for better weight and health later. You do not finish the bottle of rum now to avoid the hangover tomorrow. Many people, such as some juvenile delinquents, have not adequately learned how to behave to long delays and their behavior is often under the control of more immediate gratification, which is often undesirable in the long run. Treatment involves helping the person learn to respond to longer-range contingencies. Contingency contracting, discussed later, is a powerful behavioral tool to help bridge long delays of reinforcement.

Schedule of reinforcement refers to the pattern by which reinforcers are related to responses. The primary distinction between schedules of reinforcement is based on whether every correct response is reinforced *(continu-*

ous reinforcement) or whether only some correct responses are reinforced *(intermittent reinforcement).* Learning is faster with continuous reinforcement than with intermittent reinforcement, but time to extinction is longer with intermittent reinforcement. Therefore, it is often strategic first to teach the behavior under continuous reinforcement and then gradually switch to intermittent reinforcement to maintain it.

Facilitating generalization and maintenance

Often an operant program will be established in a specific setting, such as a clinic, half-way house, or classroom. Yet we usually want the behaviors and skills supported and acquired in this setting to carry over and be maintained in other settings. Hopefully, our programs are establishing behaviors with general usefulness. The behaviors usually will generalize, to some degree, from our specific setting to other settings; but it is usually desirable to facilitate this carry-over. Fading, discussed earlier, is one way of accomplishing this. Other ways to facilitate generalization and maintenance of behaviors include the following: Phase the client off the behavior change reinforcements onto more "natural" forms of reinforcement. Thus we start with a specific set of reinforcers and contingencies, as with mental patients in a half-way house or children in a classroom, and gradually switch to the types of reinforcers that should support the behaviors in the everyday environment, reinforcers such as social approval and self-reinforcement. A related approach involves gradually exposing the clients to the types of reinforcement contingencies that occur in the natural social environment. This is accomplished by switching from continuous schedules of reinforcement to intermittent schedules and by gradually helping the clients learn to function under long delays of reinforcement. Finally, we may wish to reprogram the other environments or enlist the help of others to support the newly acquired behaviors. For example, a school counselor and a teacher may set up a program in one classroom that helps Bobby learn social skills that improve his ability to get along with his peers and experience less conflict in the classroom. To facilitate these skills occurring in settings other than this one classroom, the counselor may talk with Bobby's parents and his other teachers about ways to support these new behaviors in various settings.

Criticisms

There are many criticisms of programs that use reinforcement, particularly when used in classrooms (O'Leary et al., 1972). For many critics it seems inappropriate to be reinforcing people for something they should be doing;

to some critics, this smacks of bribery. Another common criticism is that people will come to expect rewards for everything they do and will not work otherwise. This may foster greed or teach the person to be bad in order to be rewarded for being good.

There are a number of problems with these arguments. First, everyone operates under reinforcement contingencies. How do the students earning a reinforcement in a classroom differ from their parents working for their paychecks or the students in another classroom receiving stars or certificates for good work or good behavior? The issue should be what the student is learning and the nature of the contingencies, not whether contingencies exist. To avoid reinforcing people for behaving in some way, because they should behave in this way without reinforcement, is impractical and often to the detriment of those involved. To take the position that students should learn simply for the sake of learning will lose many students to an unrealistic ideal. An alternative is to use an operant program to provide the initial motivation for learning such things as social and academic skills. If these skills are useful to the person, they will eventually be supported by more natural forms of reinforcement. A 15-year-old special education student may never have learned to read and not want to learn. You may establish an operant program in which the student is reinforced for learning to read, being aware of the ethics of all such decisions. At first, the student may only be learning to read to be reinforced. But if things go well and he learns to read, he may find that the skill of reading and what he can do with it becomes reinforcing in itself. Finally, in all such programs, we phase the person off our reinforcement contingencies onto social and self-reinforcement.

Another criticism is based on the fact that some mixed data exist suggesting that in some situations the use of extrinsic reinforcement may reduce intrinsic motivation (Levine & Fasnacht, 1974; Notz, 1975). That is, reinforcing people for doing something may reduce their motivation to do it when not being reinforced. If children enjoy playing certain games and then we begin reinforcing them for playing the games, when we remove the reinforcement their interest in the games may be less than it was prior to reinforcement.

This is certainly important research and points out the need for more studies on intrinsic motivation and self-reinforcement. But it is not that damaging to operant behavior modification programs. First, most of the research involves situations in which the subjects are reinforced for performing behaviors that are already high-probability behaviors. But these are not the types of behaviors we usually need to reinforce in applied settings. Also, we can minimize the suggested problems by such approaches as only reinforcing a person until the behavior becomes intrinsically reinforcing, phase from extrinsic reinforcement to social and self-reinforcement, and support the development of intrinsic motivation.

CONTINGENCY CONTRACTING

A variation of operant procedures is *contingency contracting*, a program in which the operant contingencies are well-specified and clearly understood by everyone involved. These contingencies—reinforcements and punishments that can be expected for different behaviors—are formalized into a contract which is often written. Sometimes the contract is imposed on people; but often the best approach is to negotiate, as much as possible, with all people involved about the nature of the contract. Thus the role of the behavior modifier is often consultant and negotiator about contracting.

Benjamin Franklin employed many procedures for self-development that have a behavior modification flavor to them (Knapp & Shodahl, 1974). Franklin also introduced a simple form of contingency contracting when on a fort building expedition. The chaplain had low attendance at prayer meetings so Franklin suggested that the chaplain give the men their rum after prayers. This greatly increased attendance and punctuality. Franklin considered this method "preferable to the punishment inflicted by some military laws for non-attendance on divine service."

Gupton and LeBow (1971) worked with two telephone solicitors who sold service contracts on household and garden appliances. They preferred to sell renewal contracts, as opposed to new service contracts, as there were more sales with renewal. A contract was set up in which each solicitor had to make one new service sale to be given five renewal customers to call. This resulted in an increase in sale of both types of contracts. Removing the contingency resulted in a decline in sales for both types of contracts, particularly new service contracts.

Often when running a program, such as a smoking clinic or weight loss program, it is important that the clients attend the meetings and/or do homework assignments. One way to provide the necessary motivation is to have the clients deposit money or valuables, which they earn back by fulfilling a contract they agreed to (e.g., Mann, 1972). Thus a person may pay $50 for a clinic on how to stop smoking and be able to earn $30 of it back by attending meetings (e.g., $5 dollars back for each of six meetings). Or a person may give the practitioner some records and photos that can only be earned back by loss of specified weights.

Therapists may also work out contracts with their clients in which such things as procedures, goals, and expenses are carefully specified (Goldiamond, 1974). This is a good way to come to grips with legal and ethical issues. Much of therapy would dramatically change if all therapists were paid for results, specified in a contract, rather than for time spent.

Contingency contracting is powerful in classroom situations (Hayes, 1976; Homme et al., 1969; Litow & Pumroy, 1975; Mikulas, 1974a). The teacher sets up a contract, perhaps with the help of the behavior modifier, specifying what is expected of the students, academically and non-academically, and what reinforcements they may expect for behaving these ways. Thus the students may be required to bring specified supplies, abide by a list of well-specified classroom rules, and turn in their homework completed to a specified degree. Reinforcements may include opportunity to spend a certain amount of time in a reward area or opportunity to work on a special project. Ideally the teacher has negotiated all aspects of the contract with the students and all students fully understand the contract.

Consider the contingencies operative in many classrooms below the college level. Teachers have a certain amount of material they wish to cover and work they wish completed. For the students the contingent event for completing some work is more work. Hence the students learn to work well below capacity, the teachers push for more to be done, and a certain amount of antagonism develops between teachers and students. Now with contingency contracting the teacher presents the work that needs to be done and asks the students what reinforcements they would like for completing the work and what sort of classroom rules can be established to facilitate this program. This results in the students and teacher working together to establish a mutually satisfactory contract. Such an approach generally results in a decrease in behavior problems, an increase in the students liking the classroom setting, and the students doing the work much faster than would be expected. Most teachers, particularly with younger children, spend most of their time being policemen. Contingency contracting provides a behavior management system that frees the teachers to do more teaching.

Although most classroom contracts, at least at first, emphasize nonacademic behaviors, such as being in your seat by the time the second bell rings, academic behaviors can also be built into a contract. Thus a student might earn a reward for improvement in his mathematics skills, independent of his absolute level of proficiency (which may be reflected in his grade). Or the teacher may specify exactly what must be done to achieve a particular grade; this approach being currently popular at the college level.

Contracts, such as those in the classroom, may apply to all the individuals as a unit, a *group contract*. If all students turn in their homework, the whole class gets five extra minutes of recess. This results in social pressure by the group to conform and the whole group being affected by the behavior of a few. A second approach is to have a single contract, which is applied to the people individually. A third approach is to gradually evolve *individualized contracts* in which each person has a personal contract geared toward his specific skills, needs, and problems. In classrooms, this is the point at which we can begin to truly individualize instruction.

Consistency is a critical aspect of most behavior change programs, while inconsistency can generate many problems. If a parent or teacher is consistent in dealing with a child, the child can easily learn what contingencies are operative and feels comfortable understanding how part of the world works. Inconsistency, on the other hand, may produce uncertainty, anxiety, tantrums, psychosomatic illness, learned helplessness (discussed later), and related problems. A parent or teacher who responds to a child more on the adult's temporary mood than on the child's behavior is more difficult for the child to understand than a parent or teacher whose behavior is more consistently related to the child's behavior. Children and others also engage in *rule-testing,* the intentional breaking of a rule to determine if the contingency is in effect. If the system is consistent, there will be some rule-testing. If inconsistent, there will be much rule-testing. Although consistency is perhaps most important with children, it is also important with others. For example, inconsistency in a business setting may result in a drop in morale, feelings of favoritism, feeling powerless to control events, and not knowing what to expect.

A major strength of contingency contracting is that it teaches and requires people to be consistent. If one person fulfills his part of the contract, the other person must fulfill his part. This needs to be true even if the first person is taking advantage of an oversight or loophole in the contract, which will be altered later. This makes contracting in classrooms and homes popular with children because they can hold their teachers or parents responsible to an agreement, while before they may have felt at the mercy of the person in power. In classrooms, this often increases the motivation of students who may otherwise feel the teacher is biased against them.

All operant conditioning involves reciprocity, a mutual interchange of contingent events, usually reinforcements. Even teaching a rat to press a bar has this reciprocity, for the rat is reinforced with food for pressing the bar and the experimenter is reinforced for giving the rat food by the rat pressing the bar, since the experimenter wanted and is pleased by the pressing. The same is true of most human interaction situations; there is usually a mutual interchange of reinforcements. For example, in the classroom the teacher reinforces the students for various accomplishments and in turn is reinforced by these accomplishments. Contingency contracting is a way of establishing a level of reciprocity that is most satisfying for the various people involved. Thus it has proved a useful tool in marriage counseling (Azrin et al., 1973; Glisson, 1976; Hops, 1976; Jacobson & Martin, 1976; Stuart, 1969; Wieman et al., 1974) and families in general (Mikulas, 1976b; Stuart, 1971; Stuart & Lott, 1972; Weathers & Liberman, 1975).

People who live together, such as a married couple or parents and children, need a fair interchange of reinforcements. Often the reciprocity gets out of balance and a standoff develops with various people holding back what is reinforcing to others. For example, during marriage counseling a husband may say he has no desire to rush home from work to a complaining woman dressed as a slob; instead he often goes for drinks with various friends. The wife, on the other hand, reports she does not care how she looks for a man who comes home when he wants and then immediately turns on the television. Or a mother may report that her son does not let her know where he goes, does not do his chores around the home, and is generally too irresponsible to be allowed to do what he wants. The son, on the other hand, sees no reason to cooperate with his mother, since she does not let him do things all his friends are allowed to do. Situations such as these lend themselves to contingency contracting, emphasizing problem-solving rather than fault-finding. Thus a contract involving the mother and her son would involve clear specification of the son's chores around the house and privileges the mother agrees to let him earn by doing the chores.

Basically, the behavior modifier acts as a negotiator discussing with the various people involved what they would like and expect from the others. This is combined, discussed, and negotiated into a formal, written, well-specified contract in which the various people agree to behave in specific ways. The contract provides a powerful way to get a fair reciprocity reinstated. As the various ways of interacting catch hold and support each other, the contract is gradually phased out. Through contracting the people learn when they are rewarding others and when they are being rewarded, how to provide feedback to each other, and how to negotiate with each other. Negotiation can be facilitated by the practitioner arranging hypothetical situations the clients can practice negotiating (Kifer et al., 1974).

In most cases of contracting the contract needs to be altered over time, adding new provisions or qualifications, plugging up loopholes, or renegotiating. However, the contract should usually not be changed retroactively, but only for the future. Contracts often have to be altered to find a good balance between behaviors and reinforcement. If too little reinforcement is given for a behavior, the behavior may not occur; if too much reinforcement is given, the system is inefficient and perhaps wasteful. Contracting is often most effective when accompanied by graphs, signs, reminders, and checklists posted in conspicuous places. Nothing should be left to memory. All aspects of the contract should be written and whenever someone completes part of the contract, it should be marked off or indicated in some written manner. This eliminates disagreements based on people's different memories or perceptions of what is expected or took place.

Since contracting generally involves behavior change in all the people involved, it is an effective way of changing a person's behavior even when that person sees most of the fault being with the others. For example, it is not uncommon for a teacher or parent to bring or refer a child to a practitioner because the child is misbehaving in some sense. Assessment may show that it is the teacher or parent who is responsible for much of the child's misbehavior. Contracting then is an effective way to reasonably and honestly alter the adult's behavior even though the adult sees it primarily as a way to change the child's behavior.

Throughout this text remember that approaches such as desensitization and covert sensitization are being discussed independently, when in fact most actual problems will involve a combination of approaches and procedures. This is certainly true of contracting. Thus contracting may be a critical part of marriage counseling, but the practitioner may also need to deal with such things as sexual dysfunctions, communication problems, or difficulty in handling finances. Or a teacher may use contracting to handle basic class-room behavior and motivation, but still deal separately with many students' problems or individual needs. A strength of contracting is that it provides a motivational framework into which other change programs can be fitted. For example, you may be doing contracting with a family. In addition, you may be helping the mother to stop smoking and desensitizing the daughter. Here the various aspects of the smoking program and desensitization can be incorporated into the contract.

Extrapolating from the discussion of families it can be seen that contract-ing could be a useful component of experimental communities, such as Twin Oaks (Kincaid, 1973), which was basically founded on Skinner's *Walden Two* (1948), a novel of a utopian community using operant procedures. Of the many different types of experimental communities that rise and fall, a major cause of failure is not getting the work done (e.g., "I can't plow the field until I get my head straight about Sally"). This leads to interpersonal problems and some people doing more than their share of work. Through contracting each person can agree to do a certain number of units of work in exchange for community resources and privileges. The system can be made broad enough to handle individual differences in skills and interests and allow flexibility in when the work is done. Miller (1976) describes a commu-nity in which contracting is the basis for a variety of activities, including sharing work, leadership, and self-government. This helps create a truly democratic self-governing system in which roles such as coordinator do not become power positions.

Contracting is also applicable in institutions such as prisons, mental hospitals, and halfway houses, although most of these use token economies, which are discussed later.

Finally, contracting can often be done by people with themselves, perhaps as a component of self-control (e.g., Epstein & Peterson, 1973; Mikulas, 1976a). Here even simple contracts are often effective, requiring the completion of one activity to engage in a preferred activity. For example, first, I will finish the work in the yard, then I will go for a bike ride. For each set of five shirts I iron, I get to read a chapter in the novel. The reason this is effective is that many people have the tendency to do the opposite. Thus a person may have a tendency to watch television until in the mood to study, when contracting would require studying before television. More complex contracting may involve rewards for reaching specific points along the path to the goal, such as buying a new record when 20 chapters of a text have been read and outlined in a specified manner. Contracting provides a source of motivation for whatever program is set up, and this motivation may or may not be sufficient for behavior change. For example, contracting may be sufficient to get the windows around the house washed, but not sufficient for weight loss. In the latter case, we need to add various behavior modification procedures to change the eating habits, with the contracting providing the motivation for doing the program. Although operant procedures in general, including contracting, should emphasize reinforcement, some people find they need a punishment contract to motivate them. That is, the contract specifies a punishment, such as doing extra chores, if the person does not do what is required. For example, a graduate student having motivational problems completing his thesis may give his professor several checks in stamped envelopes made out to an organization the student dislikes. Each time the student turns in part of his paper to a specified criterion by a specified date he gets back one of the checks to destroy. Each time the student misses, his check is mailed to the organization.

TOKEN ECONOMIES

In some contingency contracting programs the client is reinforced with *tokens* (e.g., poker chips, marks on a chart, punch holes in a special card) that can later be exchanged for a choice of reinforcers. Contingency contracting programs using tokens are called *token economies*. There are now a large number of such programs in a wide variety of settings (Kazdin & Bootzin, 1972). The tokens a person earns by completing his part of the contract are eventually exchanged for a choice of reinforcers from a *reinforcement menu*. By having a large number of items and privileges on this menu the tokens are reinforcing for most of the people most of the time, even though people will buy different things at different times. This reduces problems of a person satiating on any particular reinforcer or continually trying to determine what is currently reinforcing to any person.

A strength of token systems is that they deal with the issue of delay of reinforcement discussed earlier. The tokens are often easily dispensed and can be given farily immediately after the desired behavior. For example, a teacher may walk around a classroom putting checks on each student's small clipboard for appropriate behavior and accomplishment. These checks are immediately reinforcing, even though they will not be cashed in until later. They can also be dispensed without greatly disrupting the student's work. Token systems are often used in home situations (e.g., Christophersen et al., 1972). A child may earn tokens every day, which maintains his behavior, even though his purchased reinforcement does not come until the weekend. Or the child may use some of his tokens for small daily rewards (e.g., staying up an extra half hour) and save others over a period of time for a larger reward (e.g., a new model airplane).

Most situations in which contracting is applicable also lend themselves to token economies. This includes classrooms, businesses, mental hospitals, prisons, half-way houses, homes, communities, and the military. The staff of an institution using a token system may also be on a token system.

Token economies in classrooms have been effective with a wide range of academic and social behaviors (O'Leary & Drabman, 1971; Payne et al., 1975; Walker & Buckley, 1974). This is particularly true if the teacher has positive expectations about the system and has been trained how to use praise, attention, and reprimands to aid in the shaping of behavior (O'Leary & Drabman, 1971). In addition, there are often changes in behaviors not specifically treated, such as increases in attention and class attendance. The tokens themselves may be used to teach math or simulate aspects of the real economy. Token systems are particularly useful when working with students who are behavior problems or have little motivation. Similarly, they are useful when working with retarded children (e.g., Welch & Gist, 1974).

A classic example of a token economy in a half-way house is Achievement Place, a family-style residential treatment program for pre-delinquent youths (Phillips et al., 1971, 1973). This is a home with two adults and six to eight boys who have gotten into trouble with the law. The boys live on a token economy in which they can earn tokens for learning social skills, academic skills, self-help skills, and pre-vocational skills. The tokens can be exchanged for such things as games, snacks, allowance, permission to go downtown, and special privileges. While the boys live in Achievement Place they go to regular school; and the practitioners consult and work with the boys' parents and teachers. Eventually the boys are phased back into their homes. Follow-up suggests that as a result of this program there is a decrease in the probability the boys will later get in trouble with the law and an increase in the probability they will continue in school. Achievement Place has provided a model for similar programs elsewhere (e.g., Liberman et al., 1975).

Token economies have also been established in prisons (Musante, 1975), a domain of great potential significance, for they could provide the basis for truly rehabilitative programs. To date, unfortunately, most of these programs have been quite poor and have often merely been new names for standard, questionable disciplinary procedures, such as putting a person in solitary and requiring him to earn his way out by conforming to the guards' wishes.

The best-known and one of the most important applications of token economies is in mental hospitals (Atthowe & Krasner, 1968; Ayllon & Azrin, 1968b; Carlson et al., 1972; Foreyt, 1975; Kazdin, 1975b, 1977; Schaefer & Martin, 1975; Ulmer, 1976). In many mental hospitals there is an inadequate number of staff to deal with all the patients, particularly if therapy is a long process only carried out by a few of the staff. This often results in the hospital being more of a custodial institution in which most of the patients are kept on drugs and receive little therapy. On many wards the patients do little more than sit, pace about, or watch television, for the contingencies are such that there is much they can do that will result in punishment, but little they can do for reinforcement. A token economy can dramatically change all of this.

With a token economy the patients can be gradually shaped to do more and more—such as taking care of themselves, learning social and vocational skills, attending and participating in physical or psychological therapy, and generally taking control of their lives. With their tokens they may buy such things as recreational opportunities or commissary items. The ward attendants and other staff can be trained to implement the program, thus providing considerable treatment for all the patients. This also frees the practitioner to supervise the overall program and tend to specific needs of individual patients. One report (Greenberg et al., 1975) suggests that such programs can be made even more effective by having the patients involved in decision making about treatment procedures.

As a patient gradually improves he may be moved to situations or wards where he has greater responsibilities and greater privileges. Eventually the client may be phased out of the hospital and phased off the tokens onto more natural sources of reinforcement. By this time self-reinforcement and the reinforcement from improvement may be sufficient and the tokens are more for back-up support. Transition into the real world needs to be gradual and carefully considered. Such a transition may be aided by a half-way house, a living situation in the community whose living conditions are half-way between the hospital system and the outside community. Or a community-based program may help the transition (e.g., DeVoge & Downey, 1975).

Although token economies have made dramatic and successful changes in mental hospitals, there are many problems in evaluation of such programs (see Carlson et al., 1972; Gripp & Magaro, 1974). For example, in addition to the token system, the patients also may receive more attention or better physical environments. Although these effects can be factored out in controlled experiments, little such research has been done. The controls that have been used are often superficial and/or not well specified. We need research factoring out the effects of different components of token systems, the effects of different parameters of these components, and comparisons with various different types of treatment.

Although there have been many successful token economies with psychiatric patients, there have also been many problems and failures (see Atthowe, 1973; Hall & Baker, 1973; Kazdin, 1973b). These problems include the following: There is often an enormous heterogeneity of patients, making it difficult to devise a program complex enough to help them all. The program may be missing important needs and problems of the patients and thus the program should be more individualized. Some patients remain unresponsive; we need more information about such patients. Some of the staff may be uncooperative, be responding incorrectly to the patients, or need more training. Similarly, antagonistic or uncooperative administrators or outside communities may hurt the program. Finally, it is important to pay more attention to the global system and look at it in terms of basic economic principles such as wages, prices, and savings. All these problems can be seen to apply, in varying degrees, to other types of token economies.

In any behavior change program there are always important ethical, and sometimes legal, issues to be considered. In the case of token economies, particularly in mental hospitals and prisons, legal constraints are related to the person's personal rights (see Wexler, 1973). The courts have decided, and will be deciding for a while, that patients and prisoners have basic constitutional rights, including having a comfortable bed and adequate meals, opportunity to attend religious services, receive visitors, interact with members of the opposite sex, and go on regular trips outdoors. Also, a patient who does work related to hospital functioning must be paid minimum wage, even if such work is considered therapeutic. Thus a patient cannot be required to earn tokens to buy a meal; the patient has a basic right to the meal.

Operant reinforcement strategies are some of the most powerful behavior change approaches available. Contingency contracting and token economies are ways of formalizing these approaches and thus often making them more effective. Now I turn to operant approaches for decreasing undesired behaviors. But remember that in most situations in which you are decreasing one behavior, you should be reinforcing and increasing another so that desired behaviors are encouraged and the person continues receiving reinforcement.

EXTINCTION

Establishing a contingency between a behavior and a contingent event is operant conditioning; terminating this contingency is operant *extinction*. Reinforcing a behavior increases the probability of that behavior; withholding the reinforcement decreases the probability. A patient in a mental hospital may learn to emit psychotic talk because it gets him extra attention from the staff and other patients. Not reinforcing this type of talk may cause it to extinguish and thus occur less. Williams (1959) reported the case of a 21-month-old male whose tantrums were reinforced by parental attention. After he was put to bed, if the parents left before he went to sleep, he would scream until they returned to the room. This tantrum behavior was easily extinguished by simply letting him scream and rage at night without reinforcing him—that is, by not returning to the room. Eventually, there were no more nighttime tantrums.

However, a person does not learn a simple behavior to a stimulus, but rather learns a whole hierarchy of behaviors. The behavior on the top of the hierarchy is the most probable to occur, the second behavior the next most probable, and on down. The position on the hierarchy and the distance between items on the hierarchy are functions of how many times the behaviors have been reinforced. If the top behavior is extinguished, then the second behavior will occur. And if this behavior is considered undesirable, it will have to be extinguished. Thus the problem with the extinction procedure is that considerable time may be spent going through the entire hierarchy or until a desirable behavior is reached. For this reason the extinction procedure is generally inefficient unless the hierarchy is small, as with many problems with children. It is generally better to emphasize reinforcing a desired behavior in place of the undesired behavior.

Another problem is that it may be difficult or undesirable not to attend to some behaviors, such as destructive or disruptive behaviors. Extinction may also have emotional side effects such as frustration, anger, or confusion. These side effects are minimized if we are simultaneously reinforcing alternative behaviors.

Cautela (1971) has suggested *covert extinction* in which the client imagines doing the undesired behavior and not being reinforced. At the present there is little evidence on the effectiveness of this approach and when it would be most applicable. Cautela suggests it would be useful when you cannot control the environmental contingencies or when the client will not cooperate with regular extinction.

REDUCING NERVOUS HABITS

Many people have a nervous habit such as a tic, biting fingernails, some forms of stuttering, and some typing errors including repeating a letter. Two ways of dealing with these habits are negative practice and habit-reversal.

Negative practice is the reduction of a nervous habit by continually repeating the response in as realistic a way as possible (Dunlap, 1932). A person with a nervous twitch in the mouth would intentionally make this twitch repeatedly until fatigued. Wooden (1974) described the case of a 26-year-old man who for 25 years had been banging his head into his pillow while asleep, resulting in restless sleep and damage to the skin of his forehead. Negative practice consisted of banging his head over and over in the manner he did when asleep, as observed and photographed by his wife. The negative practice was done before he went to sleep and done to the point of being aversive. Four such sessions basically eliminated the habit and resulted in peaceful sleep and less fatigue and anxiety during the day.

The data on the effectiveness of negative practice are mixed (see Rimm & Masters, 1974, p. 325). There are many reports of successful and unsuccessful cases. It is also not clear why it works. My bias is that it is primarily discrimination learning. The practice causes the person to learn to detect the stimuli associated with the habit. Later, when the habit is occurring or beginning to occur, the person will be more able to stop or reduce it. Other explanations and components include extinction, due to the habit occurring without being reinforced, and the suppressive effects of punishment and fatigue that result from the excessive practice.

Habit-reversal is a more complicated program for dealing with nervous habits (Azrin & Nunn, 1973). The client is first taught to be aware of each occurrence of the habit. Then the client is taught to make a response which is incompatible with the undesired response, such as clenching your fists at your sides is incompatible with nail-biting. This incompatible response is made whenever the undesired habit occurs or is about to occur, and the client is taught how to do this in everyday situations. Finally the practitioners increase the client's motivation to decrease the habit and carry out the program. This involves increasing social support for the change and reducing any reinforcement supporting the habit. Habit-reversal was reported as effective with habits such as nail-biting, thumb-sucking, and head-jerking. The habits were reduced by an average of 95 percent after the first day of training, with no recovery during the several months of follow-up. A variation of this approach has been successfully used with stuttering (Azrin & Nunn, 1974).

PUNISHMENT

The most common approach people use to reduce undesired behaviors, particularly in others, is punishment. This consists in applying a contingent event to a behavior that results in a decrease in the probability of the behavior. As mentioned earlier, there are two types of punishment, positive and negative.

Positive punishment is a contingent event whose onset or increase results in a decrease in the probability of the behavior it is contingent upon. If each time Richard starts eating his mother's house plants she shows disapproval and if this disapproval reduces the probability of Richard eating the plants in the future, then the disapproval is positive punishment. Disapproval, criticism, pain, and fines are common forms of punishment.

There are many theories about punishment and its effects (Church, 1963; Johnston, 1972; Solomon, 1964). The effects of punishment include the following: By definition, the punishment has a suppressive effect on behavior—it reduces its probability of occurrence. This does not necessarily mean the behavior will extinguish more readily, only that it is suppressed. The punishment elicits various emotional reactions and possible motor reactions. The punished person may learn whatever behavior is associated with the offset of the punishment (negative reinforcement). And the punished person associates the effects of the punishment with the situations and people involved with the punishment (respondent conditioning). Varying importance is given to these factors in the different theoretical accounts of punishment.

As a behavior change procedure punishment has many disadvantages and possible bad side effects: Punishing an undesirable behavior does not necessarily result in desirable behaviors. Punishing a child in a classroom for throwing things during self-work time does not necessarily result in the child shifting to working alone. Perhaps self-work behaviors are not in the child's repertoire. Punishment may condition in reactions such as fear, anxiety, or hate to the people who administer the punishment or the situations in which it occurs. Thus children may fear their parents, students may dislike school, criminals may resent society, and workers may not fully cooperate with their foreman. Related to this is that the person may learn to escape or avoid these people or situations, resulting in such possibilities as a school phobia or an increase in absenteeism from work. Attempted punishment of an escape or avoidance response may rather increase the strength of the avoidance. Punishing a child with a fear of the dark for not going into the basement at night alone may actually increase the fear. The punished person may spend some time making up excuses and passing the blame to others. The punishing agents may act as models (Chapter 8) for aggressive behavior. Children may model after their parents and learn to hit people when mad; workers may model their supervisors and become overcritical of the errors of their subordinates. Finally, punished people may become generally less flexible and adaptable in their behaviors.

For reasons such as these, it is usually desirable to minimize or avoid the use of punishment. However, our culture is very punishment oriented. One reason is that people often punish out of their own anger or inability to handle a situation. Also the immediate suppressive effects of the punishment are reinforcing to the punishing agent, even though the long-term effects of the punishment may be undesirable. This is another example of how a short delay of reinforcement has a greater effect on behavior than do longer delays. You will run across many situations, particularly with parents and teachers, in which they want to know effective ways of stopping undesired behaviors, such as more effective forms of punishment. In most of these situations you need to turn it around and emphasize ways of increasing desirable behaviors, as with reinforcement procedures.

If punishment is to be used, it needs to be applied immediately after the behavior and applied consistently. The earlier in the response chain the punishment occurs the better, for then it may stop or disrupt a sequence of undesired behaviors. Punishment should generally be coupled with extinction and reinforcing of alternative behaviors. If possible the punishment should be viewed, by all people involved, as part of a contractual agreement rather than a personal attack. Despite all my qualifications about punishment, many situations exist in which it seems effective and desirable (Baer, 1971; Lovibond, 1970).

Lang and Melamed (1969) worked with a nine-month-old child weighing 12 pounds whose persistent vomiting prevented weight gain. Various types of treatment (e.g., dietary changes, use of antinauseants, small feedings at a time, establishing a warm secure feeling in the child) had been ineffective and there was a chance the child would die. Lang and Melamed used an electromyogram (EMG), which measures the activity of muscles, to determine the beginning of vomiting. The child received shock to the leg when the EMG showed vomiting beginning, and the shock went off when the vomiting stopped. A total of nine such punishment sessions ended the problem, and one month later the child weighed 21 pounds. In a similar case, a six-month-old child was punished for vomiting by squirting lemon juice in her mouth (Sajwaj et al., 1974). This effectively stopped the vomiting.

Kushner (1968) worked with a 17-year-old girl who could not stop sneezing, averaging a sneeze about once every 40 seconds. Neurologists, allergists, psychiatrists, hypnotists, and others had been no help. Kushner hooked her up to a device which gave her electric shock to the fingers every time she sneezed. After four and a half hours of treatment the uncontrolled sneezing was gone for good.

Punishment is often used more for its disruptive effects than suppressive effects. As part of a self-control program a person may wear a rubber band around his wrist which he snaps on the underside of his wrist to disrupt unwanted thoughts or feelings. (A parallel of this is thought stopping discussed in Chapter 9.) Also just wearing the rubber band then acts as a reminder about his behavior. This disruptive effect of punishment is a key in most behavioral treatments of autism.

Childhood autism is a poorly defined diagnostic category, but in its extreme includes behavioral characteristics such as the following: The child has little or no speech; some children will imitate sounds, some will not. Similarly they do not respond to language or other social cues. People often seem to be just objects to the autistic child. Part of the problem may be overselective attention. The child may appear deaf or visually impaired when he is only not responding to that sense mode. Autistic children generally engage in some type of self-stimulating behavior, such as whirling or flapping of arms. Autistic children may also engage in tantrums and self-mutilating behaviors, such as chewing their shoulders or biting off fingers. Such children are often kept bound spread-eagle on a bed. Many autistic children will spend the rest of their lives in institutions.

Lovaas and his associates have probably made the most progress in the treatment of autism (Lovaas et al., 1973; Schreibman & Koegel, 1975). They use basically an operant approach utilizing shaping, modeling, and guidance to gradually teach the child to imitate, speak, read, and write. This then leads to learning more complex personal and social behaviors. At first they have to use very basic reinforcers, such as food and hugs, until the child is responding to social reinforcers like approval. Punishment—in the form of slaps or electric shock—is necessary to disrupt tantrums or self-mutilating behaviors. That is, the punishment disrupts these behaviors so that the practitioner has the opportunity to shape and reinforce desirable behaviors. All children improved as a result of this treatment program, some much more than others. After eight months of treatment some children showed spontaneous use of language and spontaneous social interactions. Children who were returned to parents who had been trained in behavior modification continued to improve. Children whose parents sent them to institutions regressed to their old behaviors.

Similarly, Tanner and Zeiler (1974), working with a 20-year-old autistic woman who injured herself, reduced her slapping herself with the punishment of fumes from ammonia capsules. On the other hand, self-injurious behavior may be reduced by building in alternative behaviors (Azrin et al., 1975). And some people working with autistic children are teaching them sign language as a goal in itself and as a first step to possible normal speech (Offir, 1976).

Azrin and his associates have been experimenting with a form of punishment they call *overcorrection* (e.g., Foxx & Azrin, 1973a). In *positive practice overcorrection* the client is required to practice correct behaviors each time an episode of the undesired behaviors occurs. A child marking on the wall might be required to copy a set of patterns with pencil and paper. In the case of an autistic or hyperactive child who is pounding objects or himself, he would be told of his inappropriate behavior which would be stopped. Then the child would be given verbal instructions, and physical guidance if necessary, for the overcorrection behavior; in this case a few minutes of instruction for putting hands at sides, then over head, then straight out, and so forth.

In *restitutional overcorrection* or *restitution,* clients must correct the results of their misbehavior to a better-than-normal state. A child who marks on the wall may be required to erase the marks and wash the entire wall as well. A child who turns over chairs may be required to set up those chairs and straighten up the rest of the furniture. Screaming may require a period of exceptional quiet. Creative judges sometimes use restitution in their sentences. Thus if two juveniles vandalized the home of an elderly couple, a good sentence might involve the offenders repairing what they did, as well as doing other work around the vandalized house. This would make the juveniles more aware of the results of their misdeeds on others.

Azrin and Wesolowski (1974) used restitution to stop food stealing by retarded adults. If a client were caught stealing, he not only had to return the stolen object, but also give the victim an additional object of the same kind. This stopped food stealing in three days and was more effective than a simple correction procedure in which the person only returns the stolen object. Also working with institutionalized retardates Webster and Azrin (1973) found that an effective way of treating agitative-disruptive behavior was to require of the client two hours of relaxing in bed. If the client was disruptive during the last 15 minutes, 15 additional minutes were added to the two hours. This resulted in a rapid reduction in such things as self-injury, threats, physical aggression, and screaming.

Covert punishment would consist of carrying out the punishment in the imagination. There is almost no information on such an approach. Moser (1974) worked with a 24-year-old male "paranoid schizophrenic" who had auditory and visual hallucinations of his deceased brother and mother. The hallucinations were eliminated by teaching the client to punish them with thoughts of eating cottage cheese which the client disliked. Also Cautela's conceptualization of covert sensitization (Chapter 6) is covert punishment.

The discussion of punishment so far has emphasized positive punishment. I turn now to *negative punishment,* a contingent event whose offset or decrease results in a decrease in the behavior it is contingent on. This generally consists of taking away something that is reinforcing from a person when he misbehaves. The procedure of negative punishment generally also results in positive punishment and/or extinction. Hence at the present it is not possible to specify exactly what effects are specifically due to negative punishment. In behavior modification there are two major forms of negative punishment, response cost and time out.

Response cost is the withdrawal or loss of a reinforcement contingent on a behavior. This may be the loss or fine of tokens in a token system, such as a fine for the use of the word "ain't" in Achievement Place. Response cost has been used to suppress a variety of behaviors such as smoking, overeating, stuttering, psychotic talk, aggressiveness, and tardiness (Kazdin, 1972). Possible advantages of response cost are that it may have fewer aversive side effects than positive punishment and it leaves the person in the learning situation, which time out does not. But much more research is needed in this area.

Time out (or *time out from reinforcement*) is the punishment procedure in which the punishment is a period of time during which reinforcement is not available. For example, time out has been an effective punishment procedure in classrooms. If a child misbehaves, he may be sent to spend ten minutes in a time-out area, perhaps a screened-off corner in the back of the classroom. For time out to be effective the area the client is removed from must be reinforcing to him. The classroom should be a reinforcing place and being in time out may result in a period of time in which the student cannot earn tokens. Also the time-out area should not be reinforcing. In a home sending a child to his room may not be a good time out, as the room may be filled with reinforcers. Usually just a few minutes in time out is sufficient; and it often gives the punished person a chance to cool off.

Cayner and Kiland (1974), working with three hospitalized patients diagnosed as chronic schizophrenics, used a time out which consisted of five minutes in a ward bedroom that only had a bed in it. This time out effectively eliminated behaviors such as screaming and swearing, tantrums, and self-mutilation.

Again much research is needed on time out. MacDonough and Forehand (1973) have suggested the following parameters that need to be investigated: whether a reason is given for time out, whether the person was first given a warning, ways of getting the person into the time-out area, duration of time out, presence or absence of a signal to indicate onset or offset of time out, whether the time-out area is isolated from where the misbehavior occurred, schedule of time out (e.g., continuous versus intermittent), and whether the person must behave in some way to be released from time out.

Finally, there is also the possibility of *covert negative punishment,* negative punishment carried out in the imagination. But there is currently almost no information on this. One study reported reducing some eating behaviors by having the clients imagine the loss of something reinforcing, such as having a car stolen (Tondo et al., 1975).

STIMULUS SATIATION

So far in this chapter I have discussed two major ways of reducing undesired behaviors, extinction and punishment. A third way is to reduce the reinforcing effects of the events supporting the undesired behavior. Aversive counterconditioning (Chapter 6) is a way to do this. A related approach is *stimulus satiation* in which the client is flooded with the reinforcer repeatedly until it loses much or all of its reinforcing effect. A child who keeps playing with matches might be sat down with a large number of matches to strike and light. This would be continued until lighting matches lost their reinforcing effect. It is not known how or why stimulus satiation works, but it seems to contain components of aversive counterconditioning and respondent extinction of reinforcing effects.

Ayllon (1963) worked with a 47-year-old, hospitalized female diagnosed as a chronic schizophrenic. One of her problems was hoarding towels; she had 19–29 towels in her room at one time with the nurses removing towels twice a week. Treatment consisted of intermittently giving her towels during the day, starting with 7 per day and up to 60 per day by the third week, and not removing towels from her room. When the number of towels in her room reached 625, she started taking them out and no more were given her. During the next year, she only averaged 1.5 towels in her room per week.

Stimulus satiation has been used in the treatment of smoking by dramatically increasing the number of cigarettes smoked (Resnick, 1968) and/or the rate of smoking the cigarettes (Lichtenstein et al., 1973). In one study a metronome was used to have the clients smoke every six seconds (Lichtenstein et al., 1973). This stimulus satiation produced a significant reduction in smoking with 60 percent of the subjects abstinent at six months. The treatment was equally effective as aversive counterconditioning, using hot cigarette smoke blown in the face, and as a combination of stimulus satiation and this aversive counterconditioning. Others (e.g., Lando, 1975) have not been as successful using a variation of stimulus satiation with smokers. Also, rapid smoking should not be used with some clients with respiratory or cardiac problems.

COMBINING PROCEDURES

Many operant procedures have been discussed separately in this chapter. However, it must be remembered that in any operant program or operant analysis of a situation it is necessary to consider and combine the range of operant variables and procedures discussed in this chapter. This includes stimulus control, reinforcing desirable behaviors, contracting, extinguishing and punishing undesirable behaviors, and changing the reinforcing effects of some events. More important is the necessity of often combining operant procedures with other approaches and procedures, including those in the rest of this book. For example, let us think about operant conditioning together with respondent conditioning (Chapters 3–6).

We begin with the stimuli, external and internal, as perceived and interpreted by the person. Internal stimuli include thoughts and cues associated with emotions and bodily activity. Some of the external and internal stimuli will be conditioned stimuli eliciting a range of conditioned responses of various strengths. Some of the stimuli will be discriminative stimuli cuing various possible operants. Part of our job is identifying and perhaps altering these different types of stimuli. Next is the motivation of the person. Part of the motivation may be based on conditioned responses, such as anxiety or anger, which can be altered respondently. Part of the motivation may be based on anticipation of reinforcements and punishment, which can be altered operantly. In the presence of specific stimuli and specific motivation, the person will behave in some way based largely on past learning. Here we can provide training in alternative ways to behave in such situations. Finally, there are certain consequences to people because of their behavior, including reinforcement and punishment. Dealing with the contingencies of these consequences is operant conditioning, while altering the reinforcing or punishing effects of an event may involve respondent conditioning.

NON-DEPENDENT EVENTS

Operant conditioning is based on the effects of contingent events, events contiguous with some behavior. Now we distinguish between two different types of contingent events, dependent and nondependent. A contingent event is a *dependent* event when it occurs only if a specified behavior occurs first; otherwise it is a *non-dependent* event. That is, dependent events only occur if the person acts a certain way, while non-dependent events occur independent of what the person does. Operant conditioning only requires that the event be contingent, dependent or non-dependent. However, most examples of operant conditioning, most of this chapter, and perhaps all applied operant programs are based on dependent contingent events. Here I consider the effects of non-dependent events.

If the non-dependent event is a reinforcement, the person may be reinforced for doing something not causally related to the reinforcement. Such behavior is called *superstitious behavior* (Herrnstein, 1966). For example, a therapist may decide to try some new therapy on his clients. And the clients may improve for reasons other than the specific form of therapy, perhaps because of placebo effects or personal changes outside of therapy. Here the improvement of the clients may be a reinforcement for the therapist's superstition of doing the new therapy. Because superstitions are often maintained on an intermittent schedule of reinforcement, they are difficult to extinguish.

If the non-dependent event is a punishment, the result may be *learned helplessness,* a passive-resigned state resulting from learning the independence of behavior and consequences (Seligman, 1975). That is, if the person learns that things happen to him regardless of how he behaves, he may become passively resigned to simply take what happens with little trying to influence the outcomes. This is true of uncontrollable reinforcers as well as uncontrollable punishment; but the latter is the area in which most of the research has been done. A child in a classroom or a patient on a hospital ward who perceives that his behavior has little effect on what happens to him may develop learned helplessness. This is one reason to have consistency in our operant programs. Learned helplessness may be a component in a wide range of behavior problems, including the child who is withdrawn, the adult who is unassertive and indecisive, some forms of depression, and perhaps the acceleration of death in some old people.

FEEDBACK

It is useful to keep in mind that all of operant conditioning is a subset of the general area of *feedback,* information to individuals about the effects of their behavior (see Mikulas, 1974b, chap. 6). To move your arm requires feedback from the muscles of your arm about the effects of movement. Speech utilizes feedback from the tongue and lips, as well as auditory feedback from hearing your own voice. Education is guided by feedback on tests and papers. Political positions are sometimes altered because of feedback from voters via polls or mail. Every time we do something—from a simple movement to a complex social interaction—we receive varying amounts of feedback about what effects our behavior had on ourselves, others, and our environment. This feedback guides our current and future behavior.

Feedback may have one or more of these effects: (1) The feedback may be a reinforcement or punishment. Receiving an *A* on a test may be rewarding to a student so that he maintains the same approach to studying for the next tests. (2) The feedback may produce changes in motivation, such as the goals a person sets for himself. Receiving a *D* on a test may motivate the student to work harder in the class. (3) Feedback may provide informative cues that guide learning and performance. A person who does poorly on a test may see that it is because the test emphasized the class lectures which the student ignored. (4) Feedback may provide a new learning experience or rehearsal of previous learning. When getting a test back a student may learn the correct answers to questions that he did not know.

By keeping in mind that operant conditioning is part of feedback, it keeps us from overlooking the other important effects of feedback. When parents punish their children they should also give them feedback about exactly why (punishment contingencies) they are being punished and what are preferable alternatives. Managers should not simply praise their workers, but also point out what the workers did that is praise-worthy.

One study used operant conditioning to reduce phobias by encouraging the subjects to spend more and more time in the feared situation to extinguish the fear (Leitenberg et al., 1975). There was not much initial progress using only contingent praise. However, there was dramatic improvement when the subjects were given precise feedback about their performance.

Another subset of feedback is the area of *biofeedback,* use of mechanical devices to provide knowledge of the activity of a body function for which the person has inadequate feedback (Brown, 1975; DeCara et al., 1975; Yates, 1975, chap. 8). For example, a person may be hooked up to a device that provides him continuous feedback about his blood pressure. Through such biofeedback the person may learn to raise or lower his blood pressure at will. Biofeedback has been used for a wide range of applied problems, including improving reading by decreasing subvocalization via biofeedback from the Adam's apple, reducing tension headaches by relaxing muscles in the neck and head measured by biofeedback, reducing migraine headaches by decreasing the relative flow of blood to the head, and generating specific brain waves that may facilitate relaxing. Biofeedback is a useful tool, but it is often inferior to procedures that do not require or depend on mechanical devices. For example, a person with tension headaches may profit more from extensive muscle relaxation training (Chapter 3) for these specific muscles. This way the person can discriminate and regulate these muscles without a mechanical device. On the other hand, the biofeedback may facilitate the early stages of muscle relaxation training.

Feedback is one of the major sources of variables affecting human behavior. Altering feedback is one way a behavior modifier can alter behavior. And operant conditioning deals with some powerful alterations in feedback.

SUMMARY

Human behavior is strongly affected and guided by feedback, information about the consequences of one's behavior. Feedback produces motivation and learning changes, including those of operant conditioning. The emphasis of operant conditioning is on changes in the probability of a behavior in the presence of specific stimuli as a result of events contingent on the behavior. A reinforcer increases the probability of a behavior it is contingent on; a punisher decreases the probability. The contingent event is usually dependent on the behavior and occurs because of the behavior. Non-dependent events may lead to superstitious behavior and/or learned helplessness. Behavior modification procedures based on operant conditioning include altering the stimuli that cue operant behaviors, reinforcing desired behaviors, punishing and/or extinguishing undesired behaviors, and changing the reinforcing or punishing effect of contingent events. Stimulus control, including narrowing and stimulus change, involves removing or altering stimuli that cue undesired behaviors and/or introducing stimuli that cue alternative behaviors. The first step in reinforcing behaviors is determining a reinforcer. This may involve observing or asking the client about reinforcers and perhaps letting the client try the reinforcer (reinforcer sampling). Reinforcers include tangible items, opportunities to do things such as high-probability behaviors, social approval and recognition, pleasing thoughts, and self-reinforcement. Procedures to get a behavior to occur to reinforce it include shaping, modeling, fading, punishment, and guidance. Initial learning is usually best when the reinforcer occurs immediately after every example of the correct behavior (short delay of reinforcement, continuous schedule of reinforcement). Extinction is the return of the probability of a behavior toward its initial value (baseline) after the contingent events have been removed. Use of an intermittent schedule of reinforcement increases resistance to extinction. Punishment as a change procedure should generally be avoided bacause of undesirable side effects; but it can be used effectively to disrupt or suppress an undesired behavior while a desired alternative is being strengthened. Positive punishment procedures include administering an aversive event and overcorrection, while negative punishment includes a withdrawal or loss of a reinforcer (response cost) and a period of time during which reinforcers cannot be acquired (time out). The reinforcing effects of an event can be reduced by aversive counterconditioning or stimulus satiation. Nervous habits can be reduced by negative practice and habit reversal. Contingency contracting is a formalized operant program in which the contingencies are well specified and usually negotiated. Contracting facilitates people learning to respond consistently with each other and the development of a reasonable reciprocity of expectations and demands. A token economy is contingency contracting in which the reinforcers are tokens that can later be exchanged for a choice of rewards.

THOUGHT QUESTIONS

1. Give three reasons why it would be advantageous to establish a baseline before beginning an operant program. (Some reasons are given in Chapter 2.)
2. List two different types of tokens and three different possible reinforcers that could be used in each of the following settings: a nursery school, an automobile assembly plant, the army.

3. In your life: (a) What are the three most important types of reinforcement? (b) What is an unusual reinforcer? (c) How did these events come to be reinforcing?

4. Give examples of secondary gain from two different hypothetical cases.

5. Design and describe a training exercise you would use to help teachers identify the sources of reinforcement affecting classroom behavior.

6. How should grades be used in college and high school? as reinforcers? as a measure of accomplishment, regardless of how long it took? as a measure of accomplishment within a set time period? as an estimate by the instructor of the student's basic skills and knowledge in the area? Why? What are the effects of these different grading approaches on student behavior and on people (e.g., graduate schools, businesses) that use grades in their selection processes?

7. In general, would you expect reinforcer sampling to be more useful with mental patients or college students? Why? What are the implications of your answer?

8. Design and outline a program you might set up in a prison to help the inmates learn to postpone immediate gratification and respond to contingencies of a much longer delay of reinforcement.

9. Contingency contracting generally insures that everyone understands the nature of the operant contingencies. What are the advantages of this? When might this be disadvantageous in an operant program? What ethical issues are involved?

10. Consider a mental patient with no physical disabilities who for the last five years has always been bathed, dressed, and fed by others. Outline a shaping program to help this person become more self-sufficient.

11. What are the relationships among discriminative stimuli, fading, narrowing, and operant extinction?

12. Outline a program for improving study habits that uses stimulus control, shaping, and contracting.

13. Describe an ideal high school in which all learning is totally individualized via contracts. What traditional social and educational ideas and values would be challenged by such an approach?

14. Draw up a contract for a hypothetical couple you have been working with in marriage counseling.

15. Assuming you are the head of a token economy half-way house for drug-abusers, describe some of the things you would do to facilitate the behavior changes from the half-way house carrying over to the real world to which the clients are returned.

16. Outline the steps you would go through in establishing a token economy in a kindergarten.

17. What are some important considerations in establishing a token economy in a prison? Would it be desirable, practical, and socially acceptable to allow prisoners to earn their way out of prison by acquiring personal, social, and vocational skills?

18. Set up a contract for yourself for at least one week. What did you do? How did it work? What would you do differently next time?

19. What are the procedural differences between operant punishment of this chapter and aversive counterconditioning of the last chapter? Describe a situation in which these differences would be significant.

20. Distinguish between positive punishment and negative reinforcement. Give an applied example in which the same event is used for both.

21. Give a classroom example of positive practice overcorrection and a business example of restitutional overcorrection.
22. What are the practical similarities and differences between response cost and time out? When would you use each one? Give examples of each for an elementary classroom and a ward in a mental hospital.
23. What are the implications of having a punishment-oriented culture? What may be done to change this? How about punishing people who use too much punishment?
24. Give three different examples, other than those in the text, of situations in which you would use operant extinction as your major change approach.
25. Describe a habit reversal program for nail-biting.
26. Give two examples, other than those in the text, of situations in which you would use stimulus satiation. Design and describe a self-control approach we might call "covert stimulus satiation." Give an example of how this would be used.
27. Outline the operant components in a program for an alcoholic.
28. What is the relationship between phobias and avoidance conditioning? Give an example and show the interrelationships between operant and respondent variables.
29. In the context of reducing fear, what are the similarities between operant procedures (shaping, fading, reinforcement) and respondent procedures (use of hierarchy, incompatible response)? What does this mean in terms of separating operant and respondent variables? What are the practical implications?
30. Design and outline a general self-control strategy that incorporates the ideas of covert reinforcement, covert punishment, covert extinction, and covert sensitization. When would this approach be part of your general program?
31. Including ideas of learned helplessness, briefly describe the genesis of extreme social withdrawal in a hypothetical case of a 10-year-old girl. If not corrected, how might this problem lead to depression in later life?
32. Make up and briefly describe "feedback therapy" in which all therapeutic approaches are conceptualized in terms of feedback.

SUGGESTED READINGS

Gentry, W. D. (ed.). *Applied behavior modification*. St. Louis: C. V. Mosby, 1975.

Kazdin, A. E. *Behavior modification in applied settings*. Homewood, Ill.: Dorsey Press, 1975.

Malott, R. W., Ritterby, K., & Wolf, E. L. C. (eds.). *An introduction to behavior modification*. Kalamazoo, Mich.: Behaviordelia, 1973.

Schaefer, H. H. & Martin, P. L. *Behavioral therapy*. 2d ed. New York: McGraw-Hill, 1975.

Skinner, B. F. *Science and human behavior*. New York: Macmillan, 1953. Free Press Paperback, 1965.

Skinner, B. F. *Walden Two*. New York: Macmillan, 1948. Macmillan paperback, 1962.

Sundel, M. & Sundel, S. S. *Behavior modification in the human services: A systematic introduction to concepts and applications*. New York: Wiley, 1975.

Whaley, D. L. & Malott, R. W. *Elementary principles of behavior*. New York: Meredith Corporation, 1971.

Modeling

A person's behavior often changes merely as a result of observing the behavior and behavior consequences of someone else. A teenager may adopt some of the dress and mannerisms of his socially successful peers. A new employee in an organization may best learn his job by observing an older employee. Behavior change that results from the observation of the behavior of another is called *modeling* (Bandura, 1969, chap. 3, 1971a; Marlatt & Perry, 1975; Rachman, 1972; Rosenthal, 1976). It is also called observation learning, imitation, vicarious learning, and social learning. What is "observed" is the behavior of the model, the consequences of this behavior, and verbal cues and instructions of the model. Modeling covers a wide range of behaviors, including these described by Bandura (1969, p. 118):

> . . . one can acquire intricate response patterns merely by observing the performances of appropriate models; emotional responses can be conditioned observationally by witnessing the affective reactions of others undergoing painful or pleasurable experiences; fearful and avoidant behavior can be extinguished vicariously through observation of modeled approach behavior toward feared objects without any adverse consequences accruing to the performer; inhibitions can be induced by witnessing the behavior of others punished; and finally, the expression of well-learned responses can be enhanced and socially regulated through the actions of influential models.

The more influential model is often a person who is significant to the observer. Thus children often model after parents, students model teachers, and clients model therapists (which many therapists interpret as improvement). Or the model may be a purposed expert, celebrity, or simply someone who is effective at doing or achieving what the observer wishes. Often the model is someone similar to the observer so that the consequences of the model's behavior are seen as relevant to what may happen to the observer for acting similarly. The model may also be presented on film or television, be a real person or fictional character, or be a character in a book or cartoon. Thus modeling arises in a wide range of situations from watching people to reading a book. This gives modeling a broad field of importance and application, but also makes its exact nature and boundaries a little hazy.

The influence of the mass media, such as movies and television, gives modeling particular social importance. The movie *Deliverance* showed men rafting down a dangerous southern river. After seeing this movie, many more people attempted to raft such rivers leading to many people getting hurt. Television is much more powerful because of the number of people it reaches. Currently 96 percent of all households in the United States have at least one television. On the average the television is on for about six hours every day with children and adults watching about two hours a day. By the time the average teenager graduates from high school he will have spent more time watching television than any other activity (including school) except sleeping. Thus the impact of television content on our culture is probably quite significant, which leads to some issues such as violence on television.

Although someone may model many behaviors from one model, as a girl may model her mother, it is common for the observer to take diverse combinations of behaviors from different models, often abstracting basic strategies of responding (such as being more cooperative with teachers or being less aggressive socially) rather than specific behaviors. The effects of modeling are also often transient and easily changed. For if the new modeled behavior is not useful (e.g., reinforcing) to the person, it will be altered or abandoned. This is why modeling and operant procedures often fit together well. We are all continually involved in these types of processes, picking up behaviors and strategies from various models, trying out different behaviors, and keeping those that currently "work" for us.

Modeling is very prevalent, it is a key part of many behavior change programs, but there is no theoretical agreement on how it works. An operant analysis of modeling might be based on the person being reinforced for imitating others' behavior. But such an approach is sometimes strained to account for the initial acquisition of novel responses, acquisition when there is no overt response to be reinforced, and situations in which there is no apparent reinforcement or the reinforcement is delayed for a long time. Bandura (e.g., 1971a) argues for a social learning theory approach to modeling. Here modeling is seen as providing information that the person acquires as symbolic representations of the modeled event. Bandura suggests four processes are involved: attentional processes, retention processes, motor reproduction processes, and incentive or motivational processes.

Attentional processes regulate the sensory input and perception of the modeled event. Included here are attributes of the model that attract attention and incentives (e.g., possible reinforcement) to attend to the event. *Retention processes* refer to coding processes by which the observed event is translated into a guide for future performance. Note that what is stored is not simply what was observed, but a coded representation, perhaps abstracting information from several events or sources. Retention processes also include rehearsal of the experiences within the symbolic system. Retention may be facilitated by having the client or model summarize or describe what happened and/or have the client practice the modeled behavior. *Motor reproduction processes* refer to the integration of various constituent acts into new response patterns, while *incentive or motivational processes* determine whether observationally acquired responses will be performed. According to Bandura, the role of reinforcement and incentives is to facilitate attention to the modeled event and encourage rehearsal and translation into overt behavior. Thus it is often desirable to have the model receive reinforcement for his behaviors or have the model the one who controls the reinforcement the observer may receive.

I turn now to some of the applications of modeling to behavior change. But it is important to remember that modeling, like most other approaches, is most effective when coupled with other procedures. For example, in reducing fears contact desensitization (see Chapter 5), a combination of modeling and guided participation, is generally more effective than just modeling. And in operant conditioning (see Chapter 7) modeling is an effective way to get behaviors to occur, while reinforcement maintains the behavior after it occurs. Similarly, much of the reasoning and strategies of behavior change discussed in previous chapters are applicable to modeling. For example, the gradual approach of hierarchies and shaping is often useful. In acquiring new social skills the client may be exposed to models that behave in gradual approximations to the final complex behaviors. Or in reducing a fear the client may be exposed to models that gradually approach the feared object.

INITIATING AND ENHANCING BEHAVIOR

Modeling is often an effective way to get behaviors to initially occur, for the person can simply be shown what to do and encouraged to imitate. Thus modeling plus reinforcement is a more effective way to teach a child to tie his shoes than is shaping. Modeling plus reinforcement is also sometimes less dangerous than shaping, as in teaching a person to swim or drive a car. In clinical settings role-playing and *behavioral rehearsal* are useful adjuncts to modeling. Here the client is exposed to a model demonstrating the desired behaviors. Then the client practices the modeled behaviors in situations simulated in the clinic. From here the client can be gradually faded into similar situations in the real world.

Children pick up many behaviors by modeling their parents. Modeling plays an important role in the acquisition of language, social and sexual roles, and simple mannerisms. When Benita was two she saw that her pregnant mother said "ooh" whenever she bent over. Soon Benita was saying "ooh" whenever she bent over. Similarly, children acquire many of their parents' fears and prejudices. Teachers are also important models for many children, which points out the need for a wider variety of types (e.g., sex and race) of elementary school teachers to provide significant models for students of different types.

O'Connor (1969) used modeling to overcome severe social withdrawal in some nursery schoolchildren. The children were shown a film depicting increasingly more active, positive, social interactions among children. The narrative soundtrack emphasized the appropriate behavior of the models. Viewing this film increased the observers' social interaction to a level equal to other children. In a later variation of this study, O'Connor (1972) compared the effects of seeing the modeling film or a control film coupled with the presence or absence of later social reinforcement for social interaction. He found that modeling by itself was faster than social reinforcement by itself and the behavior changes following modeling, with or without reinforcement, were more stable than the changes following just social reinforcement. This suggests that adding reinforcement did not significantly change the effects due to modeling alone. But perhaps there was a ceiling effect: there was little more room for improvement following modeling.

Altruistic behavior can also be enhanced by modeling. If children are exposed to models who show altruistic behavior, such as giving or helping, the children will often imitate this type of behavior (Bryan & London, 1970). Bryan and Test (1967) have reported a number of naturalistic studies of altruism with adults. In one study an undergraduate female was stationed beside a control car with a flat tire so that she was conspicuous to passing traffic. In the model condition another car, located one-quarter mile down the road, had a girl watching a male changing a flat tire. In the no-model condition there was only the control car. Significantly more people (mostly men) stopped their cars to help the control girl in the model condition than in the no-model condition.

Social and vocational skills can be taught via modeling. Juvenile delinquents may learn by modeling and behavioral rehearsal such skills as how to apply for a job or how to resist social pressure for undesired activities (Sarason & Ganzer, 1973). People on welfare may learn personal and vocational skills. And this training can be incorporated into broader programs such as a token economy.

In therapeutic contexts live and filmed models may be used to facilitate a client talking about his problems or verbalizing more in group settings (see Marlatt & Perry, 1975). This is similar to model-reinforcement counseling mentioned in the previous chapter.

From the discussion so far it would probably be expected that exposing people to scenes of violence would increase the observers' tendency to act violently. This seems to be the case as supported by studies by researchers such as Berkowitz (1971) and Bandura. For example, in one experiment (Bandura et al., 1961) some nursery schoolchildren watched an adult model be aggressive toward a large, inflated plastic doll; others watched the same model act nonaggressively toward the doll; and others had no exposure to models. After being mildly frustrated, the children were given access to the doll. The children who had seen the aggressive model imitated many of the model's aggressive behaviors; the other children showed significantly less aggressive behavior. Observation of the news over the last few years shows how types of violent acts occur in clusters: mass killings, burning slums, campus riots, sky-jackings, and political kidnappings. Although there are many reasons for these different acts, the time and way in which they occur suggest that exposure to models may be important in the occurrence of these events.

On the other hand, many theorists argue for a catharsis theory, which suggests that viewing violence may act as an outlet for observers and hence they will tend to be less aggressive. Although this may be true to some degree in some situations, overall the evidence does not seem to support this position (Bryan & Schwartz, 1971). Some theorists are developing more specialized variations of the catharsis theory. For example, Manning and Taylor (1975) distinguish between hostility and aggression. Aggression is inflicting harm without intention, while hostility is the emotional response resulting from a situation perceived by the individual as anger inducing. They suggest that viewing violence may increase aggression and/or decrease hostility.

If viewing aggression may increase aggression, this has important implications for television where violence attracts viewers and sponsors. The average viewer may see several acts of violence each day, and shows often increase violence in competition with each other. Congress at various times has been concerned with this issue and often suggests a reduction in television violence. Although the data are mixed, with the qualifications given below there seems to be good evidence that viewing violence on television increases aggression in some children (Goranson, 1975; Liebert & Neale, 1972; Murray, 1973), with some of the effect perhaps more with boys than girls (Eron et al., 1972). In October 1973 the movie *Fuzz* was shown on television in Boston. The movie was a police drama set in Boston in which teen-agers burn a derelict to death for "kicks." Two nights later six youths in Boston set upon a young woman carrying a can of gasoline to her car and burned her to death.

A number of qualifications need to be made regarding the literature on viewing violence. First, examples such as the Boston one do not show that seeing the movie made the youths more aggressive. It does suggest that modeling may have affected the form their aggression took. Laboratory studied have often frustrated or irritated the subjects to accentuate the effects of the modeling. Also, the fact that a model increases a person's tendency to be aggressive does not mean the person will act more aggressively. This is just one factor affecting the person's behavior. The person's final behavior will also depend on other circumstances and learning. Thus a child in a laboratory setting in which sanctions against aggression have been minimized will tend to be more aggressive after aggressive modeling, while one of you leaving a violent movie may not act more aggressive because of other influences on your behavior. The effects of viewing a particular act generally decrease with time, although we do not know how effects from many exposures to violence may cumulatively build up over time. There is also some evidence (e.g., Meyer, 1972) that viewing justified violence has a greater tendency to increase aggression than viewing unjustified violence. But given all these qualifications, there still seems to be evidence that viewing aggression often increases aggression.

One study compared children who had seen a lot of television and resulting violence with children who had seen much less (Cline et al., 1973). The children who had seen a lot were significantly less autonomically aroused by a violent film. Perhaps exposure to violence has a desensitization effect so that one becomes less aroused by violence. This may be one factor in the development of some people's apathy to violence and the need for more violence to be exciting. There is the famous case of the girl in New York who was assaulted, raped, and murdered over a period of one half hour while more than 40 people were aware of her distress. Yet no one came to her aid directly or indirectly, such as calling the police.

Similar modeling effects have been observed with suicides. After a suicide has been publicized in a newspaper, there is a rise in the suicide rate in the area the paper serves. The more publicity devoted to the suicide story, the larger the rise in suicides (Phillips, 1974).

ASSERTIVE TRAINING

Many people are inappropriately unassertive. They are not standing up for their rights or honestly and openly expressing their feelings and opinions. Thus they are not as personally, socially, and professionally successful as they might be. This leads to such things as feelings of inadequacy and various anxieties. Numerous questionnaires (see Chapter 2) are being devised to identify non-assertive behaviors in clients. Unassertive people include men who are overly shy about asking women for dates, workers who are afraid to approach their bosses for raises, people in their 20s and 30s who are still dominated by a parent, people who wish to change the nature of their relationship with their partners but stay stuck in the old behavior patterns, people who have trouble openly expressing their feelings, people who are overly apologetic or have trouble saying "no," people who are easily manipulated or easily hurt, and people who are intimidated by salesclerks, waitresses, or teachers. Such people profit from *assertive training*, teaching the client appropriate assertive behaviors for various situations (Alberti & Emmons, 1974, 1975; Dawley & Wenrich, 1976; Lange & Jakubowski, 1976; Smith, 1975). In a culture that primarily supports assertive behavior only in white adult males, many programs and materials are being developed especially for women (Baer, 1976; Phelps & Austin, 1975); minorities (Cheek, 1976), and children.

Assertive behavior is in between unassertive behavior and aggressive behavior. Assertive training is not intended to make the person aggressive, a common error in some group therapy programs, but to teach the person reasonable, appropriate, effective, assertive behaviors. What such behaviors are naturally vary with the clients and the situations they encounter. Assertive training then is equally applicable with clients who are too aggressive, but such cases are less frequent than unassertive cases. Much of assertive training is discrimination learning, for the client generally does not know what the appropriate assertive behavior is or is ineffectual at acting in an assertive manner. Thus modeling is often used to demonstrate the desired behavior. Assertive training is done in many different ways, so the description in this discussion is only meant to be one composite, mentioning many of the common components. Also, as generally true in behavior modification, assertive training is often best when coupled with other procedures such as anxiety-control, desensitization, or the cognitive approaches of the next chapter. Assertive training is also sometimes useful for someone related to the client, as assertive training may be desirable for the spouse of an alcoholic to help in the program to reduce drinking.

A good first step is to discuss the client's assertive rights with him, perhaps based on the client's readings of such rights (e.g., Alberti & Emmons, 1974; Smith, 1975). Examples of these rights are "You have the right to change your mind" and "You have the right to say no, without feeling guilty." Some unassertive clients feel they have no right to be assertive; and this needs to be dealt with first. For example, a woman in marriage counseling may feel she has no right to question her husband about how the family money is spent. Whether she does have the right is an ethical question for which there is no "correct" answer. But the issue probably needs to be confronted.

The next step is the actual training of assertive behavior. This includes non-verbal behaviors such as eye contact, posture, gestures, and facial expressions, as well as verbal behaviors such as the tone, inflection, and volume of the voice. Generally, most important is the content of what is said, including basic communication skills, expressions of feelings such as positive caring feelings or constructive anger, and verbalizations geared toward specific situations. Most of the training should center around simulations of actual situations in which the client needs to be more assertive. Thus for the male who is shy about asking out girls, training in the clinic may simulate a situation, such as a student union, where the client wishes to be able to approach girls. This may involve arranging furniture in the clinic to resemble the union, having a female practitioner play the part of some particular girl, and so forth.

In the simulation of a specific situation the practitioner now models the appropriate assertive behavior. Alternative modeling might use videotaped models, written descriptions of models' behavior, or covert modeling in which the client imagines the model (e.g., Kazdin, 1975a). After observing the model, the client engages in behavioral rehearsal, imitating and practicing the modeled behaviors. This is accompanied by feedback from the practitioner, including suggestions for improvement and social reinforcement. Videotapes of the client is another good form of feedback. During the training the client practices assertive behavior in different variations of the different situations, including various possible reactions of the other people involved. For example, a client may have trouble returning incorrectly cooked food in a restaurant. Assertive training for having the waitress take the food back would involve the simulation of many possible reactions of the waitress. In the clinic the client would also be taught covert rehearsal, practicing in the imagination, particularly at home, what was carried out in behavioral rehearsal. A strength of behavioral and covert rehearsal is that the client becomes prepared with things to say and do in situations that probably used to catch him off guard. During training the client may also assume the role of another person (e.g., waitress, mother), a procedure called role reversal, as practice in seeing the situations from the other's viewpoint.

As the client develops his assertive skills in the clinic he is gradually phased into the real world through a series of behavioral assignments. Here shaping and hierarchies are kept in mind as the client begins being more assertive in fairly simple situations and is gradually moved into more difficult situations. If the person has learned appropriate assertive behaviors, his experiences being more assertive will be reinforcing and naturally support his new behaviors. Therefore it is necessary that the client not learn things which will get him punished, as from someone who does not wish him to change. The client may be taught to take small steps with the people he will encounter. Related to this is that the client may have a fear, justified or not, about the consequences of his becoming more assertive.

Assertive training can also be carried out in small groups (Lange & Jakubowski, 1976; Liberman et al., 1975). Advantages to assertive training in groups include the fact that with more people you can have a greater variety of models and can better approximate some social situations, the groups can provide support and reinforcement to the individual, and the individual can learn from watching others be assertive. Possible disadvantages to using a group are that less time is spent with the individual, the program is less individualized, or working in a group is initially too anxiety-producing for the client.

Assertive training in some form is one of the most common practices currently in use by behavior therapists. In the last few years it also became popular among practitioners of many different orientations. Although there is a body of research related to its effectiveness (Hersen et al., 1973; Rich & Schroeder, 1976), it is still a relatively new field of inquiry. The practice contains so many components it will be some time before we can evaluate the relative importance of the different components, let alone begin parametric studies. Then there is the whole question of how assertive training packages with other approaches for different types of clients with different types of problems.

OVERCOMING FEARS

Modeling has been shown to be an effective way to reduce fears. Here the client observes the model gradually approach the feared situation with no bad results. For example, a girl with a fear of snakes may watch another girl gradually approach and handle snakes without the snakes hurting her. Modeling to reduce fears has several effects, including providing information that there is no real cause for fear, motivating the client to act as the model, and reducing the fear through extinction or counterconditioning.

One study involved young children with a fear of dogs (Bandura et al., 1967). One group of subjects watched a fearless peer model gradually exhibit, without adverse effects, progressively more interactions with a dog. Some of these subjects observed the model while in a positive party context; the others observed from a neutral context. One control group just observed the dog from the positive context; and another control group just participated in positive activities, but never saw the model or the dog. Subjects were then given avoidance tests with dogs. The subjects who had been exposed to the model showed less fear of dogs than subjects from the control groups, but there were no significant differences between the two modeling subgroups.

Another study investigated the effects of modeling plus gradual counterconditioning on the reduction of dental phobias (Shaw & Thoresen, 1974). The subjects were trained in relaxation and shown videotapes of models in dental chairs. The subjects were to imagine themselves in the modeled situations, which were presented in a hierarchial order, in which the rate of moving through the scenes was determined by the subject's report of fear. Other subjects were given a variation of desensitization, which was the same as the modeling group, except the scenes were presented on audiotape and imagination was interrupted if anxiety was reported. Both treatments were effective as far as increasing the subjects' going to the dentist and having dental work done. The modeling was more effective than the desensitization. The two treatments also produced about equal changes in attitudes toward dentists and dental work.

Because this type of modeling can be accomplished with films, it readily lends itself to group treatment. It could also be the basis for preventative programs directed at common sources of anxiety. Similarly, cartoons and children's books could be geared toward reduction of common fears.

In practice the use of modeling to reduce fears is often most effective when accompanied by such procedures as relaxation training, gradual approaches to the feared situation (a hierarchy), guidance and encouragement to later approach the feared situation, and reinforcement for participation and progress as well as for learning alternative behaviors. Many of these components are in contact desensitization (Chapter 5). Also, because many of these components occur in various studies of fear reduction, it is often difficult to determine the relative importance of the various components.

There are mixed results on the effects of similarity of model to client in fear reduction (e.g., Bandura & Barab, 1973; Kornhaber & Schroeder, 1975). However, the following is often true: If the model is very similar to the client, then the client may perceive that what happens to the model is relevant to him. Hence this is generally a good type of model. In some cases if the model is dissimilar, it may have a motivating effect. Thus an adult who watches a child model may decide that if the child can do it so can he (Bandura & Barab, 1973).

It also is not best if the model is too calm when approaching the feared situation. For this may make the model seem too unreal, may make the model too dissimilar to the client, or may make the client more anxious because he sees someone being calm where he can not be calm. Thus several researchers (e.g., Kazdin, 1973a; Meichenbaum, 1971) have found that coping models, who begin anxious and overcome their fears, are more effective than mastery models, who are always fearless.

In all modeling the models may be imagined models, an approach called *covert modeling*. This has been demonstrated in the reduction of fear of rats (Cautela et al., 1974) and fear of snakes (Kazdin, 1973a). A gradual covert modeling coupled with relaxation becomes very similar to imaginal desensitization. A major difference is whether the client imagines himself or someone else gradually approaching the feared situations. Also in desensitization he should live the scenes rather than picture himself in the scenes.

Finally, there are some studies on vicarious desensitization suggesting that test anxiety can be reduced by having the subjects watch videotapes of models going through desensitization for test anxiety (Hall & Hinkle, 1972; Mann, 1972). More research is needed to determine what is going on. Part of the effect may be because of modeling and/or the subject actually going through desensitization with the model.

ENHANCING EMOTIONAL RESPONSES AND INHIBITIONS

A person's emotional reactions may be acquired or enhanced by watching models in pleasurable or painful situations. For example, the movie *Jaws* depicted shark attacks on swimmers. The result of this popular movie was that many people acquired a fear of swimming in the ocean, and others stayed closer to shore than they had before. Similarly, people acquire attitudes and prejudices toward people they have never met and places they have never been partly from models in books, television, and movies.

Inhibitions may also be induced in a person from watching a model being punished. After seeing someone being given a ticket on the highway, we may slow down, even though it may now be less probable we will be stopped because the police are involved with the other person.

Overall, modeling is a powerful and useful component of behavior modification, particularly when coupled with other approaches. It is not clear whether modeling is a totally different type of learning than that discussed in previous chapters or whether it is merely these types of learning occurring at a more cognitive or symbolic level. This will perhaps become clearer in the next chapter when I consider approaches specifically geared toward cognitions.

SUMMARY

Modeling refers to behavior changes that result from the observation of a model, generally another person or fictional character. The model may be live, imagined (covert modeling), or presented via television, film, books, and so forth. People incorporate behaviors and strategies from various models into their own behavioral repertoire, modifying them according to their experience. Modeling can be used to initiate and enhance behaviors: It plays a key role in the socialization of children and affects the fears and altruistic behaviors they acquire. Modeling can be used to teach social and vocational skills to juveniles and adults. There is evidence that viewing violence may tend to make some people more aggressive; however, whether the person acts aggressively or not depends on the situation and other determinants of behavior. Modeling can also be used to help overcome fears by observing a model approach a feared situation without adverse effects. There is some evidence here that a coping model, who begins anxious and overcomes his fears, may be more effective than a mastery model, who is always fearless. Finally, modeling may also enhance emotional responses and/or inhibitions. Modeling is usually a major component in assertive training, which may include other components such as discrimination learning, teaching communication skills, behavioral rehearsal and covert rehearsal, feedback, shaping, role reversal, and behavioral assignments.

THOUGHT QUESTIONS

1. Describe the characteristics of effective models for each of the following: teaching social behaviors to juvenile delinquent boys, helping women on welfare overcome anxiety related to job interviews, and using short films on television to encourage people who just became of legal age to vote in an election.
2. How much impact do you think television has on the behaviors in our culture? Why?
3. Give four naturalistic examples of modeling you have observed in the real world, including one emotional reaction that was acquired or enhanced.
4. List three behaviors you have recently acquired via modeling.
5. Parents often act in ways appropriate for adults, but not for children. What are the implications of this for child rearing? List five common behaviors (e.g., smoking cigarettes, handling conflict with aggression) that you as a parent would try not to do around your children.
6. You are a counselor in an elementary school where there is a lot of fighting. How would you use modeling as part of your program to reduce fighting?
7. Describe a modeling film to be used at a summer camp to help children overcome their fear of the water.
8. Outline a program, using contact desensitization with a coping model, for a mental patient to overcome anxiety about attending group therapy.
9. Describe a laboratory situation that would maximize the subjects acting aggressively after seeing a violent movie.
10. Assuming violence on television results in more aggression in our culture, what should be done about it? Why? What about some form of censorship? What about the constitutional rights of the media?
11. Consider your answer to question number 30 of the last chapter. Expand your answer to now also include covert modeling and covert rehearsal.
12. Take an example of modeling and describe with specifics what may be happening in each of the four processes of the social learning theory account of modeling.
13. Outline a purely operant account of modeling that handles the problems given in the text for such operant theories.
14. Give three different possible explanations for vicarious desensitization of test anxiety. Describe an experiment that would help decide among these explanations.
15. For each of the following give an example of an unassertive, assertive, and aggressive verbal response: (a) saying "No" to a persistent insurance salesman,

(b) demanding to see the manager of a store to a clerk who is reluctant to get the manager, and (c) asking a friend not to drive because he is too drunk, although he refuses to admit it.

16. Your client is a woman who is totally dominated by her husband, a relationship that for years has been satisfactory to both of them. However during the last year many of her friends have been working to liberate her and change the way she acts toward her husband. The resulting conflict brought her to you. Is your assertive training geared toward her behaviors toward her husband and/or her friends? Why? What if your client is a man dominated by his wife?

17. Outline an assertive training program for a hypothetical case of a young college man who lives with his mother, takes courses his mother selects, and has to meet his girlfriend secretly since his mother does not approve of her. Be sure to be understanding and compassionate toward the mother.

SUGGESTED READINGS

Bandura, A. *Principles of behavior modification*. New York: Holt, Rinehart, & Winston, 1969. Chapter 3.

Bryan, J. H. & Schwartz, T. Effects of film material upon children's behavior. *Psychological Bulletin,* 1971, *75,* 50–59.

Marlatt, G. A. & Perry, M. A. Modeling methods. In Kanfer, F. H. & Goldstein, A. P. (eds.), *Helping people change.* New York: Pergamon Press, 1975.

Rachman, S. Clinical applications of observation learning, imitation and modeling. *Behavior Therapy,* 1972, *3,* 379–397.

Rosenthal, T. L. Modeling therapies. In Hersen, M., Eisler, R. M., & Miller, P. M. (eds.), *Progress in behavior modification. Vol. 2.* New York: Academic Press, 1976.

9 Cognitions

Cognitive processes or *cognitions* refer to a range of processes within the individual that has varying degrees of effect on the person's behavior. Included are perceptions; beliefs; thoughts; images; and systems of processing, coding, and retrieving information. In this chapter I discuss some ways of altering cognitions as part of a behavior change program.

Because cognitions are internal events they are less accessible to measurement and study than are overt behaviors. We have to study them indirectly via the person's overt behaviors. We generally do not know what people are thinking except by way of some behavior such as what they say they are thinking. Thus we are always dealing with behaviors, whether or not we make inferences about cognitions. This is basically the position of behaviorism. Some researchers and theorists argue that the best approach is to restrict our studies and discussions to what we can observe and measure and not make unnecessary inferences to such constructs as cognitions. We should restrict ourselves to people's verbal behavior rather than extrapolate to their thoughts. Although this is a reasonable scientific strategy, it has created the impression that such theorists are somehow denying the existence or importance of cognitions. Other theorists, including many behaviorists, readily incorporate cognitions into their models and discussions. This is particularly true of the cognitive and information-processing approaches in the psychology of learning and in the behavior modification approaches discussed later in this chapter. For simplicity I will freely talk about cognitions in this chapter, but we must remember they are usually inferences from observable behavior.

Most cognitions can be treated, researched, and formulated as behaviors (Ullmann, 1970). That is, most cognitions are covert behaviors that follow most of the same principles as overt behaviors. Thus in a treatment program people may learn how to operantly or respondently condition their thoughts in ways similar to conditioning other behaviors. At this point behavior modification overlaps other approaches, such as meditation, which deal with quieting or controlling the mind.

Many of the procedures already discussed in this book are basically cognitive procedures. This includes covert sensitization, covert reinforcement, covert punishment, covert extinction, covert modeling, covert rehearsal, and the use of imagined scenes in such practices as desensitization and implosion. All of these procedures are based on having the client imagine different events, for humans are imagers, and images are often mediating links in behavior chains. Thus people often do not respond directly to a situation, but rather respond to the image they have of the situation. Similarly, people's behavior is often governed by what they imagine will happen if they act in different ways. Thus we can often affect behavior by procedures geared toward what people imagine. This is a very old approach that underlies a wide diversity of practices, including psychocybernetics, some yoga meditations, and perhaps some or all of modeling.

Because we cannot directly measure cognitions, there is great difficulty in evaluating and researching the various covert procedures. Hence the research in this area is currently inadequate and the procedures lend themselves for many different explanations. Similarly on a practical level a client may imagine something different from what you think he is imagining or told him to imagine (Kazdin, 1975a; Weitzman, 1967). For example, in desensitization a client may imagine a scene that is more or less anxiety-producing than the suggested scene. In such situations it is often desirable to have the client verbalize, during or after, what he is imagining.

Before considering other cognitive change approaches, I wish to review two important questions: To what extent does changing cognitions affect a range of behaviors other than those used to measure the cognitions? To what extent does changing overt behaviors affect related cognitions?

COGNITIONS AFFECTING OTHER BEHAVIORS

Most people, including most teachers, parents, and therapists, try to influence others' behavior by what they say to them. That is, their approach is basically geared toward the person's cognitions. And this often results in changes in the person's behavior. For example, the cognitive change may basically consist of acquiring new information that guides behavior. A student may be instructed in strategies to improve study habits. Or a couple in therapy may require substantial sexual education. Masters and Johnson (1970) report that a major fallacy in our culture is assuming that a man naturally knows what is pleasing to a woman and the best sexual approach with his partner. In other situations the cognitive change may involve altering a person's misconceptions or faulty assumptions.

On the other hand, many cognitive approaches are basically our behavior modification procedures mediated by language. Thus by talking with a client we may produce respondent conditioning through the pairing of concepts and their related images, alter a person's incentives and affect related operant behavior, allow certain emotions to be expressed and extinguished, verbally reinforce the person for talking in certain ways, provide discrimination training so the person's behavior becomes tied to more specific stimulus situations, and act as a model for a wide range of behaviors. Thus a practitioner may believe the changes he produces by talking with the client are due to cognitive changes, such as insight or attitude change; when in fact it might be more profitable to view the changes in terms of learning and motivational constructs such as those above.

So cognitive changes may result in general behavior changes, but often they do not. In some cases the client simply does not have the desired behavior in his repertoire. Convincing a client to be more assertive may be inadequate. He may not know what do to and could go to the other extreme and act too aggressive. It is better to provide assertive training. In some cases cognitive changes are inadequate to overcome strong behaviors. For example, it is common for a person with a strong fear to understand the nature and cause of the fear, consider the fear undesirable and irrational, and know how a non-fearful person would act in these situations; but this seldom helps reduce the fear. Rather the client needs some behavioral treatment such as desensitization. And in other cases, such as with some small children, retardates, and severely mentally ill, cognitive approaches are impractical or inefficient.

A common cognitive approach is to change people's attitudes as a way to change their behavior. However, after considerable social psychological research, it turns out that this is not an effective approach (Festinger, 1964; Wicker, 1969). After people's attitudes have been changed, there may be a slight change in behavior to match the attitudes. But if the behavior is not independently changed or supported in its change, the attitudes will drift back toward their original position. Thus someone may go into a high school and show the students horror films about not brushing their teeth. As a result, the students' attitudes may dramatically change in favor of more brushing. But although there may be an immediate change in actual brushing, over time the students will probably return to their previous brushing frequencies.

When the Surgeon General's report came out relating cigarette smoking to health problems, there was a dramatic reduction in cigarette sales. But soon the sales were greater than before. Ludwig (1968) has suggested that constructive attitude change with alcoholics might merely produce a more insightful drunk. The point is that attitude change is often inadequate to produce general behavior changes; the behaviors should be independently altered as with behavior modification. Many social psychologists (e.g., Zimbardo & Ebbesen, 1970) now combine attitude change techniques with behavior change techniques.

Another common cognitive approach is insight-oriented therapy. Here the assumption is that providing the client insight into the nature and/or etiology of his problem will produce general therapeutic change across many behaviors. In many cases insight often involves the client being able to view his behavior from a particular theoretical position. For reasons such as those already discussed, this approach has not proved effective; understanding a problem does not necessarily provide the person with the skills to overcome the problem. London (1969, p. 53) concluded that "Insight therapy is clearly a poor means of symptom control; after almost 70 years of use, there are still few indications that uncovering motives and expanding self-understanding confer much therapeutic power over most troubling symptoms." And Hobbs (1962) suggested that insight is not a cause of therapeutic change, but rather is a consequence of such change. Insight-oriented approaches dominated psychotherapy for many years, and many therapists still see insight as their major therapeutic goal. Other therapists recognize that insight is often inadequate and needs to be coupled with or replaced by other approaches, such as behavior modification.

Thus cognitive approaches may be effective ways to change cognitions. But we have to be careful about assuming that the cognitive changes will produce lasting or significant changes in behaviors (other than the behaviors used to measure the cognitions). Sometimes we will get behavior changes, often we will not. If we wish behavior changes, we should generally use procedures that directly change or support change in the behaviors, rather than getting at them indirectly through cognitions. As will be seen next, changes in behavior often result in changes in cognitions.

BEHAVIORS AFFECTING COGNITIONS

Often following a behavior change program the person's cognitions (e.g., attitudes, thoughts, self-concept) alter, even though no attempt was made to directly change them. This is not surprising since people are observers of themselves. So if a person sees himself acting differently, handling problems he could not handle before, being more successful in some area, feeling more relaxed, or some other important change, it is not uncommon for the person to think and feel differently about himself and related people and situations. The human mind also has a tendency to justify whatever the person does; so changing the behaviors changes the justifications. And it is common, perhaps the rule, for attitude change to follow behavior change (Bem, 1967). For example, in assertive training, it is usually easier and more effective to work with behaviors than attitudes, which then usually results in attitude change (Alberti & Emmons, 1974,.p. 33–35).

Cautela (1965) described three cases in which he used desensitization to treat phobias. Although no attempt was made to make the clients aware of the etiology of their anxiety, the clients made "insightful-like" statements as the treatment became effective. That is, they came to understand their fear more as the anxiety was reduced, although no attempt was made to determine if their insights were "correct." Bandura, Blanchard, and Ritter (1969) used various combinations of desensitization and modeling to reduce snake phobias. Although no attempt was made to change attitudes toward snakes, clients' attitudes about snakes became more favorable as treatment progressed. Similarly, Shaw and Thoresen (1974) reduced fear of dentists by modeling and counterconditioning and found that this produced a change in clients' attitudes toward dentists and dental work. Ryan and his associates (1976) desensitized test anxiety in college students and found this produced a change in the students' self-concepts. Dua (1970) worked with female students with anxiety concerning the ability to relate in interpersonal situations. The "action program" treatment emphasized establishing specific actions to expand the behavioral repertoire, while the "reeducation program" treatment emphasized changing attitudes, cognitive processes, and verbal interactions involved in relating to others. Both programs reduced emotionality, but the action program was more effective than the reeducation program in terms of improvement in social extraversion and increasing the sense of internal control versus external control.

Desensitization of specific concepts has also been an effective way of reducing nightmares (Shorkey & Himle, 1974; Silverman & Geer, 1968). Bergin (1970) worked with a client whose dreams often had conflict situations with authority figures. The conflicts elicited much anxiety and woke him up. Following the second session of desensitization related to authority figures, there was a shift in the dreams so that the conflicts continued without anxiety to a more satisfactory conclusion. Later this subject matter no longer occurred in his dreams. Ayllon and Michael (1959) worked with a female patient who refused to eat and made "delusional" statements that the food was poisoned. Although no attempt was made to deal with her delusions, they disappeared as she was encouraged to feed herself and found the food was not poisoned.

Eitzen (1975) studied the changes in attitudes in the boys living in the token economy, residential home Achievement Place (see Chapter 7). Compared to boys of a similar age in a junior high school, the boys in Achievement Place showed a greater shift from an external to internal sense of control (they were becoming masters of their own fate) and more improved self-concept, in both cases ending up better than the control group. The Achievement Place boys also improved in achievement orientation, but stayed below the control group. Grzesiak and Locke (1975) studied a token economy program with psychiatric patients. Although the program was geared toward overt behaviors, they found changes in many independent cognitive measures—such as improved adjustment, increased ego strength, and decreased impulse responses. They also found significant changes on scales for a variety of attributes, including mood, cooperation, communication, and social contact.

Thus changing behaviors often results in cognitive changes. It seems that behaviors are often "stronger" than cognitions, so that changing the behaviors draws the cognitions along, while changing the cognitions produces a temporary change with the cognitions often changing back to match the behaviors. In practice most treatments are affecting both cognitions and other behaviors; it is more a question of emphasis. It is probably best to simply consider the whole range of the client's behaviors, some of which might be called cognitive, and how they interrelate. Then a comprehensive treatment program can be developed. The rest of this chapter deals with treatment approaches that are basically cognitive.

COGNITIVE THERAPY

Cognitive therapy, as developed by Beck (1970, 1971, 1976) and others, emphasizes changing clients' internal processing. The assumption is that people often distort their perceptions (which may lead to psychopathological responses), distort information they are processing, work from faulty assumptions, and use faulty thinking. Treatment involves such practices as delineating and testing the validity and reasonableness of the clients' misconceptions, distortions, and maladaptive assumptions. Practitioners may help clients formulate their experiences more realistically, process information more veridically, and alter faulty thinking and statements clients tell themselves. For example, the treatment of depression might involve getting clients to engage in more activities and helping them to evaluate themselves and their behavior more realistically by focusing on negative self-judgments (Rush et al., 1975).

Although cognitive therapy is currently not a formal part of behavior modification, the two share many commonalities. Both focus more on overt symptoms than assumed dynamic causes, both emphasize current behavior over historical experiences, and in both the therapist actively participates in setting up a specific treatment program. Beck (1976) has suggested that behavior therapy is a subset of cognitive therapy and primarily works by changing cognitions. In the current behavior modification literature the types of change approaches of cognitive therapy are discussed under terms such as "cognitive restructuring" and "rational restructuring."

COGNITIVE RESTRUCTURING

Cognitive restructuring is basically cognitive therapy facilitated by behavioral strategies. For example, Goldfried and Goldfried (1975) outline an approach to help clients modify their internal sentences, what they say to themselves. First the client learns how his internal sentences have been causing his emotional problems. Then the client imagines problematic situations (perhaps in hierarchial order), learns to catch undesired self-statements he makes in these situations, and practices desirable self-statements in place of the undesirable ones. This whole approach might be coupled with modeling by the practitioner, behavioral rehearsal, or simulation in groups.

Goldfried and associates (1974) have described a program of self-control of anxiety based on teaching clients to modify how they approach situations: First the client is exposed to anxiety-provoking situations in imagination or by role playing. Then the client learns how to evaluate how anxious he is. The client learns to use the anxiety as a cue to determine self-defeating anxiety-provoking attitudes and expectations he has about the situation and specifically what he is telling himself. Next these self-statements are reevaluated rationally. Finally, the practitioner suggests or models change strategies, as for faulty self-statements or irrational assumptions.

Note the importance given to the clients' self-statements and assumptions in the examples above. This represents the influence of Rational-Emotive Therapy and researchers such as Meichenbaum, discussed next. Cognitive restructuring, by definition, includes a wider range of cognitive approaches.

SELF-STATEMENTS

Rational-Emotive Therapy (RET), developed by Ellis (1962, 1970), is a cognitive therapy whose major approach is modifying the client's thinking and related assumptions and attitudes. Many psychological problems and much emotional suffering are seen as due to irrational ways of perceiving the environment, irrational thinking, and related self-statements. Part of therapy consists of identifying and correcting irrational beliefs—such as the belief that it is necessary to be loved or approved by everyone or the belief that one should be thoroughly competent in all that he does if he is worthwhile. Another part of therapy consists of helping clients correct undesired self-statements, on the assumption that what people say to themselves affects the way they feel and act.

RET is seen by some as part of modern behavior modification and by others as closely related to behavior modification. It certainly has influenced the interest of the last few years in cognitive behavior modification. The addition of behavioral techniques to RET, as in cognitive restructuring, has made it more powerful. A good example of this is the research by Meichenbaum (1974a, 1974b). While RET relies heavily on logical self-examination, Meichenbaum incorporates such behavioral components as modeling, graduated tasks, specific training, and self-reinforcement. Through his approach to altering self-statements Meichenbaum has been able to produce desirable changes in hyperactive and impulsive children, and in people wishing help with creativity, worrying, stress, and snake- and test-related anxiety.

The following is a typical sequence of training Meichenbaum might employ: First the model (e.g., the therapist) performs the task while talking out loud to himself, modeling self-statements. Then the client performs the task with instructions from the model. Next the client performs while instructing himself out loud. Then the client performs while whispering. Finally, the client performs while giving himself the self-instructions covertly. The verbalizations and related images that are rehearsed are specific to the problem or task, but may include questions (and answers) about the nature of the task; instructions guiding the performance; self-reinforcement; or coping self-statements to deal with frustration, uncertainty, or anxiety. A hyperactive child may tell himself to "Go slowly" or "Stop and think before I answer." A college student trying to be more creative may tell himself to "Defer judgments" or "Use different analogies."

Meichenbaum and Cameron (1973) used such an approach to give institutionalized schizophrenics extended training in self-instructions. Via operant conditioning the patients learned to pause and think before responding and use self-statements such as pay attention, listen, repeat instructions, and disregard distraction. The patients also learned to be sensitive to others' cues about their behavior and use this information to act more "appropriately." This involved self-statements such as be relevant, be coherent, and make oneself understood. The result of this training was that the patients showed an increase in "healthy talk" in a structured interview and showed improvement in several cognitive and attention tasks.

Another study involved the treatment of speech anxiety (Meichenbaum et al., 1971). Here the subjects were taught to identify maladaptive self-statements and encouraged to produce more adaptive self-statements. This approach and desensitization were both done in groups and both significantly reduced speech anxiety. The researchers suggest the possibility that subjects who experience anxiety in many situations profit more from self-statement approaches, while desensitization may be better for subjects whose anxiety is more specific.

Goodwin and Mahoney (1975) coupled modeling with a self-instruction approach to teach hyperactive impulsive boys to cope with verbal aggression in a verbal taunting game. The boys observed a videotape of a boy in the game remaining calm. The model was portrayed as coping via a series of covert self-instructions (e.g., "I won't get mad"), which were dubbed in on the tape. The modeling was followed by coaching and practice of the boys using these coping self-statements. This treatment resulted in increased coping in the game and an increase in non-disruptive classroom behavior.

Next I turn to behavioral approaches that apply conditioning principles to words and thoughts. This includes thought stopping to disrupt unwanted thoughts, coverant control to operantly condition desired thoughts, and respondent verbal conditioning to change the affect associated with words and related thoughts. Coupling these with the cognitive approaches already discussed gives the practitioner a more powerful treatment package. Such techniques strengthen cognitive therapies. For example, rather than simply telling the client to use certain positive self-statements, coverant control provides a way of shaping and reinforcing these statements.

THOUGHT STOPPING

Thought stopping, a procedure suggested by Bain (1928) and popularized by Wolpe (1958, 1969), is a simple but effective way to disrupt unwanted thoughts. Consider a client who is continually bothered by thoughts related to an unpleasant past event. The thoughts come into his mind with some regularity, he has little control over the thoughts, and the thoughts trigger undesired reactions such as unpleasant emotions. Treatment would involve the client being instructed to close his eyes and think the thoughts. Then the practitioner would shout "STOP!" and point out to the startled client how this caused the thought to stop. The practitioner does this a couple of times and then has the client do it himself, shouting out loud. The client practices this at home, first shouting out loud and gradually "shouting" covertly. Very quickly the client learns to be able to disrupt unwanted thoughts simply by telling them to stop. With time the process becomes more automatic and the client can simply "will" the thoughts away.

As simple as thought stopping sounds, it is quite effective and can be learned quickly to stop such thoughts as those that interfere with studying (Mikulas, 1976a). It is particularly effective when used to disrupt irrational, perhaps obsessive, thoughts or thoughts in a behavior chain leading to fear. The disruptive effect of the "STOP" can be enhanced by pairing it with such things as electric shock or pounding a fist on the table. But thought stopping is merely a disruptive tool and is thus best when coupled with other procedures such as coverant control.

Anthony and Edelstein (1975) worked with a client with a fear of epileptic seizures, although because of anti-seizure medication there had not been any seizures for two years. Excessive thoughts about seizures led to severe anxiety attacks four to five times a week, accompanied by nausea and vomiting. Thought stopping eliminated these problems in three weeks and there were no anxiety attacks during the six month follow-up.

Samaan (1975) worked with a 42-year-old woman, one of whose problems was auditory and visual hallucinations of her mother. For example, whenever she took a shower she saw the water change into blood while an image of her mother watched at the shower door and shouted threats. Thought stopping effectively stopped her hallucinations. Other parts of her treatment program for other problems included flooding, relaxation training, and working with the family.

Rosen and Schnapp (1974) used thought stopping as part of marriage counseling. The husband had obsessional thoughts regarding his wife's affair. Both the husband and wife were trained to yell "STOP" whenever the husband's thinking or speaking ran out of control on this topic.

Rimm and associates (Rimm, 1973; Rimm et al., 1975) have found that thought stopping coupled with covert assertion is an effective way to treat some phobias. *Covert assertion* consists of the client saying forceful and assertive things to himself, perhaps contradicting the problem. Thus in phobic situations the client uses covert assertion, following thought stopping, as a way to reduce anxiety. For example, a woman fearing men hiding in the closet may tell herself, "There is nobody in that stupid closet." Covert assertion is similar to the self-statements discussed earlier and coverant control discussed next.

COVERANT CONTROL

It is often useful to consider thoughts as covert responses that can be altered by operant conditioning. Homme (1965) suggested the term *coverant* as a contraction of "covert operant" and *coverant control* as an approach to operantly condition thoughts. In its simplest form coverant control consists in first identifying thoughts or self-statements we wish to increase in the client in different situations. Then the client is taught to emit these coverants when in the appropriate situation and reinforce himself for doing this. The coverants should generally be short believable statements. Johnson (1971) had his client put the statements on separate 3 × 5 index cards and carry them along. Todd (1972) used coverant control as part of his treatment of a 49-year-old depressed female whose description of herself was all negative. They found six positive statements about her and put these on a card in her cigarette pack. She then read one or two statements before smoking a cigarette and gradually added new statements to the list. This led to a general increase in positive thoughts and a decrease in depression.

If the coverants to be increased are fairly general, not tied to specific situations, then the client's life is filled with reinforcers that can be used. For example, the client might require himself to emit the coverant "I am in charge of my own behavior" before eating an apple, calling a friend, or opening the magazine that came in the mail. If the coverant needs to be tied into specific situations, we need more "portable" reinforcers—such as cigarettes or self-reinforcing thoughts or images. Historically, many people (e.g., Homme) involved in coverant control have used Premack's theory of reinforcement (see Chapter 7). The assumption here is that any high probability behavior can reinforce any lower-probability behavior. In this case low-probability coverants are reinforced by high-probability responses such as answering a telephone when it rings or opening a door you have your hand on. Johnson (1971) used urination as the high probability behavior with his client.

Homme (1965) suggested the use of coverants in favor of some behavior coupled with coverants opposed to other behavior. Thus to reduce undesired behaviors we would identify the stimuli for these behaviors. In the presence of these stimuli the client would emit a coverant against the undesired behavior, followed by a coverant for some desired behavior, followed by reinforcement. For example, to reduce smoking a client in the presence of cigarettes may say to himself "Smoking causes cancer," followed by "My health will be better if I don't smoke," followed by drinking some juice.

Although coverant control seems logical from an operant orientation and has been reported to be a useful therapeutic tool, several problems exist in evaluating it (Knapp, 1976; Mahoney, 1970, 1972). Most of the literature is case studies with little good controlled research. Homme's more complex approach, described in the preceding paragraph, has not been investigated. And there is a lack of research on the Premack principle with humans, particularly as it is being applied here. It may be that much of the effect of coverant control is simply getting the client to practice self-statements, but this is worthwhile in itself.

RESPONDENT VERBAL CONDITIONING

While operant conditioning may be used to increase or decrease the probability of certain thoughts, words, or verbalizations, respondent conditioning may be used to change their affect, such as the emotional reactions elicited by specific words. Studies below suggest that changing the affect of certain words produces changes in related behaviors. We need much more research to determine when and how this happens. Perhaps words are part of complex behavior chains, so that changing the words alters the chain. Perhaps conditioning based on words generalizes to or results in conditioning of images or other constructs that affect behavior. Research in these areas will help us understand part of what goes on in talk therapies and how to make them more effective.

Hekmat and Vanian (1971) suggested a procedure they called *semantic desensitization,* which consists of counterconditioning the negative affect of phobic-related words. They had college students with snake phobias associate the word "snake" with a pleasant word (e.g., "beautiful") by creating an image combining the two words (e.g., imagining a beautiful snake). They report that this procedure resulted in the word "snake" being evaluated less negatively (on a semantic differential), less fear of snakes reported on the Fear Survey Schedule, as well as greater behavioral approach to a live snake. Hekmat and Vanian also call their procedure "semantic counterconditioning," which may be more accurate. They suggest that their results are due to counterconditioning of meaning and suggest that other behavior modification procedures may reduce to semantic desensitization. However, their use of images allows other interpretations of their results, such as counterconditioning of mediating images. In a later study Hekmat (1973) found that semantic desensitization and systematic desensitization were equally effective in reducing phobias; and both were more effective than implosive therapy. However, semantic desensitization required less time than systematic desensitization to achieve the same results.

DiCaprio (1970) suggested an implosion approach, called *verbal satiation therapy,* to reduce the effects of specific words as an approach to deal with behaviors in which the words may be part of the behavior chain. Treatment consists of continued repetition (satiation) of the words in various forms, primarily verbal. Treatment possibilities include the client repeating the word, repeating syllables of the words or words resembling the word, repeating synonyms of the word, writing the word repeatedly, or repetitively perceiving the word presented visually or orally. For a person with a fear the repeated words would be those that elicit anxiety. For an obese person the word "cake" may be a critical word. Presently there is little evidence on the effectiveness of verbal satiation therapy.

To finish this discussion of covert procedures, consider the following case report by Wisocki (1973), which combines several covert approaches of this and previous chapters. The client was a 26-year-old man with a three-year addiction to heroin and negative feelings toward himself and society. Covert reinforcement was used for imagining refusing drugs and for thoughts antagonistic to heroin use. Thought stopping disrupted positive thoughts about heroin use. Covert sensitization associated imagining scenes related to getting or using heroin with aversive scenes, including being attacked by spiders or immersed in sewage. Vomiting could not be used as an aversive scene since it was positively associated with a good grade of heroin. To deal with the client's poor "self-concept" thought stopping was used to disrupt undesired thoughts (e.g., that he looked "ugly and nasty"), while covert reinforcement was used to reinforce desired thoughts in their place. Thought stopping and covert reinforcement were also used to deal with social anxieties. Therapy lasted four months. At an 18-month follow-up the client was drug free, had a new job, and had an active social life.

ATTRIBUTION

An important contribution to behavior modification from social psychology is the concept of *attribution,* the perception and explanation of causes of events. People perceive various factors affecting their lives; and this perceived causality (attribution) may affect their behavior. Essentially everyone, in varying degrees, misperceives himself and his environment in complex ways. Such misperceptions can lead a person to attribute causes to minor or irrelevant factors and thus overlook more significant variables. For example, a person who has trouble getting along with his neighbors may attribute this to religious differences, when in fact it may be because of inadequacies in his general interpersonal behaviors. Thus an important part of many counseling therapy programs is to identify and perhaps "correct" the client's attributions. This is generally done at a fairly basic level, for following misperceptions and faulty attributions to their extremes leads into the subtlest domains of consciousness.

One implication of attribution research relates to the importance of emphasizing self-control approaches in behavior modification. It appears that you often get greater behavior and attitude change in a client if he attributes the changes to himself rather than to an external agent, such as a drug or some treatment done *to* him (Davison & Valins, 1969; Winett, 1970).

In an early study Davison and Valins (1969) gave subjects a placebo drug and told them it was a "fast-acting vitamin compound" that would increase their ability to withstand painful electric shocks. In fact the experimenters simply reduced the amperage of the shock after giving the subjects the drug. Later half of the subjects were told the drug was a placebo, thus the subjects themselves were responsible for any tolerance change. On a final test, the half that knew the drug was a placebo withstood shock better than the half that attributed changes to the drug.

Another study investigated the effects of drug attribution on being able to fall asleep (Davison et al., 1973). All subjects were helped to fall asleep faster via self-produced relaxation, scheduling procedures (e.g., going to sleep at about the same time each night), and taking the drug chloral hydrate. Half the subjects were told they had been given the maximum dose of the drug; half were told they had the minimum dose. All subjects were then taken off the drug, but continued relaxing and scheduling. There was a greater maintenance of therapeutic gain for those subjects who did not attribute most of the effect to the drug (i.e., minimum dose subjects).

Thus when drugs are used as part of a treatment program, it is important that clients not attribute most of the effects to the drug, although treatment procedures, such as desensitization, have been successfully accomplished even when clients attribute effects, such as relaxation, to drugs (e.g., Wilson & Thomas, 1973). Generally, clients should view the use of a drug as an aid to acquiring self-control skills and/or as a transient tool which will produce long-term effects (e.g., counterconditioning) that will last after the drug is withdrawn.

A change procedure which has come from the attribution literature is the approach of *misattribution,* getting the client to believe the source of his anxiety is one that is not affectively charged (Ross et al., 1969). A client with a specific phobia may be exposed simultaneously to the phobic object and some other stimulus, such as a loud noise. Misattribution therapy would consist of getting the client to believe his feeling of anxiety was because of the tone rather than the phobic object. There is some evidence (e.g., Loftis & Ross, 1974) that misattribution procedures actually affect physiological responses to a conditioned source of arousal, rather than just affecting subjective feelings, reports, misperceiving, and denial of internal states. However, current research on the effectiveness and parameters of misattribution is mixed (e.g., Calvert-Boyanowsky & Leventhal, 1975).

Misattribution by itself is probably not an effective way to deal with problems such as strong or long-standing fears, for outside of laboratory experiments people's personal experiences probably force them to attribute the cause of their fear to at least the general categories of situations that elicit the fear. Hence attribution effects are probably more significant in more ambiguous situations, such as those involving drugs.

Overall then, cognitive approaches, such as those discussed in this chapter, are often useful adjuncts to a complete behavior modification program. The recent interest in this general area has brought behavior modification closer to other change models that emphasize cognitive variables.

SUMMARY

Cognitions refer to a wide range of internal events and processes, including aspects of perceptions, images, assumptions, beliefs, attributions, attitudes, thoughts, self-statements, insights, and understanding. Cognitions are not directly measurable, but can only be inferred from overt behavior, causing practical problems in research, interpretation, and application. Cognitive therapy is an approach geared primarily at changing cognitions. Rational-Emotive Therapy is a form of cognitive therapy that emphasizes changing thoughts, self-statements, and related assumptions. Cognitive restructuring is the combination of cognitive therapy with behavioral procedures. Although changing cognitions may result in changes in many related behaviors, often the cognitive changes are insufficient and need to be coupled with more direct behavioral approaches. This is particularly true when the client does not have the desired behaviors in his repertoire. On the other hand, changing behaviors often results in changes in cognitions such as attitudes and self-concept. In practice almost all change procedures affect both cognitions and behaviors; differences among approaches are usually more of emphasis on one or the other. Also many cognitive approaches can be viewed as behavioral strategies mediated by language. Many covert behavior modification procedures, such as covert modeling, covert reinforcement, covert sensitization, and the use of imagined scenes in desensitization are basically cognitive procedures. Other behavior modification practices dealing with cognitions include thought stopping to disrupt unwanted thoughts, coverant control to operantly condition desired thoughts, and respondent verbal conditioning to change the emotional affect elicited by specific words and thoughts.

THOUGHT QUESTIONS

1. Give a general definition of cognition. Discuss this definition from a behaviorist position. How can a person be both a behaviorist and concerned with cognitions? Give a definition of cognitive behavior modification.
2. Discuss the idea that all cognitions are covert behaviors.
3. Give three different situations, other than those in the text, in which a change in cognitions results in widespread behavioral changes.
4. Give three different situations, other than those in the text, in which cognitive changes would be inadequate to deal with the major behavioral problem.
5. When would you expect changes in overt behavior to produce changes in cognitions?
6. Give two different theoretical explanations for the effects of thought stopping. Describe an experiment that would help decide between these two theories.
7. Give a different hypothetical case example for how coverant control might be coupled with each of the following: desensitization, assertive training, and covert sensitization.
8. When would you use semantic desensitization as opposed to standard desensitization described in Chapter 5? Why?
9. Outline a cognitive therapy program for a hypothetical case of paranoia in which the client feels people are out to ruin him because he is so much smarter than everyone else. How does the idea of attribution relate to this case? How may thought stopping and coverant control be used with this client?
10. Combining cognitive restructuring, RET, the work of Meichenbaum, and coverant control, outline a general self-control approach a person can use to identify and change self-statements that are causing trouble.
11. Discuss the interrelationships among attribution, self-control, and self-concept. What are the implications for general assessment procedures?

SUGGESTED READINGS

Beck, A. T. *Cognitive therapy and the emotional disorders.* New York: International Universities Press, 1976.

Goldfried, M. R. & Davison, G. C. *Clinical behavior therapy.* New York: Holt, Rinehart, & Winston, 1976. Chapter 8.

Mahoney, M. J. *Cognition and behavior modification.* Cambridge, Mass.: Ballinger Publishing Co., 1974.

Meichenbaum, D. *Cognitive behavior modification.* Morristown, N.J.: General Learning Press, 1974.

Meichenbaum, D. *Cognitive-behavior modification: An integrative approach.* New York: Plenum, 1977.

Rimm, D. C. & Masters, J. C. *Behavior therapy: Techniques and empirical findings.* New York: Academic Press, 1974. Chapter 10.

10 Overview

So far in this book I have tried to present a general picture of the current domain of behavior modification, defined in its broadest terms. Now it is time to consider the field as a whole: how its various components combine, criticisms of behavior modification, and how behavior modification interrelates with other psychological change models.

PRACTITIONER SKILLS

A strength of behavior modification is that it provides the practitioners with many concrete things they can do. Practitioners have available to them a number of tools of great potential power, if they learn to use them well. The trap in this is that many people simply become technicians, learning the behavior modification techniques, but lacking psychological breadth, interpersonal skills, or practical knowledge of the givens and limitations of various situations. Although a need for such technicians exists at the paraprofessional level, the optimal behavior modifier is broader and more fluid. Practitioners need to know a lot about the settings in which they will be working and the types of people they will be working with. This includes social, political, beaucratic, economic, and physiological constraints. As much as possible, practitioners need to be able to understand the people they work with, to see from their point of view. They need the interpersonal skills to be able to interrelate with, communicate with, and perhaps influence these people. Practitioners need to be able to view the flow of human behavior in its broadest sense, understanding its relationships with other behaviors and various situations. And as much as possible, they should do all this from an empathic, non-judgmental position.

Breadth in various areas of psychology, such as social psychology and physiological psychology, strengthen the effectiveness of the behavior modifier. My bias is that a strong background in the psychology of learning and motivation (principles and paradigms, not classical theorists) is currently the most useful to behavior modification. Being able to see the contingencies and principles of learning and motivation in all human behavior, including your own, is an enormously useful vantage point, beyond most technicians. From this position behavior modification is less a set of discrete techniques and more an empirically testable set of special-case manifestations of principles of human behavior coupled with practical suggestions for implementation.

For some psychological approaches, such as some client-centered therapy, the relationship between the practitioner and client is seen as the primary tool for therapeutic change. For some theorists the therapeutic relationship is the necessary and sufficient condition for therapeutic change. In behavior modification this relationship is seen as not always necessary and seldom sufficient. Certainly, situations exist in which the relationship is sufficient for satisfactory change. Perhaps a client learns from the relationship with the practitioner effective ways of interacting with people. Perhaps a client wishes to explore or expand aspects of his consciousness and needs a practitioner who is an experienced guide or mirror. And many people who enter therapy or counseling are primarily just purchasing a friend they can talk to. But across the range of psychological problems, the relationship as a therapeutic change tool is generally insufficient or at best inefficient. Here is where approaches such as desensitization and contracting are useful adjuncts.

Similarly, there are many situations in which the therapeutic relationship is unnecessary or detrimental. For example, with some autistic children, retardates, psychotics, and catatonics, a therapeutic relationship (except in the simplest sense of the term) is not possible. And attempting to establish such a relationship in the early stages of therapy may actually impair progress. In other situations, such as group desensitization of test anxiety or a problem that can be handled via a programmed handout, imposing a required personal relationship could dramatically impair the effectiveness of the program. And of course, this whole discussion of therapeutic relationship is less applicable to some non-clinical settings in which behavior modification is applied, such as most weight-loss programs.

On the other hand, a good therapeutic relationship is often a decided advantage to the behavior modifier (Goldstein, 1975). A good relationship may lead to a better understanding and assessment of the client; improvement in helping the client decide on goals; overcoming resistance and misunderstandings about some aspect of therapy; the client being freer and more open to discuss problems and explore feelings; the client being more motivated; the practitioner being a more effective model and source of reinforcement; and the opportunity to minimize factors that often impair therapeutic progress, such as pre-conceptions and social roles. Although the research suggests that behavior modification generally works better than simple expectancy effects—such as placebo treatments—it is desirable to have any expectancy effects working in the desired direction. And certainly the relationship is a major determinant of expectancy.

COMBINING PROCEDURES

A total program for a client may include many components in addition to the psychological change program, components such as medical aid, physical therapy, extensive physiological assessment, changing nutrition, legal and financial aid, vocational training, money management, training in problem solving, parent training, or religious or spiritual counseling. The psychological change procedures of the total program consists of behavior modification plus whatever is part of your approach.

My concern here is the breadth of the behavior modification component. For it is important to be able to draw from the total domain of behavior modification a combination of procedures logically combined together in a program geared toward your client. Many behavior modifiers unfortunately only draw from a small subset of behavior modification, such as practitioners who are basically entirely operant in approach or clinicians who see most of therapy in terms of reciprocal inhibition. Although such limited approaches are successful with restricted types of behaviors or settings, I suspect that most people practicing behavior modification, especially clinicians, could significantly improve their effectiveness by increasing their breadth of knowledge and skills in behavior modification. This is particularly true since the field is currently evolving and expanding rapidly. The reader who is interested in staying current should follow journals such as those given in the next chapter. The importance of combining procedures creates research problems, for if the research only investigates the effects of a single procedure or small number of procedures, the effectiveness may be well below that of a more comprehensive approach, particularly with difficult and complex problems. On the other hand, research on more comprehensive or more individualized programs may have difficulty evaluating the relative importance of the different components.

   The combining of procedures can be seen by looking at general problem areas like alcoholism. But it must be remembered that the ideal program for one person who is alcoholic may be very different from the ideal program for another alcoholic.

   Consider behavioral treatments of homosexuality (Barlow, 1973; Barlow & Abel, 1976; Wilson & Davidson, 1974). First is the ethical question, discussed earlier (Chapter 2), of whether you should change such behaviors. Should you help the client become primarily heterosexual? Should you help him be more effective and comfortable as a homosexual? Assuming you choose to move toward heterosexuality, a treatment program may include some form of aversive counterconditioning—perhaps covert sensitization—to reduce sexual responses to homosexual stimuli; some approach—maybe desensitization—to reduce anxiety associated with heterosexual situations; procedures—like respondent conditioning of specific images with masturbation—to increase heterosexual responses; and social skills-training and assertive training geared toward heterosexual situations.

   Although much research is needed, many behavior approaches have been applied to the abuse of drugs other than tobacco and alcohol (Callner, 1975; Miller & Eisler, 1975). Procedures used include altering environmental cues, aversive counterconditioning, desensitization, overt and covert reinforcement of incompatible behaviors, contingency contracting, thought stopping, and assertive training.

   Many successful behavioral programs have been developed to reduce overeating (Abramson, 1973; Foreyt, 1976; Hall & Hall, 1974; Jeffrey, 1976; Leon, 1976; Mahoney & Mahoney, 1976; O'Leary & Wilson, 1975, chap. 12; Yates, 1975, chap. 6). Weight control has three components: exercise, diet, and eating behaviors. Exercise improves health and uses up calories. Diet controls the input of calories and other components that affect health, behavior, and weight. Although control of the diet, relative to the person's metabolism and amount of exercise, is a possible way to control weight, it often is not effective. For many problem eaters can lose weight by one diet or another, but they usually gain it back. Long-term weight control often requires changing eating behaviors via behavior modification.

   Behavioral approaches to deal with eating behaviors include stimulus control, such as restricting eating to one particular place in the house (no eating while reading, watching TV, etc.); reduction of anxiety that triggers eating, as by desensitization; aversive counterconditioning, perhaps covert sensitization, geared toward control of overeating; decreasing the reinforcing value of some foods, as with stimulus satiation or by only preparing difficult meals; covariant control and thought stopping to deal with thoughts related to eating; reinforcing alternative incompatible behaviors to eating in various situations; enlisting family and friends to provide support and social reinforcement of behavior change and weight loss; and contingency contracting to reinforce carrying out the program and losing weight. Changes during the actual eating of a meal might include putting small quantities on the plate; slowing down the actual eating; not putting more food on a utensil while still chewing; paying more attention to eating, so enjoyment may not decrease, even though quantity consumed may; and stopping just before being full and then quickly removing the food from the table.

Essentially no approach from any orientation has been proven to have more than temporary success in reducing or eliminating cigarette smoking, although many programs will work for a month or two or work with some types of clients. For cigarette smoking gets tied into too much of the person's daily behavior, in addition to being physiologically addicting. There is often social support for smoking; and many people, particularly teen-agers, usually begin for this reason. Smoking becomes tied in with many situations and activities such as the cup of coffee after a meal, cocktails, talking on the telephone, parties, or feeling anxious. Smoking may reduce anxiety and/or give the person something to do with his hands. About one third of everyone in the United States smokes. And many, perhaps most, of these people are not able to stop smoking for more than a short period of time.

Many behavioral programs have been geared toward smoking (Bernstein, 1969; Flaxman, 1976; Keutzer et al., 1968; O'Leary & Wilson, 1975, chap. 12; Yates, 1975, chap. 5). Several programs have shown good initial promise, but much more research is needed. Most of the programs so far have primarily emphasized only one or two procedures, such as stimulus satiation or covert sensitization. I suspect that a program more comprehensive in approach will be more effective. Behavioral procedures that have been applied to smoking include stimulus control, such as removing cues associated with smoking or only smoking in a special room; aversive counterconditioning, as with hot stale cigarette smoke or covert sensitization; stimulus satiation, as by rapid smoking; reduction of related anxiety or other negative emotions leading to smoking; motivational changes as by contracting and peer support; learning alternative behaviors; and thought stopping and coverant control to decrease thoughts leading to smoking and increasing anti-smoking thoughts. This may be an area in which a gradual approach, such as gradually reducing the number of cigarettes smoked, is sometimes inferior to a non-gradual approach, such as stopping all smoking immediately. A program for smoking should also deal with client behaviors that result from removing the smoking, problems such as the client becoming more irritable or aggressive, increased eating, or the client needing something to do with his hands and mouth.

Alcoholism is a major health problem in the United States. Half of all fatal automobile accidents involve a drunken driver. By one common definition there are about 10 million alcoholics in the United States. Some types of treatments, such as Alcoholics Anonymous, have been successful with some types of people. But most treatment programs have not been successful. Many hospitals and mental health centers will not work with alcoholics.

Drinking is encouraged and reinforced by many facets of our culture. Drinking is a critical part of many social situations; inebriated and uninhibited behavior following drinking is often reinforced; and many parents are worried their teenagers are smoking marijuana, then relieved if they are only drinking alcohol. Many men equate part of manlihood with drinking and drinking capacity. This makes it more difficult for many men to admit they are too drunk to drive or admit they need therapy. Alcohol reduces such emotional responses as anxiety and boredom and thus is reinforcing. The reinforcing effects of drinking are fairly soon after drinking behavior, while the adverse effects of drinking and being alcoholic are often temporally more distant. Alcohol often is physiologically addicting and withdrawal may produce nausea, vomiting, and fever.

Many behavioral programs, some quite successful, have been established to treat alcoholism (Miller, 1976; Miller & Eisler, 1976; O'Leary & Wilson, 1975, chap. 13). Several programs have used a variety of behavioral tools and approaches. The specific procedures that could be used depend on the individual clients and include, among others, all the procedures mentioned above relative to drug abuse, cigarette smoking, and overeating. In addition, Hunt and Azrin (1973) show the importance of altering vocational, family, and social reinforcers. For a long time it was assumed that a cured alcoholic must stay totally abstinent or he would become an alcoholic again. Now researchers are suggesting that for some alcoholics controlled drinking is a possible and desirable goal (Lloyd & Salzberg, 1975). A person learns, perhaps in a simulated bar, how to have one or two drinks and stop. One way to help clients learn self-control over how much they drink is to teach them how to estimate their blood alcohol level from the number of drinks they had and emotional and physiological cues (Silverstein et al., 1974). This training requires booster training sessions. Some researchers treat alcoholic drinking as an operant behavior. Treatment then emphasizes determining situations in which the client drinks and teaching alternative behaviors to these situations. Sobell and Sobell (1973, 1976) successfully coupled this approach with an emphasis on controlled drinking.

One example of a behavioral program is reported by Voger and his associates (1975) for chronic in-patient alcoholics. The patients while sober saw videotapes of their drunken behavior in order to motivate change. Controlled drinking, rather than abstinence, was the goal; and the patients were given training in estimating their blood alcohol level. The patients were sometimes punished with electric shock for overconsumption. There was training of alternative behaviors to drinking. And some of the above treatment took place in a simulated bar. All patients were also given a general education about alcohol and behavioral counseling, which included relaxation training, assertive training, and learning interpersonal skills related to drinking situations (e.g., refusing drinks). After leaving the hospital the patients came back for an occasional booster-treatment session. At a one year follow-up 62 percent of the patients were abstinent or maintaining controlled drinking. There was also a change in what they drank (usually toward lower alcoholic content), when they drank, and whom they drank with.

CRITICISMS

There have naturally been a number of criticisms of behavior modification (see London, 1972; Mahoney et al., 1974; Mikulas, 1972b). Some of the criticisms have been discussed in the first chapter, such as the misunderstanding that behavior modification only deals with peripheral behaviors and the contention that it does not deal with underlying causes. Here I consider some other common criticisms.

Many writers in behavior modification talk about the field being based on learning theory. But as some critics rightly point out, there is little consensus among learning theories; hence the theories do not make a solid base. To the extent that behavior modification draws on the learning literature, it is based more on empirical relationships of learning, for which there is some consensus, rather than theories of these relationships. For example, we know much about the effects, parameters, and applications of reinforcement, even though there are numerous different theories of reinforcement.

Also many behavior modification practices are substantially more complex than the experimental paradigms on which they are based. Laboratory studies of respondent conditioning usually use well defined and readily measurable stimuli (CS and UCS) and responses (CR). While desensitization usually uses imagined scenes—which consist of flows of imagery—and some subjective sense of relaxation, both generally assessed by the client's self-report, a questionable measure. Now desensitization works well and may be based on respondent conditioning, but there are many gaps between laboratory and practice that need to be filled by research. Similarly, many laboratory studies are based on experiments with non-human animals. Extrapolation from such studies to human behavior has proven useful, even though it offends some people. But such studies may not be the best approach for understanding some variables of human behavior, such as aspects of cultural socialization and symbolic processes.

Another related criticism is that behavior modification is oversimplified; it reduces complex human behavior to a few principles, such as respondent and operant conditioning. Behavior modification is oversimplified; it is a relatively new field in the science of psychology, which itself is a new, oversimplified discipline. Human behavior is currently the most complex field of study; and most of our scientific investigation of it has been in the last few decades. But behavior modification is less oversimplified than approaches that assume that a generally sufficient approach to behavior change can be based on insight, interpersonal feedback, or a primal scream. A strength of behavior modification is the degree to which its constructs can be interrelated. Without devaluating the uniqueness of a client, it is possible to break that client's behaviors down into a complex, interrelated set of components which provides a useful conceptualization when designing a treatment program.

Another objection to behavior modification is that it is dehumanizing, mechanical, and dictatorial. It is sometimes argued that the client is conditioned in the same way one might train a dog. These critics argue that other orientations are more responsive to the client's human qualities. Such criticisms certainly apply to some practitioners of behavior modification, as well as to practitioners from many other orientations. But these are not properties of behavior modification, which is more a technology and functional conceptualization than a philosophy of man or style of interpersonal relating. Behavior modification may be one of the most humane things you can do with a client, whether you regard that client as an animal, biocomputer, person moving toward self-actualization, or one who is consciously evolving on a spiritual path. The practitioner's philosophy, attitudes, and behaviors are significant to the degree they affect the client, regardless of how the practitioner may conceptualize what he does.

Some critics see behavior modification as too controlling and argue for change models, such as client-centered therapy, which minimize control of the client and are geared toward the client becoming "self-directing" (Rogers & Skinner, 1956). In one sense a self-control approach with behavior modification gives the client more control of his own behavior. But in another sense the whole issue of control is spurious. Anyone (e.g., teacher, counselor, therapist, parent, minister) who influences another is involved in control. And this is true regardless of what the controller believes he is doing or his awareness of the extent of his influence. Any influence of a person, including toward being "self-directing," involves control. To the extent a practitioner does not influence the client, he is not an effective change agent and may be leaving the control of much of the client's behavior to undesirable sources. By not recognizing the ever-present issue of control or philosophically denying it, the practitioner may not adequately confront ethical decisions about the direction of behavior change and/or not realize important ways he is influencing the client (e.g., modeling and social reinforcement).

The next issue concerns the current research evidence on behavior modification. Although it is still a young field, there are more controlled studies on behavior modification than any other therapeutic model and most other behavior change models. But there is great need for considerable more research in most areas of behavior modification. The major strength of the field is that it is continuing to evolve and expand through research. Currently some areas of behavior modification, such as some of operant conditioning, have been well researched and shown to be effective. Research in these areas is more on issues of implementation and the comparison of variations of approaches. Other areas, such as desensitization, have proven effective and generated considerable research. But there are still many basic questions about what is going on that need to be answered. Some areas—for example, aversive counterconditioning—have resulted in considerable research with mixed results, partly because these procedures may be most effective when part of a more complex treatment program. Some areas, such as contracting in marriage counseling, have generated procedures that are used often and reported to be effective. But there is currently little research in these areas. Finally there are areas—such as most of the covert approaches—for which there is too little evidence to evaluate. All of this, particularly my examples, is currently changing. But for a while we can conclude that research on behavior modification is encouraging, mixed, and needed.

Researchers using a single-subject research design, mostly operant conditioners, have demonstrated treatment effects across a wide range of settings and subjects. (Some theorists even define behavior modification in terms of this approach.) Other forms of controlled research have often relied heavily on relatively healthy subjects, such as college students with test anxiety, while behavior modification with more extreme clients, such as mental patients, is often more in the form of a case study. Thus we need more controlled research in a wider range of clients and settings. Behavior modification practice is also more complex than the theory and the reports by the practitioner, particularly journal articles. Hence we need more research on what successful behavior modifiers do, not what they say they do.

INTERRELATIONSHIPS WITH OTHER APPROACHES

The student of psychology is confronted with a bewildering mass of models and theories about the nature of man and his behavior. Some are useful, some are detrimental, some are silly, some are common sense translated into psychological jargon; but psychologists do not agree on which are which. Most psychologists who work as change agents drifted toward those psychological models that seemed to fit their interpretations and preconceptions of their own experiences and how they would like man to be. Clients often choose practitioners for similar reasons, and the effectiveness of counseling or therapy often depends on the match between client and practitioner.

Many students and practitioners adopt an eclectic approach in which they intend to draw from a wide range of psychological models and approaches. Although this is desirable in theory, and I suggest some interrelationships below, it is difficult in practice, for many approaches (e.g., aspects of behavior modification and psychoanalysis) are incompatible in terms of assumptions and change strategies. Thus a combination may be less effective than one or both approaches taken separately. Also, being an eclectic generally requires a detailed knowledge of the various approaches being combined. Learning about behavior modification superficially and adopting a few of its techniques may leave the eclectic less effective than a practitioner who has mastered behavior modification.

One problem in discussing combining behavior modification with other approaches is that it is not an area with specific assumptions and boundaries. In this text, particularly in this and the first chapter, I have tried to convey the current status of behavior modification and some of its working assumptions and strategies. But behavior modification is more a movement toward better specification, measurement, and research. As an evolving approach, which should draw from all experimental areas, behavior modification will not combine with other areas as much as incorporate parts of them. Although many people define behavior modification in a more restricted sense—and thus some people propose variations such as cognitive behavior modification and multimodal-behavior therapy—in its broadest sense behavior modification is simply the application of the systematic study of behavior. In this sense one could question whether there really is an area called "behavior modification" and the pros and cons of making such a distinction. Given these qualifications I will suggest some interrelationships between the current practice of behavior modification and a few other approaches. A detailed discussion here is far beyond the scope of this book and I mean the following to just be a sample of ideas.

Throughout the book I have suggested relationships between behavior modification and other approaches, such as Rational-Emotive Therapy and the cognitive therapies in the last chapter. Gestalt therapy, a potpourri of approaches, overlaps with behavior modification in that both often help clients get in touch with their feelings (e.g., relaxation training, anxiety management, assertive training), deal with affective responses, and use role playing and imagery techniques. Others have suggested relationships between behavior modification and group therapy (Johnson, 1975; Rose, 1977); psychodrama (Sturm, 1970, 1971); and Morita therapy (Gibson, 1974). But I wish to consider relationships with psychoanalysis, humanistic psychology, transpersonal psychology, and multimodal therapy.

Psychoanalysis

In psychoanalytic or psychodynamic approaches, discussed as the medical model in chapter one, the emphasis is on resolving assumed underlying causes, often deep within the client's unconscious. Therapy generally centers around the relationship between the practitioner and client with the therapist helping the client gain insight into the causes of his behavior and interpret this behavior from a psychoanalytic orientation. Psychoanalysis is basically a verbal therapy using such tools as dream interpretation and word association to discover intrapsychic conflict and other psychodynamic influences on behavior. Resolution of these underlying causes, many of which are found in the client's psychosexual history, is the basis of therapy.

Many behavior therapists (e.g., Levis, 1970; Rachman, 1970) consider psychoanalysis and behavior modification incompatible and suggest combining the two would weaken one or both approaches. Differences between the two orientations include the following: Psychoanalysis is basically geared toward "underlying causes," perhaps in the unconscious, while a behavioral approach avoids such constructs, which are difficult to define and measure. Psychoanalysis usually traces historical causes of current problems, while behavior modification emphasizes interrelationships among current behavior. Psychoanalysis gives more weight to the treatment effects of understanding and insight, while behavior therapy emphasizes structured new learning.

On the other hand, others see behavior modification and psychoanalysis as similar (e.g., Sloan, 1969) and/or compatible (Birk, 1970; Feather & Rhoads, 1972a, 1972b; Hersen, 1970; Marmor, 1971). It is suggested that if you look at what successful psychoanalysts and successful behavior therapists do, not what they say they do, there are many similarities in approach. One argument is that the two approaches are applicable to different types of clients or problems. Or the two approaches are complementary, dealing with different aspects or levels of people's complex problems. In either case, it is not clear what each approach deals with that the other does not. Stampfl's implosive therapy (Chapter 4) incorporates psychoanalytic scenes as sources of anxiety; but it is not clear that this is necessary or useful.

Another possibility is that behavior modification procedures produce wider range changes than is assumed, perhaps including changes in psychodynamic conflicts. There is not sufficient data to suggest this is true, but the following studies are examples of support for this position. Kamil (1970) used desensitization to reduce snake fears in college males. In psychoanalytic theory fear of snakes is often seen as related to castration anxiety. Kamil found that the desensitization produced a decrease in castration anxiety as measured by the TAT (Thematic Apperception Test) but not a decrease as measured by the Rorschach inkblot test. Kamil suggests that desensitization had an effect down to the level of interpersonal themes assessed by the TAT, but not down as far as the castration anxiety measured by the Rorschach. However, Kamil suggests that desensitization does go far enough to strengthen the ego and thus avoid symptom substitution.

Silverman and associates (1974) suggest that part of the effects of desensitization are due to activating unconscious merging fantasies. They view the therapist during desensitization as a mother substitute. This coupled with the client's relaxed state and perhaps prone position encourages regression and an unconscious fantasy of merging with the therapist as mother. The client then uses aspects of the merging experience to counter his fears. To test this, Silverman and associates treated women with insect phobias with their own variation of desensitization. Instead of having the client relax when experiencing anxiety, they quickly flashed ("tachistoscopic subliminal exposure") to the client the visual phrase "MOMMY AND I ARE ONE." Reporting this as an effective procedure, they see this as support of their theory. In a partial replication of this study, Emmelkamp and Straatman (1976) found no differences between subjects who viewed "Mommy and I are one" and subjects who viewed "Snake and I are one," questioning the specificity of any merging fantasy.

Humanistic psychology

Humanists view humanism as a "third force" in psychology, with behaviorism and psychoanalysis the other two forces. They often view behaviorists as determinists who only deal with the peripheral behaviors of humans, while they view humanists as dealing with people's human characteristics, their will, and what goes on inside them. Such straw man arguments generate many apparent conflicts between humanism and behaviorism (see Matson, 1973), with most of the disagreements centering around models of people that humanists postulate behaviorists must hold to. In fact, the fields of humanism and behaviorism both contain a wide range of models and approaches, some compatible and some not.

Consider some of the goals often cited as important to the humanistic approach in psychology: reverence for the unique in the individual; appreciation of the dignity and worth of people; and dealing with meaning, value, choice, experience, creativity, and self-understanding. Goals for the client include experiencing life more harmoniously, greater self-determination and responsibility, ability to communicate better, ability to act more compassionately, and extended awareness. Now I basically agree with all of these goals, as I imagine most of you do. Hence we all can be humanists, and some of us are behaviorists. Many behavior modifiers (e.g, Thoresen, 1973) see themselves as humanists and sometimes speak of behavioral humanism. Skinner, a favorite target of humanists, was voted Humanist of the Year in 1972 by the American Humanist Association because he is a person concerned about human behavior and the destiny of humanity.

The compatibility of behavior modification and humanism can be seen in areas of behavior modification such as the development of self-control and related awareness, dealing with cognitive processes, and the general attitude that a person is capable of changing. Often the most humanistic thing you can do for a person is to provide that individual with help via behavior modification. Unfortunately, some humanists have gone to the extreme of minimizing or disregarding scientific studies of human beings. Others have confused how they would like things to be with how things might really be.

A popular humanistic psychology is the *client-centered therapy* of Rogers (e.g., 1958). According to Rogers, everyone has a natural motivational force toward self-actualization. Counseling centers on the relationship between the client and practitioner. Here the proper attitude of the counselor (genuineness, empathetic understanding, unconditional positive regard) helps the client in self-exploration and altering his self-concept, which leads to positive personality changes. Some client-centered therapists see this relationship as the necessary and sufficient condition for therapeutic change, while many behavior modifiers, as discussed above, see such a relationship as often facilitory, not always necessary, and seldom sufficient.

However, in many counseling or therapy situations client-centered therapy and behavior modification are compatible (Dustin & George, 1973; Martin, 1972; Naar, 1970). The client-centered approach provides practitioners with useful skills in developing a facilitory relationship with clients, while behavior modification provides specific programs to deal with behavioral problems.

Transpersonal psychology

The field of transpersonal psychology (e.g., Tart, 1975) is fairly new and not well defined (which is considered desirable by many transpersonalists). It is the intersection of psychology with such phenomena and experiences as peak experiences, mystical experiences, transcendence of the self, altered states of consciousness, meditation, spiritual paths, and ultimate human potentialities. As a western psychology, transpersonal psychology arose as a "fourth force" out of humanism; thus writers in this area often perceive themselves as further from behaviorism than the humanists are. However, behavior modification is compatible with many aspects of transpersonal psychology.

People in quest of transpersonal goals often find the necessity of dealing with behavior problems that are impeding progress. It is common for a spiritual leader to require a disciple to first straighten out problems of daily living. Although transpersonal experiences may provide more clarity or freedom from the behavioral problems, the problems still often have to be dealt with. And here behavior modification provides useful tools. As a person progresses transpersonally he generally must confront his self or ego, a subjective sense of individualized and separate existence. From a transpersonal point of view, this self is an illusion, basically a product of learning, which needs to be superceded if one is to reach the ultimate human potential. An understanding of learning then provides a conceptualization of the processes of the self and how it can be "unlearned." Note that behaviorists generally avoid constructs such as the "self" and prefer to deal with the processes that affect a person's behavior. Humanists often exalt the self and want to strengthen or actualize it. Then the transpersonalists complete the circle, see the self as an obstacle, and run back into many of the processes studied by the behaviorist.

Through various disciplines, such as meditation, a person may come to be a more objective witness of himself and the world, including his own confusions, problems, behaviors, and processes of the mind. Eventually the types of effects on behavior discussed in this book fall into the natural flow of things; and cause and effect have more a sense of "happening." With more progress this witnessing orientation and the related self dissolve into the flow.

Indries Shah (Hall, 1975) when discussing *Sufism,* a transpersonal approach primarily associated with the mystical aspects of the Moslem religion, said, "Nobody is trying to abolish conditioning, merely describe it, to make it possible to change it, and also to see where it needs to operate, and where it does not . . . As a consequence of Sufi experience, people—instead of seeing things through a filter of conditioning plus emotional reactions, a filter which constantly discards certain stimuli—can see things through some part of themselves that can only be described as not conditioned."

Buddhism is a powerful and important psychology often overlooked by western psychologists. Although partially transpersonal in nature, Buddhism focuses on the practical problems in the here and now; thus it is very compatible with behavior modification (Mikulas, 1978). For example, Buddha observed that life is filled with suffering. People are not at peace; there is always some condition or thing they believe they must have to be happy. Yet even if a person achieves what he thought he wanted, there is always something else. Buddha understood that this basic (perhaps existential) source of suffering was based on peoples' attachments (craving) to some model of how things should be. But such attachments are relatively constant while the world is in a continual state of change (impermanence). Thus seldom does a person's model match the way things are, so there is suffering. Freedom from suffering, peace of mind, and entrance into transpersonal domains thus is based on getting free from the attachments, a process which becomes very subtle. It is not that a person necessarily stops doing many of the things he does, or that he stops trying to influence the course of events, or that he gives up all preferences. Rather, the person learns to continually live free from attachments to how things "should be," joyfully, peacefully, and compassionately accepting things as they are. The way to gain this freedom from attachments is complex, but Buddha included cleaning up one's life-style and specific practices of meditation.

Now since the attachments basically come about by learning, knowledge of learning processes and behavior modification can facilitate identifying and dealing with attachments. Similarly, Shapiro and Zifferblatt (1976) have drawn several comparisons between Zen Buddhist meditation and behavioral self-control, for both lead to being more observant of oneself and the influences on behavior. Differences are primarily in terms of what is observed, how it is observed, and the reactive effects from observing. From a behavioral standpoint, Zen meditation may facilitate relaxation, learning to focus attention, becoming self-conscious while minimizing reactive effects, desensitization of thoughts that come to "mind" during meditation, a reduction in covert thoughts and images, and a greater openness to various stimuli.

Multimodal therapy

Arnold Lazarus was a major researcher and practitioner in the early days of behavior modification. Over time he came to combine behavior modification with various other approaches and techniques (e.g., Lazarus, 1971) under different names—such as technical eclecticism, broad spectrum therapy, and multimodal therapy. Lazarus's latest statements of multimodal therapy (Lazarus, 1973, 1976) center around the acronym "BASIC ID," where each letter stands for a modality that may need to be treated. The argument is that durable treatment results often depend on the number of modalities treated. In the acronym B stands for behavior—overt behavior and appearance. A is affect—affect and emotions, such as anxiety, fear, anger, and depression. S is sensation—bodily sensations, such as sexual and sensual pleasure, pain, and spasms. I is imagery, including images, imaginations, and dreams. C is cognitions, including self-instructions, faulty reasoning, misconceptions, lack of information, insights, and philosophies. I is interpersonal relationships, ways of interacting, such as being non-assertive. D stands for drugs, allowing for the necessity or usefulness of adjunctive use of drugs.

One strength of Lazarus's approach is that he gets the practitioner to pay attention to the range of possible components (modalities) that need to be included in the treatment program. However, behavior modification in its broadest sense, as discussed in this text, covers all of these modalities. So it is not clear what is added in the term "multimodal therapy." Lazarus's works also contain many suggestions for new therapeutic tools and approaches. Unfortunately, many of these have not been adequately researched; and some may be based on change procedures which are more effectively carried out by existing behavior modification approaches. Finally, Lazarus in his broad spectrum practice easily switches from one therapeutic approach to another. Perhaps Lazarus's experience and knowledge allow him to do this effectively. But the student who reads his works probably will have trouble successfully emulating him. It may be that the new practitioner should begin by mastering a more delineated approach, such as a combination of behavior modification and client-centered skills.

It seems that anyone interested in understanding and changing human behavior, whether one's own or someone else's, will profit from learning about behavior modification. How this knowledge is used or integrated with other concerns and approaches is now left to the reader.

SUMMARY

In its broadest sense, behavior modification is the application of principles of behavior derived from systematic studies of behavior, with emphasis on specification, measurement, and research. Currently it is heavily based on the empirical relationships, not theories, of learning and motivation, although breadth in many areas of psychology is often advantageous to the practitioner and theorist. Behavior modification should incorporate ideas and procedures from any source, including other psychological change models, to the extent the ideas and procedures are verifiable and prove useful. Combining behavior modification with other procedures naturally depends on the compatibility of the different sets of assumptions and approaches. Behavior modification conceptualizations, like all conceptualizations of human behavior, are oversimplified and are useful to the degree they suggest practical courses of action. Similarly, behavior modification practice is often more complex than reports of the practice suggest and usually much more complex than the laboratory studies and paradigms on which the practice is based. Research is currently filling in these gaps. A change program usually involves psychological components, such as behavior modification, and non-psychological components, such as physiological limitations of the client and social-political restrictions of the helping organization. The optimal behavior modifier draws from the whole domain of behavior modification and related approaches to develop a change program geared toward the specific needs of the client. Although behavior therapy does not require a specific type of relationship with the client and does not assume that establishing a particular relationship is sufficient for effective behavior change, a good relationship with the client often greatly facilitates many aspects of assessment and the change program. Finally, behavior modifiers, like any influence agents, need to try to remain as aware as possible of the many influences on their clients and related ethical issues.

THOUGHT QUESTIONS

1. What is behavior modification defined in its broadest sense? Discuss the usefulness of this definition. Discuss the idea that behavior modification is not a well-defined field, but rather a movement to emphasize the importance of a more scientific study of human behavior and change programs.
2. To what extent can experiments with animals help us improve behavior modification practice with humans?
3. Does behavior modification exert more control on a client than other psychological approaches? Why? What are the implications of your answer?
4. Discuss the possibility of behavior modification procedures producing changes in psychodynamic conflicts.
5. What is behavioral humanism? Evaluate this position.
6. What are important interpersonal skills a behavior therapist should have? Describe a training program, using behavior modification technology, to teach these skills.

7. What general fields of psychology would be useful for a behavior modifier to know for working in each of the following: an elementary school, a marriage counseling center, a factory?

8. What other psychological approaches would you couple with behavior modification? Why? What would be the major problems in making such a combination?

9. What are the pros and cons of having goals of controlled eating of high-calorie foods, controlled smoking of cigarettes, and controlled drinking of alcohol, as opposed to goals of abstinence?

10. Outline a change program for a hypothetical case of depression, which uses and specifies all the modalities of multimodal therapy.

11. Outline a comprehensive program, drawing from the whole domain of behavior modification, for a hypothetical case of alcoholism.

12. Overall, what do you think of behavior modification? Why? What would you do to help improve the field?

SUGGESTED READINGS

Bandura, A. Behavior therapy and the models of man. *American Psychologist,* 1974, *29,* 859–869.

Lazarus, A. A. *Behavior therapy & beyond.* New York: McGraw-Hill, 1971.

Martin, R. *Legal challenges to behavior modification: Trends in schools, corrections, and mental health.* Champaign, Ill.: Research Press, 1975.

Mikulas, W. L. Criticisms of behavior therapy. *Canadian Psychologist,* 1972, *13,* 83–104.

Skinner, B. F. *Beyond freedom and dignity.* New York: Knopf, 1971. Bantam paperback, 1972.

Stolz, S. B., Wienckowski, L. A., & Brown, B. S. Behavior modification: A perspective on critical issues. *American Psychologist,* 1975, *30,* 1027–1048.

11 Further Reading

General texts

Bandura, A. *Principles of behavior modification.* New York: Holt, Rinehart & Winston, 1969.

Craighead, W. E., Kazdin, A. E., & Mahoney, M. J. (eds.). *Behavior modification: Principles, issues, and applications.* Boston: Houghton Mifflin, 1976.

Goldfried, M. R. & Davison, G. C. *Clinical behavior therapy.* New York: Holt, Rinehart & Winston, 1976.

Kanfer, F. H. & Phillips, J. S. *Learning foundations of behavior therapy.* New York: Wiley, 1970.

O'Leary, K. D. & Wilson, G. T. *Behavior therapy: Application and outcome.* Englewood Cliffs, N.J.: Prentice-Hall, 1975.

Rimm, D. C. & Masters, J. C. *Behavior therapy: Techniques and empirical findings.* New York: Academic Press, 1974.

Tanner, B. A. & Parrino, J. J. *Helping others: Behavioral procedures for mental health workers.* Eugene, Ore.: E-B Press, 1975.

Wolpe, J. *The practice of behavior therapy.* 2d ed. Elmsford, N.Y.: Pergamon Press, 1973.

Yates, A. J. *Behavior therapy.* New York: Wiley, 1970.

Edited books

Bijou, S. W. & Ribes, E. (eds.). *Behavior modification: Issues and extensions.* New York: Academic Press, 1972.

Eysenck, H. J. (ed.). *Experiments in behaviour therapy.* New York: Macmillan, 1964.

Feldman, M. P. & Broadhurst, A. (eds.). *Theoretical and experimental bases of the behavior therapies.* New York: Wiley, 1976.

Franks, C. M. (ed.). *Behavior therapy: Appraisal and status.* New York: McGraw-Hill, 1969.

Franks, C. M. & Wilson, G. T. (eds.). *Annual review of behavior therapy theory & practice.* New York: Brunner/Mazel, yearly beginning 1973.

Hersen, M., Eisler, R. M., & Miller, P. M. (eds.). *Progress in behavior modification.* New York: Academic Press; Vol. 1 in 1975, Vol. 2 in 1976, Vol. 3 in 1976.

Kanfer, F. H. & Goldstein, A. P. (eds.). *Helping people change: A textbook of methods.* Elmsford, N.Y.: Pergamon Press, 1975.

Leitenberg, H. (ed.). *Handbook of behavior modification and behavior therapy.* Englewood Cliffs, N.J.: Prentice-Hall, 1976.

Spence, J. T., Carson, R. C., & Thibaut, J. W. (eds.). *Behavioral approaches to therapy.* Morristown, N.J.: General Learning Press, 1976.

Thompson, T. & Dockens III, W. S. (eds.). *Applications of behavior modification.* New York, Academic Press, 1975.

Ullmann, L. P. & Krasner, L. (eds.). *Case studies in behavior modification.* New York: Holt, Rinehart & Winston, 1965.

Ulrich, R., Stachnik, T., & Mabry, J. (eds.). *Control of human behavior.* Glenview, Ill.: Scott, Foresman; Vol. 1 in 1966, Vol. 2 in 1970, Vol. 3 in 1974.

Specialized journals

Advances in Behaviour Research and Therapy
Behavior Modification
Behavior Therapy
Behaviour Research and Therapy
Behavioural Analysis and Modification
Cognitive Therapy and Research
Journal of Applied Behavior Analysis
Journal of Behavior Therapy and Experimental Psychiatry
Mexican Journal of Applied Behavior Analysis

Related learning texts

Bandura, A. *Social learning theory.* Englewood Cliffs, N.J.: Prentice-Hall, 1977.

Mikulas, W. L. *Concepts in learning.* Philadelphia: W. B. Saunders, 1974.

Staats, A. W. *Social behaviorism.* Homewood, Ill.: Dorsey Press, 1975.

Counseling

Dustin, R. & George, R. *Action counseling for behavior change.* New York: Intext Press, 1973.

Krumboltz, J. D. & Thoresen, C. E. (eds.). *Behavioral counseling: Cases and techniques.* New York: Holt, Rinehart & Winston, 1969.

Osipow, S. H. & Walsh, W. B. (eds.). *Behavior change in counseling: Readings and cases.* New York: Meredith, 1970.

Osipow, S. H. & Walsh, W. B. *Strategies in counseling for behavior change.* New York: Meredith, 1970.

Children (see also next section)

Blackman, G. J. & Silberman, A. *Modification of child behavior.* Belmont, Calif.: Wadsworth, 1971.

Browning, R. M. & Stover, D. O. *Behavior modification in child treatment: An experimental and clinical approach.* Chicago: Aldine Atherton, 1971.

Gardner, W. I. *Children with learning and behavior problems: A behavior management approach.* Boston: Allyn and Bacon, 1974.

Gelfand, D. M. (ed.). *Social learning in childhood: Readings in theory and application.* 2d ed. Belmont, Calif.: Wadsworth, 1975.

Gelfand, D. M. & Hartmann, D. P. *Child behavior: Analysis and therapy.* Elmsford, N.Y.: Pergamon Press, 1975.

Graziano, A. M. (ed.). *Behavior therapy with children.* Chicago: Aldine Atherton; Vol. 1 in 1971, Vol. 2 in 1975.

Kozloff, M. A. *Reaching the autistic child: A parent training program.* Champaign, Ill.: Research Press, 1973.

Lovaas, O. I. & Bucher, B. D. (eds.). *Perspectives in behavior modification with deviant children.* Englewood Cliffs, N.J.: Prentice-Hall, 1974.

Patterson, G. R., Reid, J. B., Jones, R. R. & Conger, R. E. *A social learning approach to family intervention, Volume 1: Families with aggressive children.* Eugene, Ore.: Castalia, 1975.

Ross, A. O. *Psychological disorders of children: A behavioral approach to theory, research, and therapy.* New York: McGraw-Hill, 1974.

Thompson, T. & Grabowski, J. (eds.). *Behavior modification of the mentally retarded.* New York: Oxford Univ. Press, 1972.

For parents and non-psychologists

Azrin, N. H. & Foxx, R. M. *Toilet training in less than a day.* New York: Simon and Schuster, 1974. Pocket Books paperback, 1976.

Becker, W. C. *Parents are teachers: A child management program.* Champaign, Ill.: Research Press, 1971.

Deibert, A. N. & Harmon, A. J. *New tools for changing behavior.* Champaign, Ill.: Research Press, 1970.

Krumboltz, J. D. & Krumboltz, H. B. *Changing children's behavior.* Englewood Cliffs, N.J.: Prentice-Hall, 1972.

Madsen, C. K. & Madsen, C. H. *Parents/children/discipline: A positive approach.* Boston: Allyn and Bacon, 1972.

Patterson, G. R. *Families: Applications of social learning to family life.* Rev. ed. Champaign, Ill.: Research Press, 1975.

Patterson, G. R. & Gullion, M. E. *Living with children: New methods for parents and teachers.* Rev. ed. Champaign, Ill.: Research Press, 1971.

Watson Jr., L. S. *Child behavior modification: A manual for teachers, nurses, and parents.* Elmsford, N.Y.: Pergamon Press, 1973.

Classrooms (see also next section)

Becker, W. C. (ed.). *An empirical basis for change in education: Selections on behavioral psychology for teachers.* Palo Alto: Science Research Associates, 1971.

Harris, M. B. (ed.). *Classroom uses of behavior modification.* Columbus, Ohio: Charles E. Merrill, 1972.

O'Leary, K. D. & O'Leary, S. G. (eds.). *Classroom management: The successful use of behavior modification.* 2d ed. Elmsford, N.Y.: Pergamon Press, 1977.

Pitts, C. E. (ed.). *Operant conditioning in the classroom: Introductory readings in educational psychology.* New York: Thomas Y. Crowell, 1971.

Ulrich, R., Stachnik, T., & Mabry, J. (eds.). *Control of human behavior: Behavior modification in education.* Glenview, Ill.: Scott, Foresman, 1974.

For teachers and non-psychologists

Buckley, N. K. & Walker, H. M. *Modifying classroom behavior: A manual of procedures for classroom teachers.* Champaign, Ill.: Research Press, 1970.

Homme, L., Csanyi, A. P., Gonzales, M. A., & Rechs, J. R. *How to use contingency contracting in the classroom.* Champaign, Ill.: Research Press, 1969.

MacMillan, D. L. *Behavior modification in education.* New York: Macmillan, 1973.

Madsen, C. H. & Madsen, C. K. *Teaching/discipline: A positive approach for educational development.* 2d ed. Boston: Allyn and Bacon, 1974.

Meacham, M. L. & Wiesen, A. E. *Changing classroom behavior.* 2d ed. New York: Intext, 1974.

Mikulas, W. L. *Behavior modification in the classroom.* Teaneck, N.J.: Behavioral Sciences Tape Library, 1974.

Payne, J. S., Polloway, E. A., Kauffman, J. M., & Scranton, T. R. *Living in the classroom: The currency-based token economy.* New York: Human Sciences Press, 1975.

Sarason, I. G. & Sarason, B. R. *Constructive classroom behavior: A teacher's guide to modeling and role-playing techniques.* New York: Behavioral Publications, 1974.

Sheppard, W. C., Shank, S. B., & Wilson, D. *Teaching social behavior to young children.* Champaign, Ill.: Research Press, 1973.

Sulzer, B. & Mayer, G. R. *Behavior modification procedures for school personnel.* Hinsdale, Ill.: Dryden Press, 1972.

Walker, H. M. & Buckley, N. K. *Token reinforcement techniques: Classroom applications for the hard-to-teach child.* Eugene, Ore.: E-B Press, 1974.

Self-control: texts and studies (see also next section)

Goldfried, M. R. & Merbaum, M. (eds.). *Behavior change through self-control.* New York, Holt, Rinehart & Winston, 1973.

Mahoney, M. J. & Thoresen, C. E. (eds.). *Self-control: Power to the person*. Belmont, Calif.: Wadsworth, 1974.

Thoresen, C. E. & Mahoney, M. J. *Behavioral self-control*. New York: Holt, Rinehart & Winston, 1974.

Watson, D. L. & Tharp, R. G. *Self-directed behavior: Self-modification for personal adjustment*. Belmont, Calif.: Wadsworth, 1972.

Williams, R. L. & Long, J. D. *Toward a self-managed life style*. Boston: Houghton Mifflin, 1975.

Self-control: for the layman

Alberti, R. E. & Emmons, M. L. *Stand up, speak out, talk back*. New York: Pocket Books, 1975.

Amit, Z., Sutherland, E. A., & Weiner, A. *Stop smoking for good*. New York: Walker & Co., 1976.

Baer, J. *How to be an assertive (not aggressive) woman in life, in love, and on the job*. New York: Signet, 1976.

Coates, T. J. & Thoresen, C. *How to sleep better: A drug-free program for overcoming insomnia*. Englewood Cliffs, N.J.: Prentice-Hall, 1977.

Fanburg, W. H. & Snyder, B. M. *How to be a winner at the weight loss game*. New York: Simon & Schuster, 1975. Ballantine Books paperback, 1976.

Fensterheim, H. & Baer, J. *Don't say yes when you want to say no*. New York: David McKay, 1975. Dell paperback, 1975.

Heiman, J., LoPiccolo, L., & LoPiccolo, J. *Becoming orgasmic: A sexual growth program for women*. Englewood Cliffs, N.J.: Prentice-Hall, 1976.

Jeffrey, D. B. & Katz, R. *Take it off and keep it off: A behavioral program for weight loss and exercise*. Englewood Cliffs, N.J.: Prentice-Hall, 1977.

Mahoney, M. J. & Mahoney, K. *Permanent weight control: A total solution to the dieter's dilemma*. New York: Norton, 1976.

Miller, W. R. & Munoz, R. F. *How to control your drinking*. Englewood Cliffs, N.J.: Prentice-Hall, 1976.

Phelps, S. & Austin, N. *The assertive woman*. San Luis Obispo, Calif.: Impact, 1975.

Rathus, S.A. & Nevid, J.S. *BT Behavior therapy: Strategies for solving problems in living*. New York: Doubleday, 1977.

Robbins, J. & Fisher, D. *How to make and break habits*. New York: Peter H. Wyden, 1973. Dell paperback, 1976.

Rosen, G. M., *Don't be afraid: A program for overcoming fears and phobias*. Englewood Cliffs, N.J.: Prentice-Hall, 1976.

Schmidt, J. *Help yourself: A guide to self-change*. Champaign, Ill.: Research Press, 1976.

Stuart, R. B. & Davis, B. *Slim chance in a fat world: Behavioral control of obesity*. Champaign, Ill.: Research Press, 1972.

Wenrich, W. W., Dawley, H. H., & General, D. A. *Self-directed systematic desensitization: A guide for the student, client and therapist*. Kalamazoo, Mich.: Behaviordelia, 1976.

References

Abramson, E. E. A review of behavioral approaches to weight control. *Behaviour Research and Therapy,* 1973, *11,* 547–556.

Alberti, R. E. & Emmons, M. L. *Your perfect right.* 2d ed. San Luis Obispo, Calif.: Impact, 1974.

Alberti, R. E. & Emmons, M. L. *Stand up, speak out, talk back.* New York: Pocket Books, 1975.

Anthony, J. & Edelstein, B. A. Thought-stopping treatment of anxiety attack due to seizure-related obsessive ruminations. *Journal of Behavior Therapy and Experimental Psychiatry,* 1975, *6,* 343–344.

Atthowe, J. M. Token economies come of age. *Behavior Therapy,* 1973, *4,* 646–654.

Atthowe, J. M. & Krasner, L. Preliminary report on the application of contingent reinforcement procedures (token economy) on a "chronic" psychiatric ward. *Journal of Abnormal Psychology,* 1968, *73,* 37–43.

Ayer, W. A. Implosive therapy: A review. *Psychotherapy: Theory, Research, and Practice,* 1972, *9,* 242–250.

Ayllon, T. Intensive treatment of psychotic behaviour by stimulus satiation and food reinforcement. *Behaviour Research and Therapy,* 1963, *1,* 53–61.

Ayllon, T. & Azrin, N. H. Reinforcer sampling: A technique for increasing the behavior of mental patients. *Journal of Applied Behavior Analysis,* 1968a, *1,* 13–20.

Ayllon, T. & Azrin, N. H. *The token economy: A motivational system for therapy and rehabilitation.* New York: Appleton-Century-Crofts, 1968b.

Ayllon, T. & Michael, J. The psychiatric nurse as a behavioral engineer. *Journal of the Experimental Analysis of Behavior*, 1959, *2*, 323–334.

Azrin, N. H. & Foxx, R. M. *Toilet training in less than a day*. New York: Simon & Schuster, 1974. Pocket Books paperback, 1976.

Azrin, N. H., Gottlieb, L., Hughart, L., Wesolowski, M. D., & Rahn, T. Eliminating self-injurious behavior by educative procedures. *Behaviour Research and Therapy*, 1975, *13*, 101–111.

Azrin, N. H., Naster, B. J., & Jones, R. Reciprocity counseling: A rapid learning-based procedure for marital counseling. *Behaviour Research and Therapy*, 1973, *11*, 365–382.

Azrin, N. H. & Nunn, R. G. Habit-reversal: A method of eliminating nervous habits and tics. *Behaviour Research and Therapy*, 1973, *11*, 619–628.

Azrin, N. H. & Nunn, R. G. A rapid method of eliminating stuttering by a regulated breathing approach. *Behaviour Research and Therapy*, 1974, *12*, 279–286.

Azrin, N. H., Sneed, T. J., & Foxx, R. M. Dry-bed training: Rapid elimination of childhood enuresis. *Behaviour Research and Therapy*, 1974, *12*, 147–156.

Azrin, N. H. & Wesolowski, M. D. Theft reversal: An overcorrection procedure for eliminating stealing by retarded persons. *Journal of Applied Behavior Analysis*, 1974, *7*, 577–581.

Baer, D. M. Let's take another look at punishment. *Psychology Today*, October, 1971.

Baer, J. *How to be an assertive (not aggressive) woman in life, in love, and on the job*. New York: Signet, 1976.

Bain, J. A. *Thought control in everyday life*. New York: Funk & Wagnalls, 1928.

Baker, B. L. Symptom treatment and symptom substitution in enuresis. *Journal of Abnormal Psychology*, 1969, *74*, 42–49.

Baker, B. L., Cohen, D. C., & Saunders, J. T. Self-directed desensitization for acrophobia. *Behaviour Research and Therapy*, 1973, *11*, 79–89.

Bandura, A. *Principles of behavior modification*. New York: Holt, Rinehart & Winston, 1969.

Bandura, A. (ed.). *Psychological modeling: Conflicting theories*. New York: Aldine-Atherton, 1971a.

Bandura, A. Vicarious and self-reinforcement processes. In R. Glaser (ed.), *The nature of reinforcement*. New York: Academic Press, 1971b.

Bandura, A. & Barab, P. G. Processes governing disinhibitory effects through symbolic modeling. *Journal of Abnormal Psychology*, 1973, *82*, 1–9.

Bandura, A., Blanchard, E. B., & Ritter, B. Relative efficacy of desensitization and modeling approaches for inducing behavioral, affective, and attitudinal changes. *Journal of Personality and Social Psychology*, 1969, *13*, 173–199.

Bandura, A., Jeffery, R. W., & Gajdos, E. Generalizing change through participant modeling with self-directed mastery. *Behaviour Research and Therapy*, 1975, *13*, 141–152.

Bandura, A., Ross, D., & Ross, S. A. Transmission of aggression through imitation of aggressive models. *Journal of Abnormal and Social Psychology*, 1961, *63*, 575–582.

Barlow, D. H. Increasing heterosexual responsiveness in the treatment of sexual deviation: A review of the clinical and experimental evidence. *Behavior Therapy*, 1973, *4*, 655–671.

Barlow, D. H. & Abel, G. G. Sexual deviation. In N. E. Craighead, A. E. Kazdin, &

M. J. Mahoney (eds.), *Behavior modification: Principles, issues, and applications*. Boston: Houghton Mifflin, 1976.

Barrett, C. L. Systematic desensitization versus implosive therapy. *Journal of Abnormal Psychology*, 1969, *74*, 587–592.

Barrett, T. J. & Sachs, L. B. Test of the classical conditioning explanation of covert sensitization. *Psychological Reports*, 1974, *34*, 1312–1314.

Beck, A. T. Cognitive therapy: Nature and relation to behavior therapy. *Behavior Therapy*, 1970, *1*, 184–200.

Beck, A. T. Cognition, affect, and psychopathology. *Archives of General Psychiatry*, 1971, *24*, 495–500.

Beck, A. T. *Cognitive therapy and the emotional disorders*. New York: International Universities Press, 1976.

Begelman, D. A. Ethical and legal issues of behavior modification. In M. Hersen, R. Eisler, & P. M. Miller (eds.), *Progress in behavior modification. Vol. 1*. New York: Academic Press, 1975.

Belliveau, F. & Richter, L. *Understanding human sexual inadequacy*. Boston: Little, Brown, 1970. Bantam paperback, 1970.

Bem, D. J. Self-perception: The dependent variable of human performance. *Organizational Behavior and Human Performance*, 1967, *2*, 105–121.

Beneke, W. M. & Harris, M. B. Teaching self-control of study behavior. *Behaviour Research and Therapy*, 1972, *10*, 35–41.

Bergin, A. E. A note on dream changes following desensitization. *Behavior Therapy*, 1970, *1*, 546–549.

Berkowitz, B. D. & Graziano, A. M. Training parents as behavior therapists: A review. *Behaviour Research and Therapy*, 1972, *10*, 297–317.

Berkowitz, L. The contagion of violence: An S-R mediational analysis of some effects of observed aggression. Nebraska Symposium on Motivation, 1971, *18*, 95–135.

Bernstein, D. A. The modification of smoking behavior: An evaluative review. *Psychological Bulletin*, 1969, *71*, 418–440.

Bernstein, D. A. & Borkovec, T. D. *Progressive relaxation training: A manual for the helping professions*. Champaign, Ill.: Research Press, 1973.

Berwick, P. & Oziel, L. J. The use of meditation as a behavioral technique. *Behavior Therapy*, 1973, *4*, 743–745.

Birk, L. Behavior therapy—integration with dynamic psychiatry. *Behavior Therapy*, 1970, *1*, 522–526.

Blanchard, E. B. Relative contributions of modeling, informational influences, and physical contact in extinction of phobic behavior. *Journal of Abnormal Psychology*, 1970, *76*, 55–61.

Blanchard, E. B. Brief flooding treatment for a debilitation revulsion. *Behaviour Research and Therapy*, 1975, *13*, 193–195.

Blanchard, E. B. & Draper, D. O. Treatment of a rodent phobia by covert reinforcement: A single subject experiment. *Behavior Therapy*, 1973, *4*, 559–564.

Borkovec, T. D., Kaloupek, D. G., & Slama, K. M. The facilitative effect of muscle tension-release in the relaxation treatment of sleep disturbance. *Behavior Therapy*, 1975, *6*, 301–309.

Boudreau, L. Transcendental meditation and yoga as reciprocal inhibitors. *Journal of Behavior Therapy and Experimental Psychiatry*, 1972, *3*, 97–98.

Boulougouris, J. C. & Bassiakos, L. Prolonged flooding in cases with obsessive-compulsive neurosis. *Behaviour Research and Therapy*, 1973, *11*, 227–231.

Brown, B. B. (ed.). *The biofeedback syllabus: A handbook for the psychophysiologic study of biofeedback.* Springfield, Ill.: Charles C. Thomas, 1975.

Bryan, J. H. & London, P. Altruistic behavior by children. *Psychological Bulletin,* 1970, *73*, 200–211.

Bryan, J. H. & Schwartz, T. Effects of film material upon children's behavior. *Psychological Bulletin,* 1971, *75*, 50–59.

Bryan, J. H. & Test, M. A. Models and helping: Naturalistic studies in aiding behavior. *Journal of Personality and Social Psychology*, 1967, *6*, 400–407.

Butler, P. E. The treatment of severe agoraphobia employing induced anger as an anxiety inhibitor: A case study. *Journal of Behavior Therapy and Experimental Psychiatry*, 1975, *6*, 327–329.

Butterfield, W. H. Instrumentation in behavior therapy. In E. J. Thomas (ed.), *Behavior modification procedure: A sourcebook.* Chicago: Aldine, 1974.

Cahoon, D. D. Symptom substitution and the behavior therapies: A reappraisal. *Psychological Bulletin*, 1968, *69*, 149–156.

Callner, D. A. Behavioral treatment approaches to drug abuse: A critical review of the research. *Psychological Bulletin*, 1975, *82*, 143–164.

Calvert-Boyanowsky, J. & Leventhal, H. The role of information in attenuating behavioral response to stress: A reinterpretation of the misattribution phenomenon. *Journal of Personality and Social Psychology*, 1975, *32*, 214–221.

Carlin, A. S. & Armstrong Jr., H. E. Aversive conditioning: Learning or dissonance reduction? *Journal of Consulting and Clinical Psychology*, 1968, *32*, 674–678.

Carlson, C. G., Hersen, M., & Eisler, R. M. Token economy programs in the treatment of hospitalized adult psychiatric patients: Current status and recent trends. *Journal of Nervous and Mental Diseases*, 1972, *155*, 192–204.

Cautela, J. R. Desensitization and insight. *Behaviour Research and Therapy*, 1965, *3*, 59–64.

Cautela, J. R. A behavior therapy treatment of pervasive anxiety. *Behaviour Research and Therapy*, 1966a, *4*, 99–109.

Cautela, J. R. Treatment of compulsive behavior by covert sensitization. *Psychological Record*, 1966b, *16*, 33–41.

Cautela, J. R. Covert sensitization. *Psychological Reports*, 1967, *20*, 459–468.

Cautela, J. R. Covert negative reinforcement. *Journal of Behavior Therapy and Experimental Psychiatry*, 1970a, *1*, 273–278.

Cautela, J. R. Covert reinforcement. *Behavior Therapy*, 1970b, *1*, 33–50.

Cautela, J. R. Treatment of smoking by covert sensitization. *Psychological Reports*, 1970c, *26*, 415–420.

Cautela, J. R. Covert extinction. *Behavior Therapy*, 1971, *2*, 192–200.

Cautela, J. R. Reinforcement survey schedule: Evaluation and current applications. *Psychological Reports*, 1972, *3*, 185–187.

Cautela, J. R., Flannery, R. B., & Hanley, S. Covert modeling: An experimental test. *Behavior Therapy*, 1974, *5*, 494–502.

Cautela, J. R. & Kastenbaum, R. A reinforcement survey schedule for use in therapy, training, and research. *Psychological Reports*, 1967, *20*, 1115–1130.

Cautela, J. R. & Wisocki, P. A. Covert sensitization for the treatment of sexual deviations. *Psychological Record*, 1971, *21*, 37–48.

Cayner, J. J. & Kiland, J. R. Use of brief time out with three schizophrenic patients. *Journal of Behavior Therapy and Experimental Psychiatry*, 1974, *5*, 141–146.

Cheek, D. K. *Assertive black/puzzled white*. San Luis Obispo, Calif.: Impact, 1976.

Christophersen, E. R., Arnold, C. M., Hill, D. W., & Quilitch, H. R. The home point system: Token reinforcement procedures for application by parents of children with behavior problems. *Journal of Applied Behavior Analysis*, 1972, *5*, 485–497.

Church, R. M. The varied effects of punishment on behavior. *Psychological Review*, 1963, *70*, 369–402.

Cline, V. B., Croft, R. G., & Courrier, S. The desensitization of children to television violence. *Journal of Personality and Social Psychology*, 1973, *27*, 360–365.

Colson, C. E. Olfactory aversion therapy for homosexual behavior. *Journal of Behavior Therapy and Experimental Psychiatry*, 1972, *3*, 185–187.

Cotharin, R. L. & Mikulas, W. L. Systematic desensitization of racial emotional responses. *Journal of Behavior Therapy and Experimental Psychiatry*, 1975, *6*, 347–348.

Danaher, B. G. Theoretical foundations and clinical applications of the Premack principle: Review and critique. *Behavior Therapy*, 1974, *5*, 307–324.

Davison, G. C. Elimination of a sadistic fantasy by a client-controlled counterconditioning technique: A case study. *Journal of Abnormal Psychology*, 1968, *73*, 84–90.

Davison, G. C. Homosexuality: The ethical challenge. *Journal of Consulting and Clinical Psychology*, 1976, *44*, 157–162.

Davison, G. C. & Stuart, R. B. Behavior therapy and civil liberties. *American Psychologist*, 1975, *30*, 755–763.

Davison, G. C., Tsujimoto, R. N., & Glaros, A. G. Attribution and the maintenance of behavior change in falling asleep. *Journal of Abnormal Psychology*, 1973, *82*, 124–133.

Davison, G. C. & Valins, S. Maintenance of self-attributed and drug-attributed behavior change. *Journal of Personality and Social Psychology*, 1969, *11*, 25–33.

Davison, G. C. & Wilson, G. T. Processes of fear-reduction in systematic desensitization: Cognitive and social reinforcement factors in humans. *Behavior Therapy*, 1973, *4*, 1–21.

Dawley Jr., H. H. & Wenrich, W. *Achieving assertive behavior*. Monterey, Calif.: Brooks/Cole, 1976.

DeVoge, J. T. & Downey, W. E. A token economy program in a community mental health day treatment center. In W. D. Gentry (ed.), *Applied behavior modification*. St. Louis: Mosby, 1975.

Diament, C. & Wilson, G. T. An experimental investigation of the effects of covert sensitization in an analogue eating situation. *Behavior Therapy*, 1975, *6*, 499–509.

DiCaprio, N. S. Essentials of verbal satiation therapy: A learning-theory-based behavior therapy. *Journal of Counseling Psychology*, 1970, *17*, 419–424.

DiCara, L. V., Barber, T. X., Kamiya, J., Miller, N. E., Shapiro, D., & Stoyva, J. (eds.). *Biofeedback and self-control 1974*. Chicago: Aldine, 1975.

Doleys, D. M. Behavioral treatments for nocturnal enuresis in children: A review of the recent literature. *Psychological Bulletin*, 1977, *84*, 30–54.

Dollard, J. & Miller, N. E. *Personality and psychotherapy.* New York: McGraw-Hill, 1950.

Donner, L. & Guerney, B. G. Automated group desensitization for test anxiety. *Behaviour Research and Therapy,* 1969, *7,* 1–13.

Dorr, D. Behavior modification in the schools. In W. D. Gentry (ed.), *Applied behavior modification.* St. Louis: Mosby, 1975.

Dua, P. S. Comparison of the effects of behaviorally oriented action and psychotherapy reeducation on introversion-extraversion, emotionality, and internal-external control. *Journal of Counseling Psychology,* 1970, *17,* 567–572.

Dunlap, K. *Habits: Their making and unmaking.* New York: Liveright, 1932.

Dustin, R. & George, R. *Action counseling for behavior change.* New York: Intext Press, 1973.

Efron, R. The conditioned inhibition of uncinate fits. *Brain,* 1957, *80,* 251–262.

Eitzen, D. S. The effects of behavior modification on the attitudes of delinquents. *Behaviour Research and Therapy,* 1975, *13,* 295–299.

Ellis, A. *Reason and emotion in psychotherapy.* New York: Lyle Stuart, 1962.

Ellis, A. *The essence of rational psychotherapy: A comprehensive approach to treatment.* New York: Institute for Rational Living, 1970.

Elwood, D. L. Automation methods. In F. H. Kanfer & A. P. Goldstein (eds.), *Helping people change.* New York: Pergamon, 1975.

Emery, J. R. Systematic desensitization: Reducing test anxiety. In J. D. Krumboltz & C. E. Thoresen (eds.), *Behavioral counseling: Cases and techniques.* New York: Holt, Rinehart & Winston, 1969.

Emmelkamp, P. M. G. & Straatman, H. A psychoanalytic reinterpretation of the effectiveness of systematic desensitization: Fact or fiction? *Behaviour Research and Therapy,* 1976, *14,* 245–249.

Epstein, L. H. & Peterson, G. L. The control of undesired behavior by self-imposed contingencies. *Behavior Therapy,* 1973, *4,* 91–95.

Eron, L. D., Huesmann, L. R., Lefkowitz, M. M., & Walder, L. O. Does television violence cause aggression? *American Psychologist,* 1972, *24,* 253–263.

Fazio, A. F. Treatment components in implosive therapy. *Journal of Abnormal Psychology,* 1970, *76,* 211–219.

Feather, B. W. & Rhoads, J. M. Psychodynamic behavior therapy. I. Theory and rationale. *Archives of General Psychiatry,* 1972a, *26,* 496–502.

Feather, B. W. & Rhoads, J. M. Psychodynamic behavior therapy. II. Clinical aspects. *Archives of General Psychiatry,* 1972b, *26,* 503–511.

Feldman, M. P. Aversion therapy for sexual deviations: A critical review. *Psychological Bulletin,* 1966, *65,* 65–79.

Feldman, M. P. & MacCulloch, M. J. The application of anticipatory avoidance learning to the treatment of homosexuality. I. Theory, technique, and preliminary results. *Behaviour Research and Therapy,* 1965, *2,* 165–183.

Fensterheim, H. & Baer, J. *Don't say yes when you want to say no.* New York: David McKay, 1975. Dell paperback, 1975.

Festinger, L. Behavioral support for opinion change. *Public Opinion Quarterly,* 1964, *28,* 404–417.

Flaxman, J. Quitting smoking. In W. E. Craighead, A. E. Kazdin, & M. J. Mahoney (eds.), *Behavior modification: Principles, issues, and applications.* Boston: Houghton Mifflin, 1976.

Foreyt, J. P. Behavior modification in mental institutions. In W. D. Gentry (ed) *Applied behavior modification*. St. Louis: Mosby, 1975.

Foreyt, J. P. (ed.). *Behavioral treatments of obesity*. Elmsford, N.Y.: Pergamon Press, 1976.

Foreyt, J. P. & Hagen, R. L. Covert sensitization: Conditioning or suggestion? *Journal of Abnormal Psychology*, 1973, *82*, 17–23.

Foxx, R. M. & Azrin, N. H. The elimination of autistic self-stimulatory behavior by overcorrection. *Journal of Applied Behavior Analysis*, 1973a, 6, 1–14.

Foxx, R. M. & Azrin, N. H. *Toilet training the retarded: A rapid program for day and nighttime independent toileting*. Champaign, Ill.: Research Press, 1973b.

Frankel, A. S. Implosive therapy: A critical review. *Psychotherapy: Theory, Research and Practice*, 1972, *9*, 251–255.

French, T. M. Interrelations between psychoanalysis and the experimental work of Pavlov. *American Journal of Psychiatry*, 1933, *12*, 1165–1203.

Friedman, D. A new technique for the systematic desensitization of phobic symptoms. *Behaviour Research and Therapy*, 1966, *4*, 139–140.

Galassi, J. P., DeLo, J. S., Galassi, M. D., & Bastein, S. The College Self-Expression Scale: A measure of assertiveness. *Behavior Therapy*, 1974, *5*, 165–171.

Gambrill, E. D. & Richey, C. A. An assertion inventory for use in assessment and research. *Behavior Therapy*, 1975, *6*, 550–561.

Gay, M. L., Hollandsworth, J. G., & Galassi, J. P. An assertiveness inventory for adults. *Journal of Counseling Psychology*, 1975, *22*, 340–344.

Geer, J. H. The development of a scale to measure fear. *Behaviour Research and Therapy*, 1965, *3*, 45–53.

Gibson, H. B. Morita therapy and behaviour therapy. *Behaviour Research and Therapy*, 1974, *12*, 347–353.

Glisson, D. H. A review of behavioral marital counseling: Has practice tuned out theory? *Psychological Record*, 1976, *26*, 95–104.

Goldfried, M. R. Systematic desensitization as training in self-control. *Journal of Consulting and Clinical Psychology*, 1971, *37*, 228–234.

Goldfried, M. R., Decenteceo, E. T., & Weinberg, L. Systematic rational restructuring as a self-control technique. *Behavior Therapy*, 1974, *5*, 247–254.

Goldfried, M. R. & Goldfried, A. P. Cognitive change methods. In F. H. Kanfer & A. P. Goldstein (eds.), *Helping people change*. Elmsford, N.Y.: Pergamon Press, 1975.

Goldfried, M. R. & Trier, C. S. Effectiveness of relaxation as an active coping skill. *Journal of Abnormal Psychology*, 1974, *83*, 348–355.

Goldiamond, I. Toward a constructional approach to social problems. *Behaviorism*, 1974, *2*, 1–85.

Goldstein, A. J., Serber, M., & Paiget, G. Induced anger as a reciprocal inhibitor of fear. *Journal of Behavior Therapy and Experimental Psychiatry*, 1970, *1*, 45–52.

Goldstein, A. P. Relationship-enhancement methods. In F. H. Kanfer & A. P. Goldstein (eds.), *Helping people change*. Elmsford, N.Y.: Pergamon Press, 1975.

Goldstein, G. S. Behavior modification: Some cultural factors. *Psychological Record*, 1974, *24*, 89–91.

Goodwin, S. E. & Mahoney, M. J. Modification of aggression through modeling: An experimental probe. *Journal of Behavior Therapy and Experimental Psychiatry*, 1975, *6*, 200–202.

Goranson, R. E. The impact of TV violence. *Contemporary Psychology*, 1975, *20*, 291–293.

Götestam, K. G. & Melin, L. Covert extinction of amphetamine addiction. *Behavior Therapy*, 1974, *5*, 90–92.

Gray, J. *The psychology of fear and stress.* New York: McGraw-Hill, 1971.

Greenberg, D. J., Scott, S. B., Pisa, A., & Friesen, D. D. Beyond the token economy: A comparison of two contingency programs. *Journal of Consulting and Clinical Psychology*, 1975, *43*, 498–503.

Gripp, R. F. & Magaro, P. A. The token economy program in the psychiatric hospital: A review and analysis. *Behaviour Research and Therapy*, 1974, *12*, 205–228.

Grzesiak, R. C. & Locke, B. J. Cognitive and behavioral correlates to overt behavior change within a token economy. *Journal of Consulting and Clinical Psychology*, 1975, *43*, 272.

Guidry, L. S. & Randolph, D. L. Covert reinforcement in the treatment of test anxiety. *Journal of Counseling Psychology*, 1974, *21*, 260–264.

Gupton, T. & LeBow, M. D. Behavior management in a large industrial firm. *Behavior Therapy*, 1971, *2*, 78–82.

Guthrie, E. R. *The psychology of learning.* New York: Harper & Row, 1935.

Hagen, R. L. Group therapy versus bibliotherapy in weight reduction. *Behavior Therapy*, 1974, *5*, 222–234.

Hall, E. The Sufi tradition. *Psychology Today*, September 1975.

Hall, J. & Baker, R. Token economy systems: Breakdown and control. *Behaviour Research and Therapy*, 1973, *11*, 253–263.

Hall, R. A. & Hinkle, J. E. Vicarious desensitization of test anxiety. *Behaviour Research and Therapy*, 1972, *10*, 407–410.

Hall, S. M. & Hall, R. G. Outcome and methodological considerations in behavioral treatment of obesity. *Behavior Therapy*, 1974, *5*, 352–364.

Hallam, R. S. & Rachman, S. Theoretical problems of aversion therapy. *Behaviour Research and Therapy*, 1972, *10*, 341–353.

Hallam, R. S. & Rachman, S. Current status of aversion therapy. In M. Hersen, R. M. Eisler, & P. M. Miller (eds.), *Progress in behavior modification. Vol. 2.* New York: Academic Press, 1976.

Hanson, R. W., Borden, B. L., Hall, S. M., & Hall, R. G. Use of programmed instruction in teaching self-management skills to overweight adults. *Behavior Therapy*, 1976, *7*, 366–373.

Harris, S. L. Teaching language to nonverbal children—With emphasis on problems of generalization. *Psychological Bulletin*, 1975, *82*, 565–580.

Hartman, W. E. & Fithian, M. A. *Treatment of sexual dysfunction: A bio-psycho-social approach.* Long Beach, Calif.: Center for Marital and Sexual Studies, 1972.

Hayes, L. A. The use of group contingencies for behavioral control: A review. *Psychological Bulletin*, 1976, *83*, 628–648.

Hearn, M. T. & Evans, D. R. Anger and reciprocal inhibition therapy. *Psychological Reports*, 1972, *30*, 943–948.

Hebb, D. O. The distinction between "classical" and "instrumental." *Canadian Journal of Psychology*, 1956, *10*, 165–166.

Hekmat, H. Systematic versus semantic desensitization and implosive therapy: A comparitive study. *Journal of Consulting and Clinical Psychology*, 1973, *40*, 202–209.

Hekmat, H. & Vanian, D. Behavior modification through covert semantic desensitization. *Journal of Consulting and Clinical Psychology*, 1971, *36*, 248–251.

Hermann, J. A., de Montes, A. I., Dominguez, B., Montes, F., & Hopkins, B. L. Effects of bonuses for punctuality on the tardiness of industrial workers. *Journal of Applied Behavior Analysis,* 1973, *6,* 563–570.

Herrnstein, R. J. Superstition: A corollary of the principles of operant conditioning. In W. K. Honig (ed.), *Operant behavior: Areas of research and application.* New York: Appleton-Century-Crofts, 1966.

Hersen, M. The complementary use of behavior therapy and psychotherapy: Some comments. *Psychological Record,* 1970, *20,* 395–402.

Hersen, M., Eisler, R. M., & Miller, P. M. Development of assertive responses: Clinical, measurement and research considerations. *Behaviour Research and Therapy,* 1973, *11,* 505–521.

Hobbs, N. Sources of gain in psychotherapy. *American Psychologist,* 1962, *17,* 741–747.

Hodgson, R. J. & Rachman, S. An experimental investigation of the implosion technique. *Behaviour Research and Therapy,* 1970, *8,* 21–27.

Hodgson, R. J. & Rachman, S. II. Desynchrony in measures of fear. *Behaviour Research and Therapy,* 1974, *12,* 319–326.

Hogan, R. A. The implosive technique. *Behaviour Research and Therapy,* 1968, *6,* 423–431.

Hogan, R. A. & Kirchner, J. H. A preliminary report of the extinction of learned fears via a short-term implosive therapy. *Journal of Abnormal Psychology,* 1967, *72,* 106–109.

Hogan, R. A. & Kirchner, J. H. Implosive, eclectic verbal, and bibliotherapy in the treatment of fear of snakes. *Behaviour Research and Therapy,* 1968, *6,* 167–171.

Holmes, T. H. & Masuda, M. Psychosomatic syndrome. *Psychology Today,* April 1972.

Homme, L. E. Perspectives in psychology. XXIV. Control of coverants, the operants of the mind. *Psychological Record,* 1965, *15,* 501–511.

Homme, L. E., Csanyi, A. P., Gonzales, M. A., & Rechs, J. R. *How to use contingency contracting in the classroom.* Champaign, Ill.: Research Press, 1969.

Hops, H. Behavioral treatment of marital problems. In W. E. Craighead, A. E. Kazdin, & A. J. Mahoney, *Behavior modification: Principles, issues, and applications.* Boston: Houghton Mifflin, 1976.

Hunt, G. M. & Azrin, N. H. A community-reinforcement approach to alcoholism. *Behaviour Research and Therapy,* 1973, *11,* 91–104.

Jacobson, E. *Progressive relaxation.* Chicago: University of Chicago Press, 1938.

Jacobson, N. S. & Martin, B. Behavioral marriage therapy: Current status. *Psychological Bulletin,* 1976, *83,* 540–556.

Janda, L. H. & Rimm, D. C. Covert sensitization in the treatment of obesity. *Journal of Abnormal Psychology,* 1972, *80,* 37–42.

Jeffrey, D. B. Behavioral management of obesity. In W. E. Craighead, A. E. Kazdin, & M. J. Mahoney, *Behavior modification: Principles, issues, and applications.* Boston: Houghton Mifflin, 1976.

Johnson, W. G. Some applications of Homme's coverant control therapy: Two case reports. *Behavior Therapy,* 1971, *2,* 240–248.

Johnson, W. G. Group therapy: A behavioral perspective. *Behavior Therapy,* 1975, *6,* 30–38.

Johnston, J. M. Punishment of human behavior. *American Psychologist,* 1972, *27,* 1033–1054.

Jones, M. C. A laboratory study of fear: The case of Peter. *Journal of Genetic Psychology,* 1924, *31,* 308–315.

Kamil, L. J. Psychodynamic changes through systematic desensitization. *Journal of Abnormal Psychology,* 1970, *76,* 199–205.

Kanfer, F. H. The maintenance of behavior by self-generated stimuli and reinforcement. In A. Jacobs & L. B. Sachs (eds.), *The psychology of private events.* New York: Academic Press, 1971.

Kanfer, F. H. & Saslow, G. Behavioral diagnosis. In C. M. Franks (ed.), *Behavior therapy: Appraisal and status.* New York: McGraw-Hill, 1969.

Kass, D. J., Rogers, H. E., & Feldman, S. E. Deconditioning anxiety by individualized inhibitors. *Journal of Behavior Therapy and Experimental Psychiatry,* 1973, *4,* 361–363.

Katz, R. C. & Zlutnick, S. *Behavioral therapy and health care: Principles and applications.* Elmsford, N.Y.: Pergamon Press, 1974.

Kazdin, A. E. Response cost: The removal of conditioned reinforcers for therapeutic change. *Behavior Therapy,* 1972, *3,* 533–546.

Kazdin, A. E. Covert modeling and the reduction of avoidance behavior. *Journal of Abnormal Psychology,* 1973a, *81,* 872–95.

Kazdin, A. E. The failure of some patients to respond to token programs. *Journal of Behavior Therapy and Experimental Psychiatry,* 1973b, *4,* 7–14.

Kazdin, A. E. Covert modeling, imagery assessment, and assertive behaviors. *Journal of Consulting and Clinical Psychology,* 1975a, *43,* 716–724.

Kazdin, A. E. Recent advances in token economy research. In M. Hersen, R. M. Eisler, & P. M. Miller (eds.), *Progress in behavior modification. Vol. 1.* New York: Academic Press, 1975b.

Kazdin, A. E. *The token economy: A review and evaluation.* New York: Plenum Publishing Corp., 1977.

Kazdin, A. E. & Bootzin, R. R. The token economy: An evaluative review. *Journal of Applied Behavior Analysis,* 1972, *5,* 343–372.

Kazdin, A. E. & Wilcoxon, L. A. Systematic desensitization and nonspecific treatment effects: A methodological review. *Psychological Bulletin,* 1976, *83,* 729–758.

Keat, D. B. Survey schedule of rewards for children. *Psychological Reports,* 1974, *35,* 287–293.

Keutzer, C. S., Lichtenstein, E., & Mees, H. L. Modification of smoking behavior: A review. *Psychological Bulletin,* 1968, *70,* 520–533.

Kifer, R. E., Lewis, M. A., Green, D. R., & Phillips, E. L. Training predelinquent youths and their parents to negotiate conflict situations. *Journal of Applied Behavior Analysis,* 1974, *7,* 357–364.

Kimble, G. A. *Hilgard and Marquis' conditioning and learning.* New York: Appleton-Century-Crofts, 1961.

Kincaid, K. *A Walden Two experiment.* New York: Morrow, 1973.

Knapp, T. J. The Premack principle in human experimental and applied settings. *Behaviour Research and Therapy,* 1976, *14,* 133–147.

Knapp, T. J. & Peterson, L. W. Behavior management in medical and nursing practice. In W. E. Craighead, A. E. Kazdin, & M. J. Mahoney (eds.), *Behavior modification: Principles, issues, and applications.* Boston: Houghton Mifflin, 1976.

Knapp, T. J. & Shodahl, S. A. Ben Franklin as a behavior modifier: A note. *Behavior Therapy,* 1974, *5,* 656–660.

Kornhaber, R. C. & Schroeder, H. E. Importance of model similarity on extinction of avoidance behavior in children. *Journal of Consulting and Clinical Psychology,* 1975, *5,* 601–607.

Krasner, L. The therapist as a social reinforcement machine. In H. H. Strupp & L. Luborsky (eds.), *Research in psychotherapy. Vol. 2.* Washington D. C.: American Psychological Association, 1962.

Krumboltz, J. D. & Schroeder, W. W. Promoting career planning through reinforcement. *Personnel and Guidance Journal,* 1965, *44,* 19–26.

Kushner, M. The operant control of intractable sneezing. In C. D. Spielberger, R. Fox, & B. Masterson (eds.), *Contributions to general psychology.* New York: Ronald Press, 1968.

Lang, P. J. & Melamed, B. G. Case report: Avoidance conditioning therapy of an infant with chronic ruminative vomiting. *Journal of Abnormal Psychology,* 1969, *74,* 1–8.

Lang, P. J., Melamed, B. G., & Hart, J. A psychophysiological analysis of fear modification using an automated desensitization procedure. *Journal of Abnormal Psychology,* 1970, *76,* 220–234.

Lange, A. J. & Jakubowski, P. *Responsible assertive behavior: Cognitive/behavioral procedures for trainers.* Champaign, Ill: Research Press, 1976.

Lando, H. A. A comparison of excessive and rapid smoking in the modification of chronic smoking behavior. *Journal of Consulting and Clinical Psychology,* 1975, *43,* 350–355.

Landouceur, R. An experimental test of the learning paradigm of covert positive reinforcement in deconditioning anxiety. *Journal of Behavior Therapy and Experimental Psychiatry,* 1974, *5,* 3–6.

Lazarus, A. A. Group therapy of phobic disorders by systematic desensitization. *Journal of Abnormal and Social Psychology,* 1961, *63,* 504–510.

Lazarus, A. A. The results of behavior therapy in 126 cases of severe neurosis. *Behaviour Research and Therapy,* 1963, *1,* 69–79.

Lazarus, A. A. *Behavior therapy and beyond.* New York: McGraw-Hill, 1971.

Lazarus, A. A. Multimodal behavior therapy: Treating the "Basic Id." *Journal of Nervous and Mental Disease,* 1973, *156,* 404–411.

Lazarus, A. A. (ed.). *Multimodal behavior therapy.* New York: Springer, 1976.

Lazarus, A. A. & Abramovitz, A. The use of "emotive imagery" in the treatment of children's phobias. *Journal of Mental Science,* 1962, *108,* 191–195.

LeBow, M. D. Implications of behavior modification in nursing practice. In M. Hersen, R. M. Eisler, & P. M. Miller (eds.), *Progress in behavior modification. Vol. 2.* New York: Academic Press, 1976.

Leitenberg, H., Agras, W. S., Allen, R., Butz, R., & Edwards, J. Feedback and therapist praise during treatment of phobia. *Journal of Consulting and Clinical Psychology,* 1975, *43,* 396–404.

Leitenberg, H. & Callahan, E. J. Reinforced practice and reduction of different kinds of fears in adults and children. *Behaviour Research and Therapy,* 1973, *11,* 19–30.

Lemere, G. & Voegtlin, W. An evaluation of the aversion treatment of alcoholism. *Quarterly Journal for the Study of Alcoholism,* 1950, *11,* 199–204.

Leon, G. R. Current directions in the treatment of obesity. *Psychological Bulletin,* 1976, *83,* 557–578.

Levine, F. M. & Fasnacht, G. Token rewards may lead to token learning. *American Psychologist,* 1974, *29,* 816–820.

Levis, D. J. Integration of behavior therapy and dynamic psychiatric techniques: A marriage with a high probability of ending in divorce. *Behavior Therapy,* 1970, *1,* 531–537.

Lewis, S. A comparison of behavior therapy techniques in the reduction of fearful avoidance behavior. *Behavior Therapy,* 1974, *5,* 648–655.

Ley, R. & Walker, H. Effects of carbon dioxide—oxygen inhalation on heart rate, blood pressure, and subjective anxiety. *Journal of Behavior Therapy and Experimental Psychiatry,* 1973, *4,* 223–228.

Liberman, R. P., Ferris, C., Salgado, P., & Salgado, J. Replication of the Achievement Place model in California. *Journal of Applied Behavior Analysis,* 1975, *8,* 287–299.

Liberman, R. P., King, L. W., DeRisi, W. J., & McCann, M. *Personal effectiveness.* Champaign, Ill.: Research Press, 1975.

Lichtenstein, E., Harris, D. E., Birchler, G. R., Wahl, J. M., & Schmahl, D. P. Comparison of rapid smoking, warm smoky air, and attention placebo in the modification of smoking behavior. *Journal of Consulting and Clinical Psychology,* 1973, *40,* 92–98.

Liebert, R. M. & Neale, J. M. TV violence and child aggression: Snow on the screen. *Psychology Today,* April 1972.

Lindemann, H. *Relieve tension the autogenic way.* New York: Wyden, 1973.

Litow, L. & Pumroy, D. K. A brief review of classroom group-oriented contingencies. *Journal of Applied Behavior Analysis,* 1975, *8,* 341–347.

Litvak, S. B. A comparison of two brief group behavior therapy techniques on the reduction of avoidance behavior. *Psychological Record,* 1969, *19,* 329–334.

Lloyd, R. W. & Salzberg, H. C. Controlled social drinking: An alternative to abstinence as a treatment goal for some alcohol abusers. *Psychological Bulletin,* 1975, *82,* 815–842.

Loeber, R. & Weisman, R. G. Contingencies of therapist and trainer performance: A review. *Psychological Bulletin,* 1975, *82,* 660–688.

Loftis, J. & Ross, L. Effects of misattribution of arousal upon the acquisition and extinction of a conditioned emotional response. *Journal of Personality and Social Psychology,* 1974, *30,* 673–682.

London, P. *Behavior control.* New York: Harper & Row, 1969.

London, P. The end of ideology in behavior modification. *American Psychologist,* 1972, *27,* 913–920.

Lovaas, O. I., Koegel, R., Simmons, J. Q., & Long, J. S. Some generalization and follow-up measures on autistic children in behavior therapy. *Journal of Applied Behavior Analysis,* 1973, *6,* 131–166.

Lovibond, S. H. *Conditioning and enuresis.* New York: Macmillan, 1964.

Lovibond, S. H. Aversive control of behavior. *Behavior Therapy,* 1970, *1,* 80–91.

Lowe, J. C. Excitatory response to music as a reciprocal inhibitor. *Journal of Behavior Therapy and Experimental Psychiatry,* 1973, *4* 297–299.

Lowe, J. C. & Mikulas, W. L. Use of written material in learning self-control of premature ejaculation. *Psychological Reports,* 1975, *37,* 295–298.

Lubetkin, B. S. & Fishman, S. T. Electrical aversion therapy with a chronic heroin user. *Journal of Behavior Therapy and Experimental Psychiatry,* 1974, *5,* 193–195.

Ludwig, A. M. Relationship of attitude to behavior: Preliminary results and implications for treatment evaluation studies. In J. M. Shlien (ed.), *Research in psychotherapy. Vol. 3.* Washington, D.C.: American Psychological Association, 1968.

Luthans, F. & Kreitner, R. *Organizational behavior modification.* Glenview, Ill.: Scott, Foresman, 1975.

Luthe, W. (ed.). *Autogenic therapy.* New York: Grune & Stratton, 1969.

MacDonough, T. S. & Forehand, R. Response-contingent time out: Important parameters in behavior modification with children. *Journal of Behavior Therapy and Experimental Psychiatry,* 1973, *4,* 231–236.

Mager, R. F. *Preparing instructional objectives.* Belmont, Calif.: Fearon, 1962.

Mager, R. F. & Pipe, P. *Analyzing performance problems or 'You really oughta wanna.'* Belmont, Calif.: Fearon, 1970.

Mahoney, M. J. Toward an experimental analysis of coverant control. *Behavior Therapy,* 1970, *1,* 510–521.

Mahoney, M. J. Research issues in self-management. *Behavior Therapy,* 1972, *3,* 45–63.

Mahoney, M. J. *Cognition and behavior modification.* Cambridge, Mass.: Ballinger, 1974a.

Mahoney, M. J. Self-reward and self-monitoring techniques for weight control. *Behavior Therapy,* 1974b, *5,* 48–57.

Mahoney, M. J., Kazdin, A. E., & Lesswing, N. J. Behavior modification: Delusion or deliverance? In C. M. Franks & G. T. Wilson (eds.), *Annual review of behavior therapy: Theory and practice. Vol. 2.* New York: Brunner/Mazel, 1974.

Mahoney, M. J. & Mahoney, K. *Permanent weight control: A total solution to the dieter's dilemma.* New York: Norton, 1976.

Maletzky, B. M. Behavior recording as treatment: A brief note. *Behavior Therapy,* 1974, *5,* 107–111.

Mandel, K. H. Preliminary report on a new aversion therapy for male homosexuals. *Behaviour Research and Therapy,* 1970, *8,* 93–95.

Mann, J. Vicarious desensitization of test anxiety through observation of videotaped treatment. *Journal of Counseling Psychology,* 1972, *19,* 1–7.

Mann, R. A. The behavior-therapeutic use of contingency contracting to control an adult behavior problem: Weight control. *Journal of Applied Behavior Analysis,* 1972, *5,* 99–109.

Manning, S. A. & Taylor, D. A. Effects of viewed violence and aggression: Stimulation and catharsis. *Journal of Personality and Social Psychology,* 1975, *31,* 180–188.

Marlatt, G. A. & Perry, M. A. Modeling methods. In F. H. Kanfer & A. P. Goldstein (eds.), *Helping people change.* Elmsford, N.Y.: Pergamon Press, 1975.

Marmor, J. Dynamic psychotherapy and behavior therapy: Are they irreconcilable? *Archives of General Psychiatry,* 1971, *24,* 22–28.

Marquis, J. N. Orgasmic reconditioning: Changing sexual object choice through controlling masturbation fantasies. *Journal of Behavior Therapy and Experimental Psychiatry,* 1970, *1,* 263–271.

Marshall, W. L., Boutilier, J., & Minnes, P. The modification of phobic behavior by covert reinforcement. *Behavior Therapy,* 1974, *5,* 469–480.

Marshall, W. L., Strawbridge, H., & Keltner, A. The role of mental relaxation in experimental desensitization. *Behaviour Research and Therapy,* 1972, *10,* 355–366.

Martin, D. G. *Learning-based client-centered therapy*. Belmont, Calif.: Wadsworth, 1972.

Masters, W. H. & Johnson, V. E. *Human sexual inadequacy*. Boston: Little, Brown, 1970.

Matson, F. W. (ed.). *Without/within: Behaviorism and humanism*. Belmont, Calif.: Wadsworth, 1973.

McBrearty, J. F., Dichter, M., Garfield, Z., & Heath, G. A behaviorally oriented treatment program for alcoholism. *Psychological Reports,* 1968, *22,* 287–298.

McGlynn, F. D. Graded imagination and relaxation as components of experimental desensitization. *Journal of Nervous and Mental Disease,* 1973, *157,* 377–385.

McGuire, R. J. & Vallance, M. Aversion therapy by electric shock: A simple technique. *British Medical Journal,* 1964, *1,* 151–153.

Meichenbaum, D. Examination of model characteristics in reducing avoidance behavior. *Journal of Personality and Social Psychology,* 1971, *17,* 298–307.

Meichenbaum, D. *Cognitive behavior modification*. Morristown, N.J.: General Learning Press, 1974a.

Meichenbaum, D. Self-instructional methods. In F. H. Kanfer & A. P. Goldstein (eds.), *Helping people change*. Elmsford, N.Y.: Pergamon Press, 1974b.

Meichenbaum, D. & Cameron, R. Training schizophrenics to talk to themselves: A means of developing attentional controls. *Behavior Therapy,* 1973, *4,* 515–534.

Meichenbaum, D., Gilmore, J., & Fedoravicius, A. Group insight vs group desensitization in treating speech anxiety. *Journal of Consulting and Clinical Psychology,* 1971, *36,* 410–421.

Meyer, T. P. Effects of viewing justified and unjustified real film violence on aggressive behavior. *Journal of Personality and Social Psychology,* 1972, *23,* 21–29.

Migler, B. & Wolpe, J. Automated self-desensitization: A case report. *Behaviour Research and Therapy,* 1967, *5,* 133–135.

Mikulas, W. L. *Behavior modification: An overview*. New York: Harper & Row, 1972a.

Mikulas, W. L. Criticisms of behavior therapy. *Canadian Psychologist,* 1972b, *13,* 83–104.

Mikulas, W. L. *Behavior modification in the classroom*. Teaneck, N.J.: Behavioral Sciences Tape Library, 1974a.

Mikulas, W. L. *Concepts in learning*. Philadelphia: W. B. Saunders, 1974b.

Mikulas, W. L. A televised self-control clinic. *Behavior Therapy,* 1976a, *7,* 564–566.

Mikulas, W. L. *Contingency contracting in the home*. Teaneck, N.J.: Behavioral Sciences Tape Library, 1976b.

Mikulas, W. L. Four noble truths of Buddhism as related to behavior therapy. *Psychological Record,* 1978, in press.

Miller, L. K. Behavioral principles and experimental communities. In W. E. Craighead, A. E. Kazdin, & M. J. Mahoney (eds.), *Behavior modification: Principles, issues, and applications*. Boston: Houghton Mifflin, 1976.

Miller, P. M. *Behavioral treatment of alcoholism*. Elmsford, N.Y.: Pergamon Press, 1976.

Miller, P. M. & Eisler, R. M. Alcohol and drug abuse. In W. E. Craighead, A. E. Kazdin, & M. J. Mahoney (eds.), *Behavior modification: Principles, issues, and applications*. Boston: Houghton Mifflin, 1976.

Morganstern, K. P. Implosive therapy and flooding procedures: A critical review. *Psychological Bulletin*, 1973, *79*, 318–334.

Morganstern, K. P. Cigarette smoke as a noxious stimulus in self-managed aversion therapy for compulsive eating. *Behavior Therapy*, 1974, *5*, 255–260.

Morris, L. W. & Thomas, C. R. Treatment of phobias by a self-administered desensitization technique. *Journal of Behavior Therapy and Experimental Psychiatry*, 1973, *4*, 397–399.

Moser, A. J. Covert punishment of hallucinatory behavior in a psychotic male. *Journal of Behavior Therapy and Experimental Psychiatry*, 1974, *5*, 297–299.

Mowrer, O. H. & Mowrer, W. M. Enuresis—A method for its study and treatment. *American Journal of Orthopsychiatry*, 1938, *8*, 436–447.

Munjack, D. J. Overcoming obstacles to desensitization using *in vivo* stimuli and brevital. *Behavior Therapy*, 1975, *6*, 543–546.

Murphy, C. M. & Bootzin, R. R. Active and passive participation in the contact desensitization of snake fear in children. *Behavior Therapy*, 1973, *4*, 203–211.

Murphy, C. V. & Mikulas, W. L. Behavioral features and deficiencies of the Masters and Johnson program. *Psychological Record*, 1974, *24*, 221–227.

Murray, J. P. Television and violence: Implications of the Surgeon General's research program. *American Psychologist*, 1973, *28*, 472–478.

Musante, G. T. Behavior modification in prisons and correctional facilities. In W. D. Gentry (ed.), *Applied behavior modification*. St. Louis: Mosby, 1975.

Naar, R. Client-centered and behavior therapies: Their peaceful coexistence: A case study. *Journal of Abnormal Psychology*, 1970, *76*, 155–160.

Nesbitt, E. B. An escalator phobia overcome in one session of flooding *in vivo*. *Journal of Behavior Therapy and Experimental Psychiatry*, 1973, *4*, 405–406.

Nicassio, P. & Bootzin, R. A comparison of progressive relaxation and autogenic training as treatments for insomnia. *Journal of Abnormal Psychology*, 1974, *83*, 253–260.

Nolan, J. D., Mattis, P. R., & Holliday, W. C. Long-term effects of behavior therapy: A 12-month follow-up. *Journal of Abnormal Psychology*, 1970, *76*, 88–92.

Notz, W. W. Work motivation and the negative effects of extrinsic rewards. *American Psychologist*, 1975, *30*, 884–891.

O'Connor, R. D. Modification of social withdrawal through symbolic modeling. *Journal of Applied Behavior Analysis*, 1969, *2*, 15–22.

O'Connor, R. D. Relative efficacy of modeling, shaping, and the combined procedures for modification of social withdrawal. *Journal of Abnormal Psychology*, 1972, *79*, 327–334.

O'Dell, S. Training parents in behavior modification: A review. *Psychological Bulletin*, 1974, *81*, 418–433.

Offir, C. W. Visual speech: Their fingers do the talking. *Psychology Today*, June 1976.

O'Leary, K. D. & Drabman, R. Token economy programs in the classroom: A review. *Psychological Bulletin*, 1971, *75*, 379–398.

O'Leary, K. D., Poulos, R. W., & Devine, V. T. Tangible reinforcers: Bonuses or bribes? *Journal of Consulting and Clinical Psychology*, 1972, *38*, 1–8.

O'Leary, K. D. & Wilson, G. T. *Behavior therapy: Application and outcome*. Englewood Cliffs, N.J.: Prentice-Hall, 1975.

Orwin, A., LeBoeuf, A., Dovey, J., & James, S. A comparative trial of exposure and respiratory relief therapies. *Behaviour Research and Therapy*, 1975, *13*, 205–214.

Paul, G. L. Insight vs. desensitization in pyschotherapy two years after termination. *Journal of Consulting Psychology,* 1967, *31,* 333–348.

Paul, G. L. A two year follow-up of systematic desensitization in therapy groups. *Journal of Abnormal Psychology,* 1968, *73,* 119–130.

Paul, G. L. Outcome of systematic desensitization. II: Controlled investigation of individual treatment, technique variation, and current status. In C. M. Franks (ed.), *Behavior therapy: Appraisal and status.* New York: McGraw-Hill, 1969.

Paul, G. L. & Shannon, D. T. Treatment of anxiety through systematic desensitization in therapy groups. *Journal of Abnormal Psychology,* 1966, *71,* 124–135.

Payne, J. S., Polloway, E. A., Kauffman, J. M., & Scranton, T. R. *Living in the classroom: The currency-based token economy.* New York: Human Sciences Press, 1975.

Phelps, S. & Austin, N. *The assertive woman.* San Luis Obispo, Calif.: Impact, 1975.

Phillips, D. P. The influence of suggestion on suicide: Substantive and theoretical implications of the Werther effect. *American Sociological Review,* 1974, *39,* 340–354.

Phillips, E. L., Phillips, E. A., Fixsen, D. L., & Wolf, M. M. Achievement Place: Modification of the behaviors of predelinquent boys within a token economy. *Journal of Applied Behavior Analysis,* 1971, *4,* 45–59.

Phillips, E. L., Phillips, E. A., Fixsen, D. L., & Wolf, M. M. Achievement Place: Behavior shaping works for delinquents. *Psychology Today,* June 1973.

Polakow, R. L. Covert sensitization treatment of a probationed barbituate addict. *Journal of Behavior Therapy and Experimental Psychiatry,* 1975, *6,* 53–54.

Powers, R. B., Osbourne, J. G., & Anderson, E. G. Positive reinforcement of litter removal in the natural environment. *Journal of Applied Behavior Analysis,* 1973, *6,* 579–586.

Premack, D. Reinforcement theory. In D. Levine (ed.), *Nebraska symposium on motivation.* Lincoln: University of Nebraska Press, 1965.

Rachlin, H. Self-control. *Behaviorism,* 1974, *2,* 94–107.

Rachman, S. Systematic desensitization. *Psychological Bulletin,* 1967, *67,* 93–103.

Rachman, S. *Phobias: Their nature and control.* Springfield, Ill.: Charles Thomas, 1968.

Rachman, S. Behavior therapy and psychodynamics. *Behavior Therapy,* 1970, *1,* 527–530.

Rachman, S. Clinical applications of observation learning, imitation and modeling. *Behavior Therapy,* 1972, *3,* 379–397.

Rachman, S. & Hodgson, R. Studies in desensitization. IV: Optimum degree of anxiety-reduction. *Behaviour Research and Therapy,* 1967, *5,* 249–250.

Rachman, S. & Hodgson, R. I. Synchrony and desynchrony in fear and avoidance. *Behaviour Research and Therapy,* 1974, *12,* 311–318.

Rachman, S., Marks, I. M., & Hodgson, R. The treatment of obsessive-compulsive neurotics by modeling and flooding in vivo. *Behaviour Research and Therapy,* 1973, *11,* 463–471.

Rachman, S. & Teasdale, J. *Aversion therapy and behavior disorders: An analysis.* Coral Gables, Fla.: Univ. of Miami Press, 1969.

Rathus, S. A. A 30-item schedule for assessing assertive behavior. *Behavior Therapy,* 1973, *4,* 398–406.

Raymond, M. J. The treatment of addiction by aversion conditioning with apomorphine. *Behaviour Research and Therapy,* 1964, *1,* 287–291.

Resnick, J. H. Effects of stimulus satiation on the overlearned maladaptive response of cigarette smoking. *Journal of Consulting and Clinical Psychology,* 1968, *32,* 501–505.

Rich, A. R. & Schroeder, H. E. Research issues in assertiveness training. *Psychological Bulletin,* 1976, *83,* 1081–1096.

Rimm, D. C. Thought stopping and covert assertion in the treatment of phobias. *Journal of Consulting and Clinical Psychology,* 1973, *41,* 466–467.

Rimm, D. C. & Masters, J. C. *Behavior therapy: Techniques and empirical findings.* New York: Academic Press, 1974.

Rimm, D. C., Saunders, W. D., & Westel, W. Thought stopping and covert assertion in the treatment of snake phobias. *Journal of Consulting and Clinical Psychology,* 1975, *43,* 92–93.

Ritter, B. The group desensitization of children's snake phobias using vicarious and contact desensitization procedures. *Behaviour Research and Therapy,* 1968, *6,* 1–6.

Ritter, B. Treatment of acrophobia with contact desensitization. *Behaviour Research and Therapy,* 1969, *7,* 41–45.

Robbins, J. & Fisher, D. *How to make and break habits.* New York: Wyden, 1973. Dell paperback, 1976.

Robinson, C. & Suinn, R. M. Group desensitization of a phobia in massed sessions. *Behaviour Research and Therapy,* 1969, *7,* 319–321.

Rogers, C. R. A process conception of psychotherapy. *American Psychologist,* 1958, *13,* 142–149.

Rogers, C. R. & Skinner, B. F. Some issues concerning the control of human behavior: A symposium. *Science,* 1956, *124,* 1057–1066.

Röper, G., Rachman, S., & Marks, I. Passive and participant modeling in exposure treatment of obsessive-compulsive neurotics. *Behaviour Research and Therapy,* 1975, *13,* 271–279.

Rose, S. D. *Group therapy: A behavioral approach.* Englewood Cliffs, N.J.: Prentice-Hall, 1977.

Rosen, G.M., *Don't be afraid: A program for overcoming your fears and phobias.* Englewood Cliffs, N.J.: Prentice-Hall, 1976

Rosen, G. M., Glasgow, R. E., & Barrera Jr., M. A controlled study to assess the clinical efficacy of a totally self-administered systematic desensitization. *Journal of Consulting and Clinical Psychology,* 1976, *44,* 208–217.

Rosen, R. C. & Schnapp, B. J. The use of a specific behavioral technique (thought-stopping) in the context of conjoint couples therapy: A case report. *Behavior Therapy,* 1974, *5,* 261–264.

Rosenthal, T. L. Modeling therapies. In M. Hersen, R. M. Eisler, & P. M. Miller (eds.), *Progress in behavior modification. Vol. 2.* New York: Academic Press, 1976.

Ross, L., Rodin, J., & Zimbardo, P. G. Toward an attribution therapy: The reduction of fear through induced cognitive-emotional misattribution. *Journal of Personality and Social Psychology,* 1969, *12,* 279–288.

Rozensky, R. H. The effect of timing of self-monitoring behavior on reducing cigarette consumption. *Journal of Behavior Therapy and Experimental Psychiatry,* 1974, *5,* 301–303.

Rush, A. J., Khatami, M., & Beck, A. T. Cognitive and behavior therapy in chronic depression. *Behavior Therapy,* 1975, *6,* 398–404.

Russell, R. K. & Sipich, J. F. Cue-controlled relaxation in the treatment of test anxiety. *Journal of Behavior Therapy and Experimental Psychiatry*, 1973, *4*, 47–49.

Ryan, V. L., Krall, C. A., & Hodges, W. F. Self-concept change in behavior modification. *Journal of Consulting and Clinical Psychology*, 1976, *44*, 638–645.

Sajwaj, T., Libet, J., & Agras, S. Lemon-juice therapy: The control of life-threatening rumination in a six-month old infant. *Journal of Applied Behavior Analysis*, 1974, *7*, 557–563.

Samaan, M. Thought-stopping and flooding in a case of hallucinations, obsessions, and homicidal-suicidal behavior. *Journal of Behavior Therapy and Experimental Psychiatry*, 1975, *6*, 65–67.

Sarason, I. G. & Ganzer, V. J. Modeling and group discussion in the rehabilitation of juvenile delinquents. *Journal of Counseling Psychology*, 1973, *20*, 442–449.

Sargant, W. *Battle for the mind*. London: Pan Books, 1959.

Schaefer, H. H. & Martin, P. L. *Behavioral therapy*. 2d ed. New York: McGraw-Hill, 1975.

Schreibman, L. & Koegel, R. L. Autism: A defeatable horror. *Psychology Today*, March 1975.

Schwitzgebel, R. L. & Schwitzgebel, R. K. (eds.). *Psychotechnology: Electronic control of mind and behavior*. New York: Holt, Rinehart & Winston, 1973.

Seligman, M. E. P. Phobias and preparedness. *Behavior Therapy*, 1971, *2*, 307–320.

Seligman, M. E. P. *Helplessness: On depression, development, and death*. San Francisco: W. H. Freeman, 1975.

Serber, M. Shame aversion therapy. *Journal of Behavior Therapy and Experimental Psychiatry*, 1970, *1*, 213–215.

Shapiro, D. H. & Zifferblatt, S. M. Zen meditation and behavioral self-control: Similarities, differences, and clinical applications. *American Psychologist*, 1976, *31*, 519–532.

Shaw, D. W. & Thoresen, C. E. Effects of modeling and desensitization in reducing dentist phobia. *Journal of Counseling Psychology*, 1974, *21*, 415–420.

Sherman, R. A. & Plummer, I. L. Training in relaxation as a behavioral self-management skill: An exploratory investigation. *Behavior Therapy*, 1973, *4*, 543–550.

Shoben, E. J. Psychotherapy as a problem in learning theory. *Psychological Bulletin*, 1949, *46*, 366–392.

Shorkey, C. & Himle, D. P. Systematic desensitization treatment of a recurring nightmare and related insomnia. *Journal of Behavior Therapy and Experimental Psychiatry*, 1974, *5*, 97–98.

Silverman, I. & Geer, J. H. The elimination of a recurrent nightmare by desensitization of a related phobia. *Behaviour Research and Therapy*, 1968, *6*, 109–111.

Silverman, L. H., Frank, S. G., & Dachinger, P. A psychoanalytic reinterpretation of the effectiveness of systematic desensitization: Experimental data bearing on the role of merging fantasies. *Journal of Abnormal Psychology*, 1974, *83*, 313–318.

Silverstein, S. J., Nathan, P. E., & Taylor, H. A. Blood alcohol level estimation and controlled drinking by chronic alcoholics. *Behavior Therapy*, 1974, *5*, 1–15.

Skinner, B. F. *Walden Two*. New York: Macmillan, 1948. Macmillan paperback, 1962.

Skinner, B. F. *Beyond freedom and dignity*. New York: Knopf, 1971. Bantam paperback, 1972.

Skinner, B. F. *About behaviorism*. New York: Knopf, 1974. Vintage Books paperback, 1976.

Sloan, R. B. The converging paths of behavior therapy and psychotherapy. *International Journal of Psychiatry*, 1969, *8*, 493–503.

Sloop, E. W. Parents as behavior modifiers. In W. D. Gentry (ed.), *Applied behavior modification*. St. Louis: Mosby, 1975.

Smith, M. J. *When I say no, I feel guilty*. New York: Dial Press, 1975. Bantam paperback, 1975.

Smith, R. D., Dickson, A. L., & Sheppard, L. Review of flooding procedures (implosion) in animals and man. *Perceptual and Motor Skills*, 1973, *37*, 351–374.

Smith, R. E. The use of humor in the counterconditioning of anger responses: A case study. *Behavior Therapy*, 1973, *4*, 576–580.

Smith, R. E. & Sharpe, T. M. Treatment of a school phobia with implosive therapy. *Journal of Consulting and Clinical Psychology*, 1970, *35*, 239–243.

Sobell, M. B. & Sobell, L. C. Individualized behavior therapy for alcoholics. *Behavior Therapy*, 1973, *4*, 49–72.

Sobell, M. B. & Sobell, L. C. Second year treatment outcome of alcoholics treated by individualized behavior therapy: Results. *Behaviour Research and Therapy*, 1976, *14*, 195–215.

Solomon, R. L. Punishment. *American Psychologist*, 1964, *19*, 239–253.

Spiegler, M. D., Cooley, E. J., Marshall, G. J., Prince II, H. T., Puckett, S. P., & Skenazy, J. A. A self-control versus a counterconditioning paradigm for systematic desensitization: An experimental comparison. *Journal of Counseling Psychology*, 1976, *23*, 83–86.

Stampfl, T. G. Implosive therapy: An emphasis on covert stimulation. In D. J. Levis (ed.), *Learning approaches to therapeutic behavior change*. Chicago: Aldine, 1970.

Stampfl, T. G. Implosive therapy: Staring down your nightmares. *Psychology Today*, February 1975.

Stampfl, T. G. & Levis, D. J. Essential of implosive therapy: A learning-theory-based psychodynamic behavioral therapy. *Journal of Abnormal Psychology*, 1967, *72*, 496–503.

Stuart, R. B. Operant-interpersonal treatment for marital discord. *Journal of Consulting and Clinical Psychology*, 1969, *33*, 675–682.

Stuart, R. B. Behavioral contracting within families of delinquents. *Journal of Behavior Therapy and Experimental Psychiatry*, 1971, *2*, 1–11.

Stuart, R. B. Challenges for behavior therapy: 1975. *Canadian Psychological Review*, 1975, *16*, 164–172.

Stuart, R. B. & Davis, B. *Slim chance in a fat world: Behavioral control of obesity*. Champaign, Ill.: Research Press, 1972.

Stuart, R. B. & Lott Jr., L. A. Behavioral contracting with delinquents: A cautionary note. *Journal of Behavior Therapy and Experimental Psychiatry*, 1972, *3*, 161–169.

Stuart, R. B. & Stuart, F. *Marital pre-counseling inventory*. Champaign, Ill.: Research Press, 1973.

Stuart, R. B. & Stuart, F. *Family pre-counseling inventory*. Champaign, Ill.: Research Press, 1975.

Sturm, I. E. A behavioral outline of psychodrama. *Psychotherapy: Theory, Research and Practice,* 1970, *7,* 245–247.

Sturm, I. E. Implications of role-playing methodology for clinical procedure. *Behavior Therapy,* 1971, *2,* 88–96.

Suinn, R. M. The STABS, a measure of test anxiety for behavior therapy: Normative data. *Behaviour Research and Therapy,* 1969, *7,* 335–339.

Suinn, R. M. & Richardson, F. Anxiety management training: A nonspecific behavior therapy program for anxiety control. *Behavior Therapy,* 1971, *2,* 498–510.

Tanner, B. A. & Zeiler, M. Punishment of self-injurious behavior using aromatic ammonia as the aversive stimulus. *Journal of Applied Behavior Analysis,* 1975, *8,* 53–57.

Tart, C. T. (ed.). *Transpersonal psychologies.* New York: Harper & Row, 1975.

Tharp, R. G. & Wetzel, R. J. *Behavior modification in the natural environment.* New York: Academic Press, 1969.

Thompson, I. G. & Rathod, N. H. Aversion therapy for heroin dependence. Lancet, 1968, *2,* 382–384.

Thoresen, C. E. Behavioral humanism. In C. E. Thoresen (ed.), *Behavior modification in education.* Seventy-second yearbook of the National Society for the Study of Education, Part I. Chicago: Univ. of Chicago Press, 1973.

Thorpe, J. G., Schmidt, E., Brown, P. T., & Costell, D. Aversion-relief therapy: A new method for general application. *Behaviour Research and Therapy,* 1964, *2,* 71–82.

Todd, F. J. Coverant control of self-evaluative responses in the treatment of depression: A new use for an old principle. *Behavior Therapy,* 1972, *3,* 91–94.

Tondo, T. R., Lane, J. R., & Gill Jr., K. Suppression of specific eating behaviors by covert response cost: An experimental analysis. *Psychological Record,* 1975, *25,* 187–196.

Truax, C. B. Reinforcement and nonreinforcement in Rogerian psychotherapy. *Journal of Abnormal Psychology,* 1966, *71,* 1–9.

Turner, R. K. & Taylor, P. D. Conditioning treatment of nocturnal enuresis in adults: Preliminary findings. *Behaviour Research and Therapy,* 1974, *12,* 41–52.

Ullmann, L. P. On cognitions and behavior therapy. *Behavior Therapy,* 1970, *1,* 201–204.

Ulmer, R. A. *On the development of a token economy mental hospital treatment program.* Washington, D.C.: Hemisphere Publishing Corp., 1976.

Ventis, W. L. Case history: The use of laughter as an alternative response in systematic desensitization. *Behavior Therapy,* 1973, *4,* 120–122.

Vogler, R. E., Compton, J. V., & Weissbach, T. A. Integrated behavior change techniques for alcoholics. *Journal of Consulting and Clinical Psychology,* 1975, *43,* 233–243.

Wachowiak, D. G. Model-reinforcement counseling with college males. *Journal of Counseling Psychology,* 1972, *19,* 387–392.

Walker, H. M. & Buckley, N. K. *Token reinforcement techniques.* Eugene Ore.: E–B Press, 1974.

Watson, J. B. Psychology as the behaviorist views it. *Psychological Review,* 1913, *20,* 158–177.

Watson, J. B. & Rayner, R. Conditioned emotional reactions. *Journal of Experimental Psychology,* 1920, *3,* 1–14.

Weathers, L. & Liberman, R. P. The family contracting exercise. *Journal of Behavior Therapy and Experimental Psychiatry,* 1975, *6,* 208–214.

Webster, D. R. & Azrin, N. H. Required relaxation: A method of inhibiting agitative-disruptive behavior of retardates. *Behaviour Research and Therapy,* 1973, *11,* 67–78.

Weitzman, B. Behavior therapy and psychotherapy. *Psychological Review,* 1967, *74,* 300–317.

Welch, M. W. & Gist, J. W. *The open token economy system: A handbook for a behavioral approach to rehabilitation.* Springfield, Ill.: Charles C. Thomas, 1974.

Wenrich, W. W., Dawley, H. H., & General, D. A. *Self-directed systematic desensitization.* Kalamazoo, Mich.: Behaviordelia, 1976.

Wexler, D. B. Token and taboo: Behavior modification, token economies, and the law. *Behaviorism,* 1973, *1,* 1–24.

White, J. & Fadiman, J. (eds.). *Relax: How you can feel better, reduce stress, and overcome tension.* New York: Confucian Press, 1976. Dell paperback, 1976.

Whyte, W. F. Skinnerian theory in organizations. *Psychology Today,* April 1972.

Wicker, A. W. Attitudes versus actions: The relationship of verbal and overt behavioral responses to attitude objects. *Journal of Social Issues,* 1969, *25,* 41–78.

Wieman, R. J., Shoulders, D. I., & Farr, J. H. Reciprocal reinforcement in marital therapy. *Journal of Behavior Therapy and Experimental Psychiatry,* 1974, *5,* 291–295.

Wilkins, W. Desensitization: Social and cognitive factors underlying the effectiveness of Wolpe's procedure. *Psychological Bulletin,* 1971, *78,* 311–317.

Williams, C. D. The elimination of tantrum behavior by extinction procedures. *Journal of Abnormal and Social Psychology,* 1959, *59,* 269.

Wilson, G. T. & Davison, G. C. Processes of fear-reduction in systematic desensitization: Animal studies. *Psychological Bulletin,* 1971, *76,* 1–14.

Wilson, G. T. & Davison, G. C. Behavior therapy and homosexuality: A critical perspective. *Behavior Therapy,* 1974, *5,* 16–28.

Wilson, G. T. & Thomas, M. G. W. Self- versus drug-produced relaxation and the effects of instructional set in standardized systematic desensitization. *Behaviour Research and Therapy,* 1973, *11,* 279–288.

Winett, R. A. Attribution of attitude and behavior change and its relevance to behavior therapy. *Psychological Record,* 1970, *20,* 17–32.

Wisocki, P. A. The successful treatment of a heroin addict by covert conditioning techniques. *Journal of Behavior Therapy and Experimental Psychiatry,* 1973, *4,* 55–61.

Wolpe, J. *Psychotherapy by reciprocal inhibition.* Stanford: Stanford Univ. Press, 1958.

Wolpe, J. The prognosis in unpsychoanalyzed recovery from neurosis. *American Journal of Psychiatry,* 1961, *118,* 35–39.

Wolpe, J. *The practice of behavior therapy.* Elmsford, N.Y.: Pergamon Press, 1969.

Wolpe, J. & Lang, P. J. A fear survey schedule for use in behavior therapy. *Behaviour Research and Therapy,* 1964, *2,* 27–30.

Wooden, H. E. The use of negative practice to eliminate nocturnal headbanging. *Journal of Behavior Therapy and Experimental Psychiatry,* 1974, *5,* 81–82.

Yates, A. J. Symptoms and symptom substitution. *Psychological Review,* 1958, *65,* 371–374.

Yates, A. J. *Theory and practice in behavior therapy.* New York: Wiley, 1975.

Yulis, S., Brahm, G., Charnes, G., Jacard, L. M., Picota, E., & Rutman, F. The extinction of phobic behavior as a function of attention shifts. *Behaviour Research and Therapy,* 1975, *13,* 173–176.

Zenmore, R. Systematic desensitization as a method of teaching a general anxiety-reducing skill. *Journal of Consulting and Clinical Psychology,* 1975, *43,* 157–161.

Zimbardo, P. & Ebbesen, E. B. *Influencing attitudes and changing behavior.* Reading, Mass.: Addison-Wesley, 1970.

Name Index

Subject Index

Abreaction, 45
Aggression
  assertive training for, 117
  viewing violence and, 115–116
Ahistorical approach, 9–10, 27, 129, 150, 153
Alcoholism, 64, 66, 144–146, 161
Altruism, 114
Anger reduction, 38–39, 45, 132
Antabuse, 66
Anxiety
  consistency and, 90
  free-floating, 58–59
  pervasive, 58–59
  reduction by
    counterconditioning, 36–40, 135
    desensitization, chap. 5
    flooding, chap. 4
    misattribution, 137
    modeling, 119–121
    operant conditioning, 56, 83, 107
    self-control, 56–57, 130
    self-statements, 131–132
    thought-stopping, 132–133
  See also Fear
Anxiety-management training, 56–57
Approach-avoidance, 18, 50
Assertion, covert, 133

Assertive behavior
  assessment, 17
  counterconditioning anxiety, 37, 59
  covert, 118, 133
  training, 116–119, 161
Assessment, 14–20
Attitudes and behavior, 126–129
Attribution, 136–137
Autism, 101–102, 159
Autogenic training, 36
Aversion relief, 38, 68
Aversion therapy, 65
Aversive counterconditioning, chap. 6
  aversion relief, 38, 68
  covert sensitization, 71–73, 103, 135
  definition, 33, 63
  generalization, 68–69
  procedure, 63–68
  punishment vs., 65–66, 73
  theories, 69–71
Aversive imagery, 71
  See also Sensitization, covert

Baseline, 18, 78–79
BASIC ID, 154
Behavior modification
  behaviorism and, 6–8

190